ARBITRATION AND THE CONSTITUTION

Arbitration has become an increasingly important mechanism for dispute resolution, in both domestic and international settings. Despite its importance as a form of state-sanctioned dispute resolution, it has largely remained outside the spotlight of constitutional law. This landmark work represents one of the first attempts to synthesize the fields of arbitration law and constitutional law. Drawing on the author's extensive experience as a scholar in arbitration law who has lectured and studied around the world, the book offers unique insights into how arbitration law implicates issues such as separation of powers, federalism, and individual liberties.

Peter B. Rutledge is a Professor of Law and the Herman E. Talmadge Chair at the University of Georgia School of Law. A recognized figure in the field of international dispute resolution and an accomplished Supreme Court advocate, Professor Rutledge has published widely in both the United States and abroad. His articles have appeared in publications such as the *University of Chicago Law Review*, the *Vanderbilt Law Review*, and the *Journal of International Arbitration*.

Arbitration and the Constitution

Peter B. Rutledge

Herman E. Talmadge Chair of Law

University of Georgia

CAMBRIDGE
UNIVERSITY PRESS

CAMBRIDGE UNIVERSITY PRESS
Cambridge, New York, Melbourne, Madrid, Cape Town,
Singapore, São Paulo, Delhi, Mexico City

Cambridge University Press
32 Avenue of the Americas, New York, NY 10013-2473, USA

www.cambridge.org
Information on this title: www.cambridge.org/9781107006119

First published 2013

Printed in the United States of America

A catalog record for this publication is available from the British Library.

Library of Congress Cataloging in Publication Data

Rutledge, Peter B.
Arbitration and the constitution / Peter B. Rutledge.
p. cm.
Includes bibliographical references and index.
ISBN 978-1-107-00611-9 (hardback)
1. Arbitration and award. 2. Constitutional law. I. Title.
K2400.R88 2012
347′.09–dc23 2012025695

ISBN 978-1-107-00611-9 Hardback

This book is dedicated to our children
Anna, Marie, Nina, and Frank

CONTENTS

ACKNOWLEDGMENTS

This book represents the culmination of years of thinking, speaking, teaching, and writing about arbitration and, specifically, its relation to the Constitution. As with any project, it has benefited from countless conversations with professors, judges, lawyers, and students. Any attempt to list all the individuals who have had an impact on the project would inevitably be incomplete. Nonetheless, I would be remiss if I did not mention some of the many individuals and institutions whose support has made the finished work possible.

As far as individuals, first and most important thanks must go to my wife, Birgit Rutledge-Riel. She is – and always has been – the rock in my life, supporting me during long nights, late hours in the office, stressful work periods, and countless conversations about what must, at times, have seemed like an especially arid subject. She is the finest teacher I know and a thoughtful critic of ideas, legal and nonlegal. Quite simply, without her, this project would not have been possible.

Second, thanks must go to the people who have been deans over the course of my academic career as I wrote this book. As any professor knows, deans have an enormous impact on our early career. Their support on matters such as courseload, research funding, course selection, and research leave enable us to do the heavy lifting that results in publication. At Catholic University Law School, Dean Douglas Kmiec, and his successors, Bill Fox and Veryl Miles, helped me get started with a friendly teaching package, including an upper-level seminar on Arbitration and the Constitution in which I first was able to pull together the literature on this topic in a systematic fashion. More recently, at the University of Georgia School of Law, Dean Rebecca White provided invaluable support, including sponsoring my application for a Fulbright award and granting me sufficient research leave to complete this project. Without her unwavering support, this project would never have become a reality.

In that same vein, special thanks must go to individuals at the J. William Fulbright Foundation and, especially, the Austrian Fulbright Commission. During the 2010–2011 academic year, a Fulbright award helped underwrite a year in residence at the Institut für Zivilverfahrensrecht at the University of Vienna Law School. The program granted me incomparable access to a network of scholars, jurists, and lawyers, both within Austria and throughout Europe, with whom I could exchange ideas and from whom I learned a great deal. For their support of my Fulbright project, special thanks to Antoinette van Zabner, Heinz Löber, Lonnie Johnson, and Irene Zavarsky.

Third, countless colleagues commented on and contributed to this work. Gary Born, my dear friend and coauthor, has been a constant source of advice on this and other projects throughout my career. Fellow scholars including Chris Drahozal, Susan Franck, Jack Goldsmith, David Kershaw, Douglas Kmiec, Richard Nagareda (whose passing was a great loss to the legal academy), Antonio Perez, Neil Richards, Stacie Strong, Symeon Symeonides, Kent Syverud, Steve Ware, Lloyd Weinreb, and Adrian Zuckerman all have commented on various parts of this project or invited me to workshops where I could present these ideas during their formative stages. In that same vein, I send my thanks to the several anonymous reviewers who commented on the book proposal while it was under consideration at Cambridge.

Fourth, I have profited greatly from numerous students whose research assistance has ensured the depth and accuracy of the ideas presented here. Former students at Catholic University including Nicole Angarella, Bri DiBari, Barney Ford, Gordon Jimison, Maureen Smith, and Sarah Wyss all contributed during various stages of this process. More recently, a crackerjack team of students at the University of Georgia helped bring the manuscript to completion. These include Halley Espy, Amanda Holcomb, Nicholas Howell, Christopher Smith, and Julianne Thon. Without this team, which operated like a well-oiled machine in the final months, these chapters would have remained unsculpted lumps of clay.

Finally, among the individuals deserving thanks, I extend my heartfelt gratitude to those persons who helped take the ideas presented here and make them ready for publication as a book. John Berger at Cambridge University Press shepherded me through the proposal-approval process, and Carol McGeehan at Wolters Kluwer provided a valuable early endorsement of my promise as an author. Research librarians including Steve Young of Catholic University and James Donovan and T. J. Striepe at the University of Georgia unfailingly tracked down difficult sources, especially, the voluminous legislative history surrounding NAFTA's implementing legislation. Julie Kendrick, Barbara Pitzl, and, especially Cindy Wentworth have provided administrative support of immeasurable value.

Beyond the individuals, numerous institutions have supported this project, whether through financial support, administrative support, or simply an opportunity to share the ideas with members of their law faculty. To that end, I must begin by thanking my home institution, the University of Georgia School of Law, quite simply one of the finest law schools in the country. I also must acknowledge the support of the University of Vienna Law School, my "home away from home" during the 2010–2011 academic year, where many of these chapters were first drafted. Participants in workshops at Cambridge University, the University of Oslo, McGill University, Washington University, George Washington University, the University of Georgia, the University of Alabama, the University of Nebraska, Willamette University, and Kansas University, as well as the Southeast Association of Law Schools all provided enriching input on early drafts of various chapters. To all of these institutions, I owe a debt of intellectual gratitude.

This list only scratches the surface of those who have had an impact on this project. To everyone, individuals and institutions, this book is better for your contributions and support. Errors remain, and for those I take full responsibility.

Peter B. Rutledge
Athens, GA

INTRODUCTION

Arbitration and the Constitution? At first glance, these two bodies of law appear to be strange bedfellows.

Arbitration, one would think, essentially involves private conduct. In arbitration, private parties contractually exit the system of state-controlled dispute resolution in favor of a purely private system wherein they authorize a private decision maker to resolve their rights and obligations. Proceedings typically are confidential, and the parties agree in advance to be bound by the result reached by the decision maker. Under these circumstances, state institutions such as courts play little to no role. They may become involved at the front end of the dispute, when one of the parties challenges the enforceability of the agreement. Or they may become involved in the back end of the dispute, when the losing party does not voluntarily comply with the arbitrator's award. Even in these instances when state actors do become involved, they play only a limited role. In most civilized legal systems, courts presumptively enforce the parties' arbitration agreements subject to a narrow range of exceptions. Similarly, they presumptively enforce the arbitrators' awards, subject again to a narrow range of exceptions.

By contrast, systems of constitutional law generally regulate various forms of public conduct. Consider the U.S. Constitution, for example. That document governs three main types of relationships with public institutions. First, it addresses the horizontal distribution of power among branches of government (for example, the division between the president and the Senate of the power to make and ratify treaties). Second, it sometimes covers the vertical distribution of power across levels of government (for example, Article III's limited grant of subject-matter jurisdiction to the U.S. courts. with the implication that state courts enjoy exclusive jurisdiction over other matters not enumerated therein). Third, the Constitution speaks to the relationship between the State and the individual (for example, the Fourth Amendment's bar on unreasonable searches and seizures serves as a restraint on the interaction between law enforcement officers and private citizens). Tellingly, what the Constitution does not regulate (subject to a few minor exceptions) is the relationship between purely private actors. Thus, for example, the Constitution does not dictate how two neighbors (or businesses) resolve the disputes that arise between them.

This intellectual separation between arbitration and the Constitution was not always the case. Consider the following examples

- The French Constitution of 1793 specified that "[t]he right of the citizens finally to resolve their disputes through arbitrators of their choice cannot in any respect be decreased by law."[1] By the time of the Napoleonic Code, however, arbitration fell into disfavor.[2]
- The Articles of Confederation provided for resolution of interstate disagreements by jointly appointed "five commissioners or judges." In the event of disagreement, parties employed a complex list system to strike names of unacceptable candidates.[3] By the time the Constitution was adopted, this idea had dropped out.
- At one time, the law of certain German principalities such as Bavaria and Prussia granted citizens a right to arbitrate and enforce their agreements. That changed when the National Socialists came to power in the 1930s. The Nazis curtailed the use of arbitration. According to the Guidelines of the Reich regarding arbitration tribunals, "from a state-political point of view a further spread of arbitration would shatter confidence in state jurisdiction and the State itself." One intellectual sympathetic to the Nazi cause declared

[1] French Constitution of Year 1, 1793 (Art. 86).

[2] *See* GARY B. BORN, INTERNATIONAL ARBITRATION 18 (2010).

[3] Articles of Confederation Art. IX (1781). *See also* JACKSON H. RALSTON, INTERNATIONAL ARBITRATION FROM ATHENS TO LOCARNO 190 (1929).

> "that the national-socialist state rejects – contrary to the liberalists' view – arbitral tribunals" altogether.[4]

The relationship between arbitration law and constitutional law therefore raises many puzzles. Some are historical, such as trying to explain the rising and falling popularity of arbitration within and across societies (some historical research dates its earliest use back 2550 B.C.[5]). Others are jurisprudential, as we try to unpack how legal systems navigate the relationships between these two seemingly disparate fields. This book focuses on that latter set of puzzles.

At the advent of the twentieth century, these two regimes – arbitration and constitutional law – indeed would have been strange bedfellows. They comfortably occupied separate spheres. Constitutional law did not influence the design of arbitration systems, and arbitration cases had little influence on the development of constitutional law.

Several forces contributed to the "wall" separating the two fields. For much of the nineteenth century, the division was traceable to courts' refusal to enforce pre-dispute arbitration agreements at all, viewing them as illegal contracts that sought to divest courts of jurisdiction.[6] Even as countries began to soften their resistance to arbitration as an effective form of dispute resolution (an acceptance symbolized through treaties such as the Geneva Convention of 1927[7] and statutory enactments such as the Federal Arbitration Act of 1925[8]), the non-arbitrability doctrine helped to ensure that arbitration would occupy only a relatively narrow field, largely limited to private commercial disputes between businesspersons. Finally, although arbitration between states enjoyed a relatively rich historical tradition, arbitration between private companies (or individual investors) and those states had not.[9] Consequently, arbitration did not implicate any serious constitutional values.

[4] *See* Gary B. Born, *Arbitration and the Freedom to Associate*, 38 GA. J. COMP. & INT'L L. 7, 19–20 (2009).

[5] *See* Gabriel Wilner, Domke on Commercial Arbitration §2:01 (3d ed. 2006).

[6] *See, e.g.*, Kill v. Hollister, 95 Eng. Rep. 532 (K.B. 1746); Judgment of 10 July 1843 (*L'Alliance v. Prunier*), 1843 Dalloz 561 (Cour de Cassation civ.).

[7] *See* Convention on the Execution of Foreign Arbitral Awards (1927), 92 L.N.T.S. 302 (1929–1930).

[8] 9 U.S.C. § 1 *et seq.*

[9] *See* GARY B. BORN, INTERNATIONAL ARBITRATION 2–6 (2010).

Beginning in the second half of the twentieth century, a number of forces began to put pressure on the wall that had historically separated arbitration law from constitutional law. One development was the demise of the non-arbitrability doctrine. This spawned a proliferation of arbitrations in areas of "public laws" traditionally reserved to the courts (such as securities, employment, and antitrust disputes) and triggered calls for ensuring that arbitration embody fundamental principles of due process.[10] It also raised new questions under Article III about the constitutional limits on resolution of federal questions outside federal court.

A second development was the expansion of arbitration in fields such as trade and investment law.[11] The use of arbitration in these areas, coupled with extremely limited opportunity for judicial or other review of the arbitrator's action, raised concerns about whether the U.S. government is delegating too much power to democratically unaccountable actors. These developments also raised concerns about whether private arbitral tribunals, not accountable to the U.S. president, could compel the executive branch to take some sort of action. As a result of these and other forces, constitutional principles began to seep into arbitration law.

A third development was the increasing popularity of arbitration as a mechanism for resolving disputes between companies and individuals (such as employer/employee relationships, company/consumer relationships, and broker/investor relationships).[12] Critics of arbitration attacked these inroads by arbitration and, among other things, decried the apparent lack of procedural protections for the individual in these settings. This led to attempts to import principles of "due process" into arbitration – initially through litigation attempting to impose the requirements of procedural due process onto arbitration, and later (after these efforts largely failed), the development of private "due process protocols."

[10] *See, e.g.*, Scherck v. Alberto-Culver Co., 417 U.S. 506 (1974); Mitsubishi Motors Corp. v. Soler, 473 U.S. 614 (1985).

[11] *See, e.g*, Campbell McLachlan et al., International Investment Arbitration: Substantive Principles (2007).

[12] *See* I Gary B. Born, International Commercial Arbitration 781–85 (2009).

Each of these foregoing developments produced fissures in the wall that traditionally separated arbitration law from constitutional law. Consequently, today, arbitration and constitutional law are no longer the strange bedfellows that they once were.

This cross-fertilization of arbitration and constitutional law is an organic, ongoing process that affects how a growing share of disputes in our society are resolved. Despite its importance, however, the relationship between these two disciplines suffers from a complete lack of rigorous theoretical examination. The purpose of this book, then, is to fill that gap.

Its objective, therefore, is twofold. First, as a positive matter, the book aims to chart systematically the breakdown of the wall separating these two disciplines and the alloying of their various principles. Second, as a normative matter, the book also (at times) critiques these developments. Sometimes, those critiques concern the substance of the alloying, where the constitutional norm is undesirable. Other times, those critiques concern the process whereby that alloying occurs (where, for example, a norm is developed through a private rather than public process or through a judicial rather than a legislative one).

Put simply, my thesis is as follows: Over the past half century, constitutional norms increasingly have worked their way into arbitration law and, to a lesser extent, arbitration law has influenced the development of constitutional norms. Tellingly, this seepage between the two disciplines has not occurred with a great deal of systematic thought or deliberation. Instead, it has tended to take place through incremental developments in various fields of arbitration, often occurring in isolation of each other and with little consideration of the broader implications of the growing interconnectivity of these two disciplines.

Rarely has this seepage taken the form of express "constitutionalization" of arbitration; with very rare exception, courts have not expressly subjected arbitral regimes to the constitutional norms governing state-run organs of dispute resolution such as judiciaries or administrative agencies. In other words, the wall between arbitration and constitution remains, although significant porous cracks have formed. The resulting seepage takes various forms. In some cases, constitutional norms have affected arbitration law through the design of treaties or statutes by the executive and legislative branches. In other cases, constitutional norms have affected arbitration law through judicial interpretation of those treaties or statutes. Finally, and perhaps most interestingly, constitutional norms have affected arbitration law through the development of private norms, whether by arbitral institutions or the parties themselves; those norms are then incorporated by the parties into their arbitration agreements and, like any other provision of contract, shape the course of the dispute.

Before we turn to the chapters that elaborate on this thesis, a few preliminary matters are in order. First, it is necessary to articulate a more formal definition of "arbitration," as that term has many meanings depending on the context. Second, it is important to describe the methodology animating the study. Third and finally, this introduction offers a road map to the remaining chapters.

DEFINING ARBITRATION

Although scholars may quibble around the edges, there is a broad consensus about the defining features of arbitration. A classic definition posits that arbitration – at least private commercial arbitration – is the private, voluntary agreement to have a dispute resolved by a private actor whose decision is presumptively binding on the parties.[13] This definition includes certain arbitrations within self-regulated organizations ("SROs") such as the National Association of Securities Dealers ("NASD") and the New York Stock Exchange ("NYSE"). It excludes, however, certain types of court-ordered arbitration for parties who have not previously consented to the procedure.

A classic example would be a sales contract between two private parties providing, in relevant part, that any disputes related to the contract shall be resolved exclusively by a single arbitrator in New York pursuant to the rules of the American Arbitration Association and subject to New York law. To be sure, arbitration clauses do not *need* to contain all of these elements. Sometimes the clause may not specify

[13] *See* BORN, *supra* note 11, at 1–7; CHRISTOPHER R. DRAHOZAL, COMMERCIAL ARBITRATION 14–27 (2d ed. 2006).

the arbitral forum or the applicable law. In other cases, the arbitral clause may not specify the applicable rules (preferring instead ad hoc arbitration), or the number of arbitrators (leaving the matter to the parties or, otherwise, an appointing authority). In all events, though, the parties have opted to have their dispute resolved extrajudicially (in contrast to a forum selection clause) and to be bound by the outcome before they know the terms of the results (in contrast to mediation).[14]

Arbitration takes other forms beyond the private commercial setting. These variations are important because they often become the medium through which one or more constitutional norms first seeps into arbitration law. The simplest variation is a private arbitration between parties of unequal bargaining power such as employment contracts or consumer contracts. That form of arbitration involves all the hallmarks of private commercial arbitration but may raise distinct public policy concerns. These concerns prompt some countries to treat these arrangements as per se non-arbitrable (at least on a pre-dispute basis), whereas others allow them. This toleration of such private arrangements is the sort of doctrine that puts pressure on the wall separating arbitral law from constitutional law and creates the conditions for seepage of due process norms into arbitration.

Investment arbitration presents another variation. Unlike private commercial arbitration, the parties in an investment arbitration often are not in direct contractual privity (instead, the right to arbitrate arises by virtue of a treaty between the investor's state and the capital-importing state);[15] moreover, awards under investment arbitration often are subject to less judicial oversight than private commercial awards. As with consumer and employment arbitration, these variations put pressure on the wall separating arbitration law from constitutional law and stimulate the seepage of constitutional norms (such as transparency protocols) into arbitration law.

Finally, there is a long tradition of State–State arbitration as well. Such arbitrations, such as those that occurred between Ethiopia and

[14] *See* Gary B. Born, International Arbitration and Forum Selection Agreements: Drafting and Enforcing (3d ed. 2010).

[15] According to one report, over 2500 such treaties are presently in force. *See* UNCTAD, I. Bilateral Investment Treaties 1995–2006: Trends in Investment Rulemaking.

Eritrea, enjoy a long history as a mode of resolving disputes such as boundary or compensation claims between States. Like commercial arbitration, they typically involve a consensual act (the States' willingness to consent to the arbitration), but, unlike private arbitration, the results are not ordinarily enforced through national courts. Although perhaps one of the most historically significant forms, State-to-State arbitration has not been as fertile a source for the incorporation of constitutional norms into arbitration. That historical puzzle, however, lies beyond the scope of this book.

Although this book focuses primarily on commercial arbitration, an understanding of these other forms is important. This is because those forms often become the mediums through which constitutional principles first filter into the arbitration jurisprudence. Once nested into the particular branch of arbitration such as investor/state arbitration, they can eventually spread, like water, into other crevices such as commercial arbitration.

A NOTE ON METHODOLOGY

At a certain level of generality, the themes of this book are universal. As the anecdotes introduced earlier illustrate, they apply across historical eras and across cultures. The only ingredients necessary to examine them are a State organized around a system of constitutional principles and some room for private orderings of dispute resolution, which then rely upon the power of the State for their enforcement.

Consequently, there is a certain temptation to make this book a truly comparative undertaking. I have opted not to do so for a couple of reasons. For one thing, I recognize that the art of comparative constitutional jurisprudence requires a degree of linguistic expertise that simply lies beyond my ken. Merely relying on available translations of foreign law sources would paint a picture that is at best inadequate and at worst affirmatively misleading. For another thing, that undertaking would distract from my purpose – which is to focus on the act of cross-fertilization between the two disciplines rather than a comparison of how the cross-fertilization occurs (or does not) across countries. Thus, my focus is primarily on U.S. law, the system I know best.

At the same time, foreign law is not entirely irrelevant to the undertaking. One of the joys of this project has been the opportunity to explore the ideas at a theoretical level with colleagues from a variety of other countries such as Italy, Norway, Austria, Canada, and the United Kingdom, just to name a few. Those interactions have enlightened me to instances in which other legal systems have confronted similar issues, lessons that can serve both to illustrate the phenomenon and that enrich our understanding of how American courts ventilate these themes. Thus, I quite explicitly introduce such foreign examples along the way where they help to elucidate a point or deepen the reader's understanding. A broader comparative undertaking is possible and may be the subject of a future work. But now is not the time.

ROAD MAP

What remains, then, is to provide a road map to the reader about the book. The project unfolds in three parts, organized around major areas of constitutional law. The first part focuses on separation-of-powers issues. Drawing on ideas that I developed in a prior article published by the *Vanderbilt Law Review*, Chapter 1 considers the basic question raised but ultimately unresolved by the Supreme Court – namely, are there structural limits on Congress's ability to require judicial enforcement of an arbitrator's award absent de novo review of the award? This question has taken on newfound importance in light of trade and investment treaty regimes that provide for extremely circumscribed judicial review of arbitral awards (such as NAFTA and the Washington Convention). Chapter 2 then considers separation-of-powers issues raised by more specialized forms of arbitration, such as the compatibility of the arbitral appointment provisions of trade treaties with the Constitution's Appointments Clause, and the compatibility of the implementation provisions of NAFTA with the Take Care Clause, both of which were heavily litigated (but ultimately unresolved) in the *Canadian Softwood Lumber* case in the D.C. Circuit.

The second part focuses on vertical separation-of-powers principles, an important but underappreciated aspect of U.S. arbitration law. Chapter 3 will begin with the odd approach to federalism taken by the

FAA. On the one hand, the FAA tramples on state rights: Section 2 – which requires courts to enforce arbitration agreements "save upon such laws as exist at law or in equity for the revocation of any contract" – preempts inconsistent state law that discriminates against arbitration. Moreover, the Supreme Court has made clear that Section 2 applies in state court. Yet in other respects, the FAA provides states an outlet to regulate arbitration agreements. Unlike most cases of preemption, states can reassert the legislative prerogative. Because general state contract law, rather than federal law, ordinarily supplies the standard under Section 2 of the FAA for determining the enforceability of Section 2, states can employ – and have employed – contract law doctrines (such as unconscionability and public policy) in an effort to reassert control over arbitral agreements. This sets the United States apart from most nonfederalized countries, which employ a single national standard on the issue. Moreover, because state contract law (rather than statutory enactments) provides the relevant metric under Section 2, the effect of this jurisprudence has been to allocate power to state courts – as opposed to state legislatures – to police the enforceability of arbitration clauses. Chapter 4 considers the complexity presented by choice-of-law clauses. Under a line of Supreme Court jurisprudence that has been highly criticized but technically remains good law, parties can subject their arbitration clauses to state law, thereby incorporating features of that state's arbitration law, which differ from the federal practice. The availability of these choice-of-law devices has the potential to create a type of "market" for arbitration law.

The third part focuses on the relationship between arbitration and individual liberties. The explosion in arbitrations between companies and individuals (whether consumers or employees) has drawn attention to this topic. Suddenly, one can no longer assume that arbitration agreements represent contracts between parties of equal bargaining positions. Instead, they now might reflect contracts of adhesion, or arrangements where one party to the contract had not given his or her informed consent to the agreement. Chapter 5 begins by testing whether arbitration should properly be considered "state action," invoking the old *Shelley v. Kramer* line of cases under which judicial enforcement of a private agreement can satisfy the Fourteenth Amendment's state-action requirement. It then addresses how the ultimate answer to the state-action question is somewhat academic. Even in a world where arbitration technically does not encompass state action, constitutional principles (for which state action would ordinarily be a constitutional prerequisite) have nonetheless seeped into arbitral practice. This seepage has taken various forms. On the domestic side, we have witnessed the increased use of due process protocols, as well as an ongoing dialogue between courts and arbitral institutions over the minimum due process standards that arbitration must observe. On the international stage, courts have incorporated due process principles to guide their interpretation of arbitral treaties such as Article V(1)(b) of the New York Convention. In this regard, Part III will explore not simply whether due process norms have been incorporated (for they undoubtedly have), but also how they have been incorporated (whether by means of contract, statute, judicial interpretation, or constitutional law). After examining the due process issue at length, this part will then move in Chapter 6 to other constitutional liberties, specifically the jury right. Ultimately, the decision to opt into arbitration, at least in the commercial setting, amounts to a prospective waiver of the right to a jury trial (apart from the limited right under the FAA to a jury determination on the clause's enforceability). This raises important questions about why an arbitration clause suffices to waive an important constitutional right and the standards governing that waiver.

Part I ARBITRATION AND SEPARATION OF POWERS

1 ARBITRATION AND JUDICIAL REVIEW

The judicial power of the United States shall be vested in one Supreme Court, and in such inferior courts as the Congress may from time to time ordain and establish.

– U.S. Constitution, Article III, Section 1

[C]omplete preclusion of judicial review is unconstitutional.

– Brief of Petitioner Coalition for Fair Lumber Imports Executive Committee

Does arbitration violate Article III of the U.S. Constitution? Despite the critical need for a coherent theory to answer this question, few commentators or courts have made serious attempts to provide one.[1] For

[1] For literature addressing the relationship between commercial arbitration and Article III, see Jim C. Chen, *Appointments with Disaster: The Unconstitutionality of Binational Arbitral Review under the United States–Canada Free Trade Agreement*, 49 WASH. & LEE L. REV. 1455, 1456–57 (1992); Henry Paul Monaghan, *Article III and Supranational Judicial Review*, 107 COLUM. L. REV. 833, 842 (2007); Jean R. Sternlight, *Rethinking the Constitutionality of the Supreme Court's Preference for Binding Arbitration: A Fresh Assessment of Jury Trial, Separation of Powers, and Due Process Concerns*, 72 TUL. L. REV. 1, 78–80 (1997); Vicki Zick, Comment, *Reshaping the Constitution to Meet the Practical Needs of the Day: The Judicial Preference for Binding Arbitration*, 82 MARQ. L. REV. 247, 249 (1998). For a sampling of the broader literature addressing various constitutional aspects of arbitration, see Edward Brunet, *Arbitration and Constitutional Rights*, 71 N.C. L. REV. 81, 81 (1992). The U.S. Justice Department's Office of Legal Counsel has released an opinion addressing some of the constitutional complications attendant to binding federal arbitration involving the federal government. Memorandum from Walter Dellinger, Assistant Attorney General, to John Schmidt, Associate Attorney General, Constitutional Limitations on Federal Government Participation in Binding Arbitration (Sept. 7, 1995), reprinted in 7 WORLD ARB. & MEDIATION REP. 23 (1996). For a very recent treatment of these issues, see Roger Perlstadt, Article III, Judicial Power and the Federal Arbitration Act, 62 Am. U. L. Rev. ___ (2012).

much of the country's history, federal courts could conveniently avoid this nettlesome question.[2] Prior to the twentieth century, courts simply declined to enforce pre-dispute arbitration agreements as unenforceable attempts to appropriate their jurisdiction.[3] From the early decades of the twentieth century (with the enactment of the Federal Arbitration Act [FAA] in 1925) through the 1960s, the non-arbitrability doctrine prevented arbitrators from resolving issues of federal statutory law. Notably, although both of these doctrines minimized the tension between arbitration and the Constitution, neither was anchored in Article III. Instead, the "jurisdictional ouster" argument found its roots in contract law – essentially treating the arbitration agreement as a void contract that offended public policy. And the non-arbitrability doctrine operated as a statutory interpretation tool that refused to interpret the FAA to deprive a plaintiff of a federal forum on a statutory claim.

Traditional dispute resolution theory teaches that disputes can be plotted along a spectrum.[4] At one end of the spectrum lie simple forms of extrajudicial dispute resolution that do not entail any intervention by the state, such as a handshake between neighbors to resolve a minor misunderstanding. At the other end lie complex disputes between a citizen and the state (or two private citizens) that can culminate in the forcible deprivation of liberty or property, such as a criminal prosecution, an administrative hearing, or a civil trial ending in a verdict.[5] A variety of other forms of dispute resolution, such as contractual

[2] On at least one occasion, the Supreme Court has considered the compatibility of the Federal Arbitration Act with Article III, but the issues explored here were not squarely presented. In *Marine Transit Corp. v. Dreyfus*, the Court held that Congress could, consistent with Article III, grant federal courts sitting in admiralty the remedial power to order specific performance of arbitration agreements. 284 U.S. 263, 277–79 (1932). Dreyfus did not explore whether the limitations on federal judicial review of arbitral awards also comported with Article III. I thank Chris Drahozal for bringing this case to my attention.

[3] Gary B. Born, International Civil Litigation in United States Courts 993 (3d ed. 1996); 1 Ian R. MacNeil et al., Federal Arbitration Law: Agreements, Awards, and Remedies under the Federal Arbitration Act § 4.3.2.2 (Supp. 1999); Sabra A. Jones, *Historical Development of Commercial Arbitration in the United States*, 12 Minn. L. Rev. 240, 256 (1928).

[4] *See generally* Owen M. Fiss, Comment, *Against Settlement*, 93 Yale L.J. 1073, 1087 (1984) (arguing that settlement generally should not be preferred to judgment because not all cases are "equal"); Lon L. Fuller, *The Forms and Limits of Adjudication*, 92 Harv. L. Rev. 353, 355 (1978) (explaining that "certain problems by their intrinsic nature fall beyond the proper limits of adjudication").

[5] For a discussion of the varying degrees of formality in systems of dispute resolution, see Fuller, *supra* note 4, at 358–59.

settlements, consent decrees, conciliation, mediation, and arbitration, lie between these poles.[6]

Depending on its position along the spectrum, a particular form of dispute resolution will entail different procedural protections and enforceability rules.[7] For example, no formal procedural rules govern the discussions between neighbors that culminate in a handshake.[8] Perhaps unsurprisingly, therefore, that handshake is entitled to minimal judicial enforceability. Conversely, criminal trials and administrative hearings are subject to a panoply of constitutional and nonconstitutional procedural protections.[9] Reflecting those protections, the results of that criminal or administrative hearing are generally more judicially enforceable than the handshake between neighbors.[10] These examples yield a predictable principle: a direct correlation between the procedural protections in a particular system of dispute resolution and the degree of judicial enforceability of the result.[11]

However, certain forms of dispute resolution do not fit neatly within the previously described pattern. This is especially true of arbitration. In contrast to a full-blown trial, arbitration carries few procedural protections.[12] Despite this quality, the result of the dispute – the arbitration award – carries with it a high degree of judicial enforceability.[13] Indeed, this presumption of enforceability and the limited degree of judicial review represent some of the defining features of arbitration. Arbitral awards are subject to far less judicial scrutiny than a civil

[6] *See* Fiss, *supra* note 4, at 1083–84 (arguing that the drive for settlement often leads to poorly planned consent decrees that eventually bring the parties back to court); William Twining, *Alternative to What? Theories of Litigation, Procedure and Dispute Settlement in Anglo-American Jurisprudence: Some Neglected Classics*, 56 MOD. L. REV. 380, 382 (1993) (noting that standard alternatives to litigation such as negotiation, compromise, and mediation often constitute phases within litigation).

[7] I am grateful to participants in the University of Montreal/McGill University faculty matinee, especially Roderick McDonald, for their insights into these ideas. McDonald rightly reminds us that arbitration is part of a broader social phenomenon about the distribution of the social power to resolve disputes.

[8] Although formal rules may not govern the handshake, informal norms of course might.

[9] Fiss, *supra* note 4, at 1077.

[10] *See id.* (asserting that the presence of a judge can "lessen the impact of distributional inequalities").

[11] *See id.* at 1084–85 (describing differences in judicial willingness to enforce consent decrees depending on whether settlement underpins decree).

[12] GARY B. BORN, INTERNATIONAL COMMERCIAL ARBITRATION 1238 (3d ed. 2009).

[13] GARY B. BORN & PETER B. RUTLEDGE, INTERNATIONAL CIVIL LITIGATION IN UNITED STATES COURTS, 1080, 1161 (5th ed. 2011).

court judgment or an administrative determination, despite the greater degree of procedural protections in those forms of dispute resolution.[14] How can this anomaly be explained?

By far the most dominant explanation in the case law and the literature is that the parties have waived their right to an Article III forum.[15] The modern-day defense of the waiver argument springs from *CFTC v. Schor*, where the Court held that the Commodity Futures Trading Commission's (CFTC) exercise of jurisdiction over a common law counterclaim in a dispute between a customer and a commodities broker did not violate Article III.[16] Although the case technically did not involve a challenge to a system of private arbitration, but rather adjudication before an independent federal agency, it has served as the intellectual foundation for decisions rejecting constitutional attack on arbitral schemes. Central to the reasoning in *Schor* was the idea that Article III has both a personal (and thus waivable) component as well as a nonwaivable component (which would be tested against a multifactor balancing test).[17] Critical in the Court's view was the fact that the parties had affirmatively chosen to invoke the CFTC, leaving the jurisdiction of the federal courts unaffected. The Court explained:

> In such circumstances, separation of powers concerns are diminished, for it seems self-evident that just as Congress may encourage parties to settle a dispute out of court or resort to arbitration without

[14] *Id.* at 1202–03.

[15] *See, e.g.*, Belom v. Nat'l Futures Ass'n, 284 F.3d 795, 799 (7th Cir. 2002) ("Where an individual consents to arbitration, he waives the right to an impartial and independent adjudication."); Geldermann, Inc. v. CFTC, 836 F.2d 310, 317 (7th Cir. 1987) (explaining that, under the Federal Insecticide, Fungicide, and Rodenticide Act, a "follow-on" registrant "explicitly consents to have his rights determined by arbitration"); Cremin v. Merrill Lynch Pierce Fenner & Smith, Inc., 957 F. Supp. 1460, 1470 (N.D. Ill. 1997) (explaining that, unless the employee waived her right to an Article III forum, she would be entitled to "her day in court"); Illyes v. John Nuveen & Co., 949 F. Supp. 580, 582–83 (N.D. Ill. 1996) (holding that the Form U-4 the former employee signed incorporated by reference the arbitration provisions later adopted by the NASD and that the plaintiff effectively agreed to arbitrate certain disputes).

[16] 478 U.S. 833, 851–53 (1986).

[17] *Id.* at 848. The Schor Court then articulated a series of factors to determine whether a particular dispute resolution system crossed the Article III line: (1) whether the "essential attributes of judicial power" are reserved to Article III Courts, (2) what is the origin and importance of the rights to be adjudicated, and (3) what are the concerns that drove Congress to depart from the requirements of Article III. *Id.* at 851.

> impermissible incursions on the separation of powers, Congress may make available a quasi-judicial mechanism through which willing parties may, at their option, elect to resolve their differences.

In my view, this passage from *Schor* – so central to the traditional account explaining the compatibility of arbitration with Article III – is deeply flawed in three respects. First, as a matter of theory, there is a reasonable argument that *Schor* was wrong to conclude that Article III rights are waivable.[18] *Schor* provides virtually no analysis supporting its bold assertion that Article III rights are personal.[19] This is perhaps unsurprising: All of the constitutional sources point in precisely the opposite direction. Textually, it is difficult to argue that Article III confers a personal right. Nothing in the Constitution speaks in terms of a "right" to a decision in a federal forum. Rather, the language speaks in definitional terms – defining the "judicial power of the United

[18] *See* Paul M. Bator, *The Constitution as Architecture: Legislative and Administrative Courts under Article III*, 65 IND. L.J. 233, 259 (1990) ("The ideals of separation of powers seem to me structural and political ideals; it is far from clear that they were designed to generate a system of private rights.").

[19] *See Schor*, 478 U.S. at 848–49 (describing Article III's role to preserve the structure of tripartite government and to protect litigants' personal rights). The Court's analysis consists of nothing other than the assertion that Article III confers a "personal right" along with a citation to a number of disanalogous precedents on criminal rights – dicta from the opinions in *Northern Pipeline Construction Co. v. Marathon Pipe Line Co.*, 458 U.S. 50 (1982) (plurality opinion) and earlier decisions that did not confront the "personal rights" question. *Schor* also cites an article by Professor David Currie for the proposition that Article III rights are primarily "personal." 478 U.S. at 848 (citing David P. Currie, *Bankruptcy Judges and the Independent Judiciary*, 16 CREIGHTON L. REV. 441, 460 n.108 (1983)).

That citation, however, at best twists Currie's argument and, at worst, is simply wrong. Sovereign immunity is, by definition, a type of personal privilege that is specific to the litigant (namely, the state); the doctrine's primary purpose is to protect a private litigant, and, in cases where the litigant, for whatever reason, does not desire that protection, waiver of the right makes sense. Currie argues that the tenure and salary provisions serve an analogous function to the private litigant. But he does not argue that the jurisdictional grants envisioned in Article III are themselves personal rights, as the *Schor* opinion seems to imply. Elsewhere he has acknowledged that "[i]t may be, as several of our most thoughtful judges have argued, that the requirement of an independent tribunal serves purposes beyond protection of the immediate parties. . . . " David P. Currie, *The Distribution of Powers after* Bowsher, 1986 SUP. CT. REV. 19, 39. Even if *Schor* reads Currie's thesis correctly, it is nonetheless clear, as I explain that Article III, beyond the tenure and salary provisions, serves additional public purposes that are not confined to the interests of the individual litigants.

States."[20] Article III discusses the subjects over which it extends and the courts in which it is vested. As some have noted, the use of terms such as "shall extend" and "all Cases" could be read to support a mandatory view, at least for some heads of jurisdiction.[21]

Beyond the text, the structure of the Constitution likewise does not support reading Article III in terms of personal rights. The opening articles of the Constitution primarily address the structural organization of our system of government; most of the discussion of rights appears in the amendments. A few passages in the initial articles, such as the Article III, Section 2 guarantee of a jury in criminal cases, do speak in terms of rights. But those passages merely prove that, even before the drafting and ratification of the Bill of Rights, the Framers knew how to draft the Constitution in terms of personal rights. In light of this contrasting language, their failure to draft the Judicial Power Clause in terms of a personal "right" to a federal forum supports the inference that this clause was never meant to confer a personal right.

Finally, the history behind Article III does not support a "personal rights" theory.[22] It is true that evidence of the Framers' intent behind Article III is fragmentary and has prompted much debate over its meaning. Much of that debate is not relevant for my purposes. What is relevant are the terms over which the debate is waged – most commentators focus on questions of the vertical and horizontal distribution of power, the necessity of inferior federal courts, the heads of federal jurisdiction, and the scope of Congress's power to control the jurisdiction of the Supreme Court and lower federal courts. The primary sources do not suggest that the Framers drafted Article III in order to confer a personal right on anyone.[23] Alexander Hamilton's

[20] U.S. CONST. art. III, § 2.

[21] JOSEPH STORY, COMMENTARIES ON THE CONSTITUTION OF THE UNITED STATES §§ 166–77 (1833); Akhil Reed Amar, *A Neo-Federalist View of Article III: Separating the Two Tiers of Federal Jurisdiction*, 65 B.U. L. REV. 205, 211 (1985). For a critique of originalist interpretations of Article III, see Michael L. Wells & Edward J. Larson, *Original Intent and Article III*, 70 TUL. L. REV. 75, 93–121 (1995).

[22] For an exhaustive discussion of the history behind Article III's development and adoption, see Robert N. Clinton, *A Mandatory View of Federal Court Jurisdiction: A Guided Quest for the Original Understanding of Article III*, 132 U. PA. L. REV. 741 (1984).

[23] *See, e.g.*, 2 THE RECORDS OF THE FEDERAL CONVENTION OF 1787, at 37–49, 422–33 (Max Farrand ed., 1911); CHARLES WARREN, THE MAKING OF THE CONSTITUTION 325–36, 531–48 (1928).

classic defense of the values underpinning Article III, in Federalist 78, discusses the provision primarily in structural terms: "That inflexible and uniform adherence to the rights of the Constitution, and of individuals, which we perceive to be indispensable in the courts of justice, can certainly not be expected from judges who hold their officials by a temporary commission."[24] He also argues that "we can never hope to see realized in practice the complete separation of the judicial from the legislative power, in any system which leaves the former dependent for pecuniary resources on the occasional grants of the latter."[25] Indeed, the drafters' failure to include a right to a civil jury trial in Article III was among the Anti-Federalists' greatest complaints about the Article during the ratification debate (had Article III included such a right, the inclusion would have provided important evidence supporting a waiver theory).

Schor never really grapples with this history. Moreover, if *Schor* were wrongly decided, that would have substantial implications for the compatibility of Article III and arbitration. Private parties would not be able to waive their right to an Article III forum as no such right would exist! Thus, the first problem with waiver theory is that it rests on dubious textual, structural, and historical foundations.

The second problem with waiver theory is that it mistakenly conflates arbitration with settlement. Settlement differs from arbitration in several material respects. For one thing, in the case of settlement, the parties know the substantive terms of their bargain in advance of their agreement to be bound. By contrast, in the case of arbitration, the parties are bound to their bargain (i.e., an agreement to arbitrate) before they know its substantive terms. Thus, arbitration involves less party autonomy than settlement. Furthermore, most forms of settlement involve greater judicial scrutiny than arbitration awards. Generally speaking, settlement agreements are simply a species of contract; before they are enforced, they are subject to the typical judicial

[24] The Federalist No. 78 (Alexander Hamilton). Although the above-quoted passage does refer to "the rights . . . of individuals," it would be erroneous to infer from that passage that Article III rights are waivable. Rather, the reference is better understood to mean that safeguarding individual rights is one purpose, among many, of an independent judiciary – not that the independent judiciary itself is a personal, waivable right.

[25] The Federalist No. 79 (Alexander Hamilton).

review that precedes an enforcement decision.[26] Arbitration awards receive much different treatment. The FAA mandates that federal courts must give effect to the arbitral award subject to very limited exceptions. Federal courts enjoy virtually no power to review the merits of the award but instead are confined to reviewing the procedures followed by the arbitrator. Whatever review of the merits exists is practically toothless. Provided that one of the limited grounds for merit review does not apply, the court must give legal effect to the award and treat it as if it were a judicial judgment enforceable by compulsion.

The third and final problem with the waiver theory is that it fails to confront the serious structural problems posed by arbitration. The roots of this problem do not lie solely with *Schor*. There, the Court recognized that, in addition to its "personal" component, Article III also implicates a public concern about the structure of government.[27] As *Schor* explained, "[w]hen these Article III limitations are at issue, notions of consent and waiver cannot be dispositive because the limitations serve institutional interests that the parties cannot be expected to protect."[28] Yet despite the Court's recognition of this nonwaivable feature of Article III, many courts have rejected Article III challenges to arbitration by making a simple statement about waiver and a perfunctory cite to *Schor*.

This conclusory reliance on *Schor* is too facile. Although judicial enforcement of arbitral awards does not directly "aggrandize" the power of a coordinate branch of government, it diminishes the power of the judicial branch. By mandating the enforcement of the award and controlling the scope of Article III review, particularly the extent of review of the merits of federal questions, Congress is effectively stripping federal courts of the power to interpret the meaning of federal law and erecting a system by which others – namely arbitrators – can define it. It is also mandating that federal courts treat the result of this private dispute resolution system as a judgment of a federal court, with all of the accoutrements that accompany such judgments.

[26] *See, e.g.*, Sanford I. Weisburst, *Judicial Review of Settlements and Consent Decrees: An Economic Analysis*, 28 J. LEGAL STUD. 55 (1999) (describing the differing degrees of judicial deference to party-initiated settlement).

[27] 478 U.S. 833, 850 (1986).

[28] *Id.* at 851.

This separation-of-powers problem might be analogized to the constitutional limits on federal commandeering of state executive officials in cases such as *Printz v. United States*.[29] By analogy, Congress commandeers the federal courts when it mandates that they reduce an extrajudicial dispute resolution to a judgment. To be sure, the problems are not identical – whereas *Printz* involved vertical separation-of-powers issues, the problem addressed here involves horizontal ones. Nonetheless, *Printz* provides a potentially helpful analogy, demonstrating how separation-of-powers principles generally prohibit the commandeering of another branch of government.

The *Bonner Mall* line of cases also provides a helpful analogy.[30] In these cases, the Court held that parties who settle a case on appeal are not automatically entitled to the vacatur of the judgment below. This view reinforces the idea that the public may have an interest in the preservation of precedent even if the parties' private interests favor its removal. Analogously, a congressional requirement that the judicial branch must reduce arbitral awards to judgment without meaningful review of the merits deprives the public of valuable precedent. The fit here is imperfect. In *Bonner Mall*, the parties were seeking to vacate a judgment already rendered; in arbitration, Congress merely requires the courts to enforce the parties' extrajudicial resolution of the parties' dispute. Nonetheless, *Bonner Mall* supports the notion that there is a public interest in a dispute beyond the immediate interests of the parties, as well as the idea that the public interest can be undermined through efforts to undermine the judiciary's role.

Identification of a more significant separation-of-powers problem does not necessarily mean that arbitration violates Article III. Rather, it shows that the waiver account offered by the *Schor* Court (and relied on by other courts) is too facile. It does not adequately wrestle with the underlying constitutional problems presented by arbitration. Can one construct a theory that salvages the essential components of arbitration while putting it on surer constitutional footing vis-à-vis Article III?

[29] 521 U.S. 898 (1997).

[30] U.S. Bancorp Mortgage Co. v. Bonner Mall P'ship, 513 U.S. 18 (1994).

A MORE STABLE THEORY OF ARBITRATION AND ARTICLE III

Article III scholars have long debated the extent to which Article III tolerates decisions by non-Article III actors in cases that otherwise would fall within the jurisdiction of the federal courts. One ventures into this field at one's own peril. As Paul Bator once observed: "[T]he Supreme Court has been unable, in these 150 years, to find a coherent and satisfying theory for justifying the existence of legislative and administrative courts . . . [Its] opinions devoted to the subject . . . are as troubled, arcane, confused and confusing as could be imagined."[31]

Some have adopted a literalist framework, according to which Article III judges, and only Article III judges, may resolve the cases or controversies arising under the heads of jurisdiction specified in Article III.[32] Literalist theory may well be appealing as a matter of first impression. But, as several scholars have noted, there is too much precedential water under the bridge for such a theory to be viable.[33] As James Pfander tersely explained in an exhaustive inquiry into the Article III question: "[W]hile scholars continue to hold up a literal interpretation of Article III as a goal to which the law might aspire, this approach suffers from serious problems of institutional fit."[34] In some areas, Congress has foreclosed judicial review in Article III courts. Examples include administrative determinations by the Veterans' Administration, the Department of Health and Human Services, and the Justice Department.[35] The Court has consistently approved these efforts.[36]

31 Bator, *supra* note 18, at 239.

32 *See* Clinton, *supra* note 22, at 749–50; Currie, *supra* note 19.

33 *See* Richard H. Fallon, Jr., *Of Legislative Courts, Administrative Agencies and Article III*, 101 HARV. L. REV. 915, 918–26 (1988); *see also* James E. Pfander, *Article I Tribunals, Article III Courts, and the Judicial Power of the United States*, 118 HARV. L. REV. 643, 656–60 (2004); Wells & Larson, *supra* note 21, at 76–78.

34 Pfander, *supra* note 33, at 656.

35 *See* Chen, *supra* note 1, at 1473–74.

36 *See* Webster v. Doe, 486 U.S. 592, 601 (1988) (holding CIA director's decision to discharge employee was not subject to judicial review); Block v. Cmty. Nutrition Inst., 467 U.S. 340, 348 (1984) (holding that consumers of dairy products could not obtain judicial review of milk market orders); Morris v. Gressette, 432 U.S. 491, 501–02 (1977) (finding that the Attorney General's failure to make timely objection under the Voting Rights Act of 1965 was not subject to judicial review); Johnson v. Robinson, 415 U.S. 361, 367 (1974) (precluding judicial review of certain Veteran's Administration determinations).

Adoption of a literalist theory would require invalidation of numerous non-Article III schemes, including adjudication by administrative agencies. By parity of reasoning, arbitration could not survive under literalist theory – the theory would bar arbitrators, as non-Article III actors, from resolving cases or controversies falling under Article III's heads of jurisdiction.

An alternative account stresses the Articles III distinction between "cases" and "controversies" – an account originally developed by Justice Story and later formalized by Akhil Amar.[37] Under the Story/Amar account, an Article III court must have the jurisdiction to decide "cases" (including federal questions) but need not necessarily have the jurisdiction to decide "controversies" (such as diversity controversies).[38] Although this theory "has substantial historical support,"[39] it too lacks adequate explanatory value in light of intervening Supreme Court precedent. Adoption of this approach would require invalidation of federal administrative agency schemes that allow non-Article III decisionmakers to interpret federal law and allow Article III courts to defer to those interpretations, provided that the law is ambiguous and the agency interpretation is reasonable.[40] By analogy, the Story/Amar theory would require invalidation of arbitral schemes, at least to the extent that they concern claims arising under federal law. Given the large number of arbitrable federal claims following the decline of the non-arbitrability doctrine, the institutional costs of this account are too great.

Recognizing the practical limitations of the literalist and Story/Amar accounts, appellate review theory seeks, as much as possible, to salvage the textual and historical underpinnings of those accounts while not upsetting the existing doctrine.[41] The theory finds its genesis in a seminal article by Richard Fallon and traces its roots to the Supreme Court's decision in *Crowell v. Benson*.[42] "The core claim of [appellate

[37] *See* Amar, *supra* note 21, at 210–19.

[38] *Id.*

[39] Chen, *supra* note 1, at 1467–68; *see also* Wells & Larson, *supra* note 21, at 91–93.

[40] *See* Chen, *supra* note 1, at 1468.

[41] *See* Fallon, *supra* note 33, at 933 (introducing appellate review theory).

[42] *Id.*; 285 U.S. 22, 62–65 (1932).

review theory] is that sufficiently searching review of a legislative court's or administrative agency's decisions by a constitutional court will always satisfy the requirements of Article III."[43]

Fallon derived the theory from a consideration of both the values supporting non-Article III tribunals and the values underlying Article III itself. In general, the values supporting non-Article III tribunals include:

1. Expertise – making the best use of the non-Article III decision maker's substantive expertise;
2. Governmental Functions – maintenance of efficiency and order in the performance of governmental functions;
3. Flexibility – flexibility in adapting a scheme of administration and adjudication to changing needs and political priorities;
4. Fairness – producing fairer and more consistent results;
5. Sovereign Immunity – principles of sovereign immunity counsel in favor of the government's ability to control the scope of the non-Article III proceedings in which it is a party.

According to Fallon, these values must be balanced against others that underpin the need for Article III tribunals, including:

1. Separation of Powers – Article III review promotes separation of powers by ensuring principled decisions on legal questions by institutions immune from political pressure.
2. Fairness – Article III review helps ensure fairness to litigants through some combination of the independence of a life-tenured judiciary plus due process guarantees.
3. Judicial Integrity – this term captures the idea that judges, through their immunity from political pressure, can offer their imprimatur of legitimacy on the action of agencies that have a "hybrid and problematic status in our constitutional system."[44]

In Fallon's view, "adequately searching appellate review" of a federal court action by a non-Article III tribunal sufficiently reconciles

[43] Fallon, *supra* note 33, at 933.
[44] *Id.* at 937–42.

these values and is reasonably consistent with the constitutional text, Framers' intent, precedent, and underlying purposes of Article III.

Based on this balance of values, Fallon argues that the necessity and scope of "adequately searching appellate review" turn on the type of determination. With respect to pure questions of constitutional law, appellate review theory requires de novo review by Article III Courts.[45] According to Fallon, Article III review is necessary for two reasons: to protect separation-of-powers principles; and to ensure fairness to individual litigants, particularly where their constitutional rights are at stake.[46] Fallon explains that the review should be de novo in order to check against the separation-of-powers issues that are implicated when "another agency of government has strayed beyond constitutional limits."[47]

With respect to pure questions of nonconstitutional law, Fallon argues that appellate review theory also demands de novo review.[48] Fallon justifies both the necessity and scope of this review in terms of a "needed [check] against arbitrariness and self-aggrandizement by legislative courts and especially by administrative agencies."[49] In Fallon's view, those agencies are not electorally accountable or insulated from political pressures, but are susceptible to capture by "powerful private groups," and "may also have a bureaucratic tendency to expand their own power."[50]

Finally, with respect to findings of fact, Fallon distinguishes between two kinds of facts. Regarding ordinary findings of fact, Fallon does not believe that review is necessary, as such findings by a non-Article III tribunal implicate neither separation of powers nor fairness concerns.[51] However, with respect to questions of constitutional or jurisdictional fact, Fallon submits that Article III courts should have the power, though not the obligation, to review another tribunal's determination.[52] In Fallon's view, this approach ensures that Article III courts are able

[45] *Id.* at 976.
[46] *Id.* at 975–76.
[47] *Id.* at 976.
[48] *Id.* at 977–78.
[49] *Id.*
[50] *Id.* at 978.
[51] *Id.* at 989.
[52] *Id.* at 990.

to correct suspect determinations while avoiding "costly relitigation in the vast run of cases."[53]

Compared with literalism and the Story/Amar account, appellate review theory best squares with the extant precedent, prompting James Pfander to note that it has "fared best" among the modern accounts of Article III.[54] In each of the cases where the Court has rejected an Article III challenge, the judicial review scheme preserved partial or full opportunity for judicial review of the non-Article III decision maker's legal conclusions. For example, under various schemes that the Court has reviewed, the non-Article III decision maker's legal conclusions were subject to de novo review.[55] In sum, appellate review theory offers the best available tool for assessing the compatibility of Article III with a dispute resolution scheme.

Before delving further into appellate review theory, it is worth pausing to consider an obvious question. Even accepting the two premises posited so far – (1) that arbitration presents an Article III problem, and (2) that waiver theory is inadequate to address this problem –why should we look to a theory developed in the context of administrative law to supply the framework for a more coherent theory to reconcile arbitration and Article III?

Two points answer this question and justify the bridge between administrative law and arbitration. The first is to recognize, as Lon Fuller did nearly a half-century ago, that arbitration and administrative adjudication are simply different "forms" of dispute resolution.[56] That is to say, they lie along the same spectrum, just at different points. The second is to recognize that arbitration, like administrative adjudication, implicates the structural concerns discussed earlier. To be clear, the structural concerns may not be the same, but they both implicate the diminution of judicial power. To the extent that appellate review theory

[53] *Id.*

[54] Pfander, *supra* note 33, at 666.

[55] *See, e.g.*, CFTC v. Schor, 478 U.S. 833, 853 (1986); United States v. Raddatz, 447 U.S. 667, 673–74 (1980).

[56] *See* Fuller, *supra* note 4, at 354–56, 389. The parallels between the two systems do not end with the issue of judicial review. *See* Rebecca Hanner White, *Arbitration and the Administrative State*, 38 WAKE FOREST L. REV. 1283, 1323–26 (2003) (explaining that the two fields also share synergies over the extent to which courts should defer to the extrajudicial decision maker, whether an arbitrator or an agency).

seeks to set boundaries on the diminution of that power, it supplies at least a starting point for a theory (although as I later explain, arbitration sheds light on how that theory should be modified).

Despite his acceptance of the relevance of appellate review theory to arbitration, Fallon does not attempt to apply his theory in this particular context. His account does, however, offer two suggestions. Unfortunately, these suggestions are in substantial tension with each other and complicate an effort to analyze the constitutionality of arbitration in terms of appellate review theory.

First, Fallon suggests that the constitutionality of an arbitral scheme turns on the opportunity for federal courts to conduct de novo review of questions of law.[57] Under this standard, *Thomas v. Union Carbide Agricultural Prods. Co.*[58] was wrongly decided. In Fallon's view, the core defect of the scheme in *Thomas* was that:

> Decisions of federal law were committed to an arbitrator, whose rulings were subject to judicial review only for fraud or misconduct. In the absence of judicial review, investiture of authority to decide questions of law in a non-article [sic] III federal decisionmaker encroaches too deeply on the fairness and separation-of-powers values that article [sic] III embodies.[59]

The second suggestion in Fallon's analysis is that the constitutionality of arbitration turns on whether the parties have validly waived their entitlement to an Article III tribunal. This suggestion may be inferred from Fallon's analysis of *Schor*:

> [*Schor*] thus suggests a question – which would have been presented directly had full appellate review not been provided – about the legitimacy and effectiveness of waivers of article [sic] III rights in the absence of appellate review. As long as the waiver is not procured by any form of illegitimate pressure, waiver ought to be held permissible within an appellate review theory. Waiver substantially alleviates any concern of unfairness to the parties. Moreover, when both parties are satisfied that the adjudicatory scheme treats them fairly, there is substantial assurance that the agency is not

[57] Fallon, *supra* note 33, at 976.
[58] 473 U.S. 568 (1985).
[59] Fallon, *supra* note 33, at 991.

generally behaving arbitrarily or otherwise offending separation-of-powers values.[60]

Unfortunately, Fallon's two suggestions offer conflicting guidance on the constitutionality of arbitration. Had his analysis ended with his discussion of *Thomas*, the implications of his theory would have been quite clear, but also quite fatal for arbitration. Just like the scheme in *Thomas*, federal courts are precluded from conducting de novo review of the arbitrator's legal conclusions. Instead, at most, federal courts review arbitral awards only for manifest disregard of the law – a highly deferential standard on which few awards have been set aside.[61] Moreover, although the manifest disregard doctrine appeared entrenched in domestic U.S. law, the Supreme Court's recent decision in *Hall Street Associates L.L.C. v. Mattel, Inc.* cast the viability of the defense into serious question.[62] While the Supreme Court ultimately left the issue unresolved, it is difficult to reconcile the manifest disregard doctrine with the Supreme Court's holding that the FAA's statutory grounds for vacatur are exclusive.[63] Since *Hall Street*, there has been a splintering in the circuit courts regarding whether the manifest disregard doctrine is still viable, and among the circuits that answer in the affirmative, there is another split regarding whether it survives as a statutory or nonstatutory ground for review.[64]

By contrast, Fallon's second suggestion potentially salvages arbitration in many contexts. So long as the parties to an arbitration, like the parties in *Schor*, voluntarily submit their dispute to a non-Article III decision maker, the separation-of- powers concerns diminish. As noted in Part I.A, most – but not all – arbitrations are voluntary. So, subject

60 *Id.* at 991–92.

61 *See* Norman S. Poser, *Judicial Review of Arbitral Awards: Manifest Disregard of the Law*, 64 Brook. L. Rev. 471, 506 (1998) ("Consequently, although most circuit courts have adopted 'manifest disregard of the law' as a non-statutory ground for vacating or modifying an award, until recently there have been few cases in which a court has set aside an arbitral award on this ground."); Noah Rubins, *"Manifest Disregard of the Law" and Vacatur of Arbitral Awards in the United States*, 12 Am. Rev. Int'l Arb. 363, 366 (2001) (describing this doctrine as "the most widely-recognized extra-statutory ground upon which courts can set aside arbitration awards under U.S. federal law").

62 552 U.S. 576 (2008); Born, *supra* note 12, at 2640.

63 Born, *supra* note 12, at 2640–41.

64 MyLinda K. Sims & Richard A. Bales, *Much Ado about Nothing: The Future of Manifest Disregard after* Hall Street, 62 S.C. L. Rev. 407, 424 (2010).

to the exceptions discussed therein, and provided that the undertaking is truly "voluntary," arbitration presents no Article III problem.

How does one reconcile the seemingly conflicting inferences in Fallon's analysis? In my view, the flaw lies in the underdeveloped second premise – the notion that consent to a non-Article III dispute addresses the separation-of-powers problem and relieves the need for "adequately searching appellate review."

Why is this last aspect of Fallon's appellate review theory weak? First, it is inconsistent with his account of *Thomas*. One could equally say that the pesticide applicants in *Thomas* voluntarily participated in the FIFRA arbitration scheme when they chose to file the pesticide application. Under the argument inferable from Fallon's *Schor* analysis, the voluntary activity should have eliminated any Article III problem (absent any undue pressure, and there was no evidence of such pressure in *Thomas*). How, then, can Fallon conclude that *Thomas* was wrongly decided? Either his analysis of *Thomas* or his waiver argument is flawed; both cannot coexist in the theory.

More fundamentally, though, Fallon does not explain why waiver of the right to an Article III forum adequately addresses separation-of-powers concerns. As explained previously, such concerns can arise even in cases of waiver. By setting the standards of review narrowly, Congress is curtailing the power of federal courts, despite the initial voluntary undertaking by the parties.

A more extreme example proves the flaw in Fallon's argument. Suppose that the scheme in *Schor* had provided for no federal review of the CFTC's decision – essentially making the CFTC's ruling on Conticommodity's counterclaim final and unreviewable.[65] If Fallon were correct, then any separation-of-powers concerns would drop out so long as Conticommodity and Schor had voluntarily opted into that system. Yet under these circumstances, Congress is at least diminishing the power of the lower federal courts by stripping them of the ability to review a claim that otherwise might fall within their jurisdiction. Even the *Schor* Court might not tolerate such a result because it would be analogous (though, admittedly, not identical) to the "phalanx of

[65] Such a law is more than fanciful. Some countries, such as Belgium, have adopted arbitration laws that bar any judicial review. Code Judiciaire [C.Jud.] art. 1704(1) (Belg.).

non-Article III tribunals equipped to handle the entire business of the Article III courts without any Article III supervision or control and without evidence of valid and specific legislative necessities."[66] Limited federal review presents the same quality-of-diminution problems, although perhaps not as extremely as in this example. It shows, nonetheless, that separation-of-powers problems can exist even in a system into which parties have opted.

Thus, despite its significant contributions to scholarship on Article III, Fallon's appellate review theory does not provide a completely workable model for testing the constitutionality of arbitration. At least some refinements of the theory are necessary to determine the relevance (if any) of consent to the analysis and whether there are other unique features of arbitration that might warrant modification of the meaning of "adequately searching appellate review."[67]

Fallon himself plants the seeds for such a refinement. When he opted for a single, unbending set of rules governing Article III review, regardless of the underlying circumstances, Fallon rejected an alternative approach that tailors the constitutionally required degree of Article III review to the particular claim. He concedes that such an approach would be consistent with appellate review theory:

> An alternative mode of analysis, which would be consistent with the principal assumptions of [appellate review] theory, would answer questions about the necessity and requisite scope of judicial review only after weighing article [sic] III values against competing governmental interests on a case-by-case basis.[68]

This more nimble approach has two advantages over Fallon's uniform standard. First, it reflects the fact that different claims and different dispute resolution schemes will involve different sets of values. Take, for example, sovereign immunity – one of the previously noted values central to appellate review theory. In some arbitrations, such as commercial ones between purely private companies, those considerations drop out. In others, such as arbitrations under NAFTA or bilateral investment treaties ("BITs"), those considerations play a much

66 CFTC v. Schor, 478 U.S. 833, 855 (1986).
67 Fallon, *supra* note 33, at 918.
68 *Id.* at 975.

more prominent role. Varying the constitutionally required standard of review with the presence or absence of a factor such as sovereign immunity would better calibrate the constitutional rules to the actual values at stake in a particular case. Second, a more nuanced standard of review also offers better hope of harmonizing the existing case law. By contrast, Fallon's original theory – once one accepts the invalidity of his argument regarding consent – would be fatal to the constitutionality of most arbitral schemes.

Fallon rejected this approach principally on the ground that "a prescription of *ad hoc* balancing offers too little guidance about how balances ought to be struck."[69] His choice thus elevates clarity and predictability over other values that might have supported the more nuanced standard described earlier.

Fallon's choice of the categorical rule over the balancing test is a familiar one in the annals of jurisprudence.[70] In brief, "rules" offer the advantage of clarity but often come at the cost of rigidity. For example, if a rule provides "no entry into the park after 10 P.M.," it provides clarity, yet it may prevent desirable outcomes (such as an overnight camping trip in the park). By contrast, multifactor balancing tests offer the advantage of adaptability but often are vague. For example, if a rule provides "drive as fast as the circumstances demand," few people will be able to discern the appropriate speed limit, but the rule is nimble enough to accommodate both the daily commuter and the man racing to the hospital while his wife is in labor. The lesson from this simple debate – and one that Fallon inexplicably overlooks – is the need to craft a rule with sufficient clarity to permit its easy application but also with sufficient flexibility to permit its adaptation to different circumstances.

In this context, appellate review theory does not force one to choose between a rigid bright-line rule (as Fallon does) and a completely amorphous ad hoc balancing test (the only other choice Fallon sees). Rather, appellate review theory provides a middle ground – one that

69 *Id.*

70 *See* Louis Kaplow, *Rules versus Standards: An Economic Analysis*, 42 DUKE L.J. 557, 621–23 (1992) (proposing proper relative weights for "rules" and "standards"); Richard H. McAdams, *The Expressive Power of Adjudication*, 2005 U. ILL. L. REV. 1043, 1092 & n.159.

remains true to its origins, is sufficiently clear as to capture the benefits of Fallon's original set of rules, and is also nuanced enough to reflect the distinct values underpinning a particular dispute resolution regime.

How exactly, then, would such a system operate? Recall that appellate review theory is rooted in two sets of values: one underpinning the benefits of Article III courts and the other underpinning the benefits of non-Article III tribunals. Thus, to determine how such a system would operate, it becomes necessary to revisit Fallon's value balance and to determine how, in the particular context of arbitration, those values translate.

In certain respects, Fallon's theory translates well. Begin with the values supporting the use of non-Article III tribunals:

1. Expertise – arbitration potentially offers the specialized expertise that arbitrators can bring to the dispute.[71]
2. Governmental Functions – to the extent that arbitration involves purely private disputes, concerns about efficient government operation drop out; by contrast, to the extent that arbitration involves public disputes (such as NAFTA claims), this consideration is more salient.
3. Flexibility – arbitration offers greater flexibility than an Article III forum in adapting a scheme of administration and adjudication. Parties generally are free to tailor the procedures of the arbitration to their needs.[72]

[71] Bruce L. Bensen, *An Exploration of the Impact of Modern Arbitration Statutes on the Development of Arbitration in the United States*, 11 J.L. ECON. & ORG. 479, 482 (1995) (noting that expert arbitrators were a widely perceived benefit of arbitration over litigation); Terry A. Bethel, *Wrongful Discharge: Litigation or Arbitration?*, 1993 J. DISP. RESOL. 289, 298 ("Perhaps the most heralded advantage of arbitration over ordinary litigation is the special competence of the arbitrator."); Edward Brunet, *Replacing Folklore Arbitration with a Contract Model of Arbitration*, 74 TUL. L. REV. 39, 43 (1999) (noting that expertise of arbitrators historically has been regarded as a benefit to arbitration); BORN, *supra* note 12.

[72] On the procedural flexibility of arbitration, see Stefano E. Cirielli, *Arbitration, Financial Markets and Banking Disputes*, 14 AM. REV. INT'L ARB. 243, 248 (2003) ("One of the major advantages of arbitration, in fact, is that the parties can agree to numerous substantive and procedural aspects, and are entitled to choose an informal and flexible process, which can be specially adapted to fit their dispute."); Thomas B. Metzloff, *The Unrealized Potential of Malpractice Arbitration*, 31 WAKE FOREST L. REV. 203, 208

4. Fairness – whether arbitration produces fairer results is a hotly disputed proposition. As explained in greater detail in Chapter 5, a long line of literature criticizes arbitration precisely on the ground that its unfair procedures are biased in favor of the party with the stronger bargaining position.[73] More recent empirical evidence, however, casts doubt on these criticisms.[74]
5. Sovereign Immunity – as with governmental functions, the salience of this factor turns on the claim. Purely private claims do not implicate sovereign immunity; by contrast, public ones – whether under NAFTA or BITs – do implicate sovereign immunity concerns (whether of the United States, in the case of NAFTA, or a foreign sovereign, in the case of BITs).

(1996); Steven C. Nelson, *Alternatives to Litigation of International Disputes*, 23 INT'L LAW. 187, 197–98 (1989). BORN, *supra* note 12.

[73] *See, e.g.*, Mark E. Budnitz, *Arbitration of Disputes between Consumers and Financial Institutions: A Threat to Consumer Protection*, 10 OHIO ST. J. DISP. RESOL. 267 (1995); Thomas E. Carbonneau, *Arbitral Justice: The Demise of Due Process in American Law*, 70 TUL. L. REV. 1945 (1996); Robert A. Gorman, *The Gilmer Decision and the Private Arbitration of Public-Law Disputes*, 1995 U. ILL. L. REV. 635. Michael G. McGuinness & Adam J. Karr, *California's "Unique" Approach to Arbitration: Why This Road Less Traveled Will Make All the Difference on the Issue of Preemption under the Federal Arbitration Act*, 2005 J. DISP. RESOL. 61, 84–92 (2005); Hiro N. Aragaki, *Arbitration's Suspect Status*, 159 U. PA. L. REV. 1233, 1262 (2011).

[74] *See* U.S. Gen. Accounting Office, Report to Congressional Requesters (1992), *reprinted in* SECURITIES ARBITRATION: HOW INVESTORS FARE, IN SECURITIES ARBITRATION 1992, at 79 (PLI Corp. Law & Practice, Course Handbook Series No. B4–7006), WL 781 PLI/Corp 19, 79 (finding no pro-industry bias in the context of securities arbitration in industry-sponsored fora); Elizabeth Hill, *AAA Employment Arbitration: A Fair Forum at a Low Cost*, 58 DISP. RESOL. J. 9 (2003) (providing statistical analysis of AAA employment arbitrations indicating that they are not systematically biased in favor of the employer as repeat player); Gary Tidwell et al., Party Evaluation of Arbitrators: An Analysis of Data Collected from NASD Regulation Arbitrations (Aug. 5, 1999) (unpublished manuscript, presented at the National Meeting of the Academy of Legal Studies in Business, on file with author) (finding that parties in NASD arbitrations believe the fora and arbitrators are fair and unbiased); *see also* Report of the Arbitration Policy Task Force to the Board of Governors of the National Association of Securities Dealers, Inc., reprinted in [1995–1996 Transfer Binder] FED. SEC. L. REP. (CCH) ¶ 85,735 (1996) (finding securities arbitration generally "to be a relatively efficient, fair, and less costly forum for resolution of disputes involving public investors, member firms, and firm employees"). Peter B. Rutledge, *Whither Arbitration?*, 6 GEO. J.L. & PUB. POL'Y 549, 551 (2008); Alan S. Kaplinsky & Mark J. Levin, *Consumer Arbitration: If the FAA "Ain't Broke," Don't Fix It*, 63 BUS. LAW. 907, 910 (2008). Searle Civil Justice Institute, Consumer Arbitration before the American Arbitration Association (2009), *available at* http://www.law.northwestern.edu/jep/symposia/documents/JEP_CJ_2009 Drahozal2.pdf.

Now balance these values against the ones underpinning the need for Article III tribunals:

1. Separation of Powers – as discussed previously, arbitration could create separation-of-powers problems (although the problem technically is a diminution problem, as opposed to an encroachment issue present in the Article I court situation). Specifically, Congress diminishes the power of the Article III courts by vesting their decision-making power in another non-Article III institution and requiring federal courts to effectuate those decisions, subject to very limited grounds for review.
2. Fairness – this is the flip side of the fairness factor presented earlier. Depending on the state of the empirical research, arbitration, in contrast to federal litigation, might run a greater risk of unfairness to litigants. This is the case particularly in areas where the litigants are of unequal bargaining positions, and, consequently, the stronger party might prefer a forum or set of rules systematically biased in its favor.
3. Judicial Integrity – arbitration does not present a "judicial integrity" problem, as Fallon has conceptualized it, for arbitrators, unlike administrative agencies, do not have a "hybrid and problematic status in our constitutional system."

Thus, an analysis of the values underpinning appellate review theory reveals that they translate well, but that the balance is not the same as that in Fallon's model. Specifically, at least two values justifying the need for non-Article III tribunals – government function and sovereign immunity– drop out in private commercial arbitration (although remaining present in trade or investment arbitration involving governments). On the other side of the scale, one of the values justifying the need for Article III tribunals – judicial integrity – is not as salient, because of the absence of constitutionally problematic administrative agencies. The lesson from this analysis is that the standard for "adequately searching appellate review" may be less taxing in arbitrations involving sovereigns than in arbitrations between purely private parties.

The solution, then, is to identify a limited number of factors based on which the constitutionally required standard of review may vary.

These factors should be robust enough to capture the partially competing values underpinning arbitration and Article III. At the same time, they should be defined sufficiently to avoid Fallon's fear of lapsing into a vague and unpredictable "totality of the circumstances" test. Although my claim here is tentative, I believe that the two critical values are the voluntariness of the undertaking and the presence (or absence) of the sovereign in the dispute.

Voluntariness operates as a proxy for fairness. As previously noted, fairness was one of the critical values in Fallon's scheme justifying the role for Article III courts. In the administrative cases that concerned Fallon, the parties often will not have opted into the system; instead, a federal statute typically directs them there. By contrast, in a voluntary arbitration (such as a private commercial one), the parties will have chosen the preferred forum for resolving their dispute. As a theoretical matter, that choice signals a mutual faith by both parties, before any dispute has arisen, that the dispute resolution mechanism will reach a fair result. Thus, fairness concerns diminish in a voluntary arbitration and, consequently, so too does the need for plenary Article III review. Doctrines in a variety of contexts, such as forum selection agreements, choice-of-law clauses, and consent to jurisdiction demonstrate a judicial solicitude for such private choices. By contrast, in a truly involuntary arbitration, such as the BIT arbitrations, the fairness concerns remain dominant and, thus, so too does the need for Article III review.[75]

The sovereign immunity doctrine recognizes the separation-of-powers values. As noted above, where a sovereign is a party to the dispute, the law accords great deference to the political branches to control judicial jurisdiction. Absent consent, the sovereign cannot be sued in its own forum.[76] Foreign sovereigns' immunity likewise has remained firmly within the control of the legislative branch – at least in recent years.[77] Thus, in any case involving a sovereign, the political branches could cut off judicial jurisdiction almost entirely (whether through declining to waive immunity or narrowing the scope of

[75] *See* text accompanying note 117.

[76] United States v. Sherwood, 312 U.S. 584, 586 (1941).

[77] BORN & RUTLEDGE, *supra* note 13, at 231–35.

jurisdiction over foreign sovereigns). That greater power to cut off jurisdiction also implies a lesser power to regulate the jurisdiction. Consequently, Article III values are, in such cases, relatively minimal.[78]

One may legitimately question whether these are the only values by which the scope of review should vary. Specifically, should the scope of review also depend on whether the case is an international one? This argument is not without foundation, and at least two starting points are possible. One could trace back to cases such as *Dames & Moore v. Regan.*[79] Under this line of argument, treaties will govern most international arbitration cases; as treaties require cooperation between the executive and legislative branches, courts should be less inclined to interfere. The other starting point could follow the line of cases suggesting the need for judicial deference in matters of foreign affairs or foreign commerce.[80] Whichever starting point is chosen, both arguments yield the same conclusion: that the scope of constitutionally required judicial review should be lower in international cases (and conversely should be greater in purely domestic cases).

Such a course might have been possible at one time. Particularly following its decision in *Scherk v. Alberto-Culver, Inc.*,[81] the Court plausibly could have maintained a distinction between international

[78] This explicit consideration of the sovereign's presence in the litigation also helps square the modified appellate review theory with the public rights doctrine (at least in its original form). As discussed above, beginning with *Murray's Lessee v. Hoboken Land & Improvement Co.*, 59 U.S. 272 (1855), the public rights doctrine justified restrictions on the jurisdiction of the Article III courts in cases where the sovereign was a party. *Thomas v. Union Carbide Agricultural Products Co.* broke with this tradition by classifying certain claims as "public rights" even though they arose between two private parties. 473 U.S. 568, 589 (1985). As Fallon himself admits, *Thomas* remains a dubious precedent under appellate review theory and so, too, does it under the modified form offered here. With the exception of *Thomas*, the other public rights cases fit comfortably within my model.

Of course, the sovereign immunity argument can be turned on its head. Arguably, the need for judicial oversight may be at its zenith precisely when the sovereign is a party in the case. In such cases, judicial oversight is necessary as a check on governmental overreaching and to ensure neutral application of relevant legal principles. Such a position, although principled, would require overruling the public rights cases tracing all the way back to *Murray's Lessee*. I am grateful to Michael Wells for his insights on this point.

[79] 453 U.S. 654 (1981).

[80] United States v. Curtiss-Wright Export Corp., 299 U.S. 304, 320 (1936); Made in the USA Foundation v. United States, 242 F.3d 1300, 1311 (11th Circ. 2001).

[81] 417 U.S. 506 (1974).

and domestic arbitration cases. Nonetheless, by the mid-1980s, any attempt to preserve a doctrinal distinction between domestic and international cases was lost. With cases such as *Rodriguez de Quijas v. Shearson/American Express, Inc.*, the Court put domestic cases on an equal footing with international ones as a matter of doctrine.[82] Since that time, it has shown no solicitude toward efforts to separate the two types of cases. Thus, although this argument has great theoretical appeal, I ultimately reject it because it undermines the theory's explanatory value.

The upshot of this modified appellate review theory is to vary the degree of constitutionally required review along two axes. At one extreme lie involuntary private arbitrations. In those circumstances, the need for Article III review is at its zenith. At the other extreme are voluntary arbitrations involving the sovereign. In those circumstances, the need for Article III review is at its nadir. The intermediate cases are voluntary private arbitrations and involuntary sovereign arbitrations.

How does this translate onto the different types of issues under review? With respect to questions of constitutional law, de novo review still should be required. As to the necessity of review, arbitration does not affect Fallon's basic analysis: Article III review of constitutional questions is necessary, both to promote separation-of- powers principles and to provide essential fairness to individual litigants when their constitutional rights are at stake.[83] As to the scope of review, the analysis admittedly does not map perfectly. Fallon justifies de novo review of constitutional questions on the ground that "separation of powers values are deeply implicated" if "another agency of government has strayed beyond constitutional limits." Arbitration does not present a situation where an agency of government can act ultra vires. Nonetheless, anything less than plenary review could implicate separation-of-powers concerns animating Fallon's standard. If Congress could strip Article III courts of their power to review an arbitrator's findings on questions of constitutional law, such a regime would undermine separation-of-powers principles just as much as the aggrandizement of a federal

[82] 490 U.S. 477 (1989).

[83] Fallon, *supra* note 33, at 975–76.

agency's power. Requiring plenary review of constitutional questions eliminates that concern.

As to questions of law, translating the modified appellate review theory is a challenge. In some respects, the reasons justifying plenary review of legal questions in cases of Article I courts or administrative agencies do not apply in the context of arbitration. For example, arbitrators lack the capacity to expand their own power. Unlike bureaucrats, arbitrators are not necessarily repeat players in a dispute settlement procedure. Their decisions lack any precedential force that might be used to justify a more expansive conception of their power in a later case. Nor are arbitrators subject to political pressure from another branch of government, as might be the case with respect to administrative agencies or legislative courts.

At the same time, in at least three respects, arbitrators present at least some of the dangers that led Fallon to conclude that appellate review theory required Article III review of nonconstitutional legal questions. First, just like agencies, arbitrators can be arbitrary. They can get the law wrong; they also can render "compromise" awards that leave both parties relatively satisfied but, as a principled matter, lack a legal basis. Second, although individual arbitrators may lack the capacity for bureaucratic self-aggrandizement, arbitration as an institution retains that capacity. Arbitrators and arbitral institutions have a direct financial interest in being able to exercise jurisdiction over a matter – one that may give them an incentive to take an expansive notion of their jurisdiction in the run of cases.[84] Third, arbitration presents at least some risk of capture by powerful political entities, albeit in a manner different from the capture at play in the bureaucratic setting. As I have explained elsewhere, arbitrators, unlike bureaucrats or judges, often are nominated by parties to resolve a dispute, and, critically, their compensation is tied to their service.[85] In theory, this nomination process gives the arbitrators a financial incentive to decide a case in favor of the player most likely to give the arbitrator repeated

[84] Courts have some ability to control this tendency toward expansion through judicial review of the arbitrator's jurisdiction, either at the pre-arbitration stage or at the enforcement stage. First Options of Chi., Inc. v. Kaplan, 514 U.S. 938, 942–47 (1995).

[85] Peter B. Rutledge, *Toward a Contractual Theory of Arbitral Immunity*, 39 GA. L. REV. 151 (2004).

business, thereby skewing the result in favor of the more powerful party.

Thus, modified appellate review theory justifies at least some degree of Article III review of an arbitrator's legal determinations, although perhaps not as exacting as that required in Fallon's original model. Some of the values that justify plenary review in the agency or legislative court context – such as political pressure or aggrandizement – drop out here. Others – such as arbitrariness, expansive conceptions of jurisdiction, or capture – remain relevant in the context of arbitration.

Deference by Article III courts to determinations of federal law made by other non-Article III entities is a familiar concept.[86] For example, in administrative law, various doctrines allow a federal court to defer to an agency interpretation of an ambiguous statute.[87] In criminal procedure, federal courts ordinarily defer to state courts' reasonable interpretations of federal constitutional questions.[88] At the same time, both areas of the law grant federal courts some latitude to disregard the prior decision maker's "unreasonable" determinations. To be sure, the analogies here are not exact – the former involves deference to another branch of government (thereby assuring some degree of political accountability), whereas the latter involves deference to a different sovereign's courts (who occupy a different position than arbitrators). Nonetheless, doctrines such as these illustrate that our constitutional scheme can tolerate a limited degree of deference by Article III courts to another entity's construction of federal law when some underlying policy reason justifies that deference. Much as the expertise of an administrative agency or federalism and finality may justify some

[86] I am especially grateful to Laura Appleman for helping me tease out this argument. *See also* White, *supra* note 56 (exploring judicial deference to adjudication).

[87] *See, e.g.*, United States v. Mead Corp., 533 U.S. 218 (2001) (discussing degrees of judicial deference to agency statutory interpretations); Chevron U.S.A., Inc. v. Natural Res. Def. Council, Inc., 467 U.S. 837 (1984); Skidmore v. Swift & Co., 323 U.S. 134 (1944).

[88] Brian M. Hofstadt, *The Deconstruction and Reconstruction of Habeas*, 78 S. CAL. L. REV. 1125, 1168 (2005). Justin F. Marceau, *Un-Incorporating the Bill of Rights: The Tension between the Fourteenth Amendment and the Federalism Concerns That Underlie Modern Criminal Procedure Reforms*, 98 J. CRIM. L. & CRIMINOLOGY 1231, 1281 n. 260 (2008) (referencing a statutory mandate that in certain circumstances, federal courts "must defer to state court decisions that apply federal law incorrectly").

deference in these contexts, so too can the promotion of arbitration support it.

Finally, as to factual review, arbitration does not alter Fallon's analysis, but instead comports quite comfortably with it. Factual findings by arbitrators, such as those of administrative agencies or legislative courts, present no particular threat to either separation-of-powers values or fundamental fairness. As to the special categories of facts warranting separate treatment – constitutional or jurisdictional – a discretionary approach ideally balances the need to correct suspect findings against the desire to avoid costly relitigation of issues.

At this point, it is worth addressing how modified appellate review theory differs from the present doctrine. How much does the "voluntariness" prong differ from *Schor*'s waiver analysis? How much does the presence of the sovereign in the dispute differ from the nonwaivable aspects of Article III noted in *Schor*? The synergies with existing doctrine are unsurprising because, as already noted, one of the main benefits of appellate review theory (whether in its original or modified form) is that it remains in harmony with existing doctrine. Harmony, though, is not the same as duplication, and in at least three critical respects, modified appellate review theory differs from the current landscape.

First, modified appellate review theory uses an entirely different metric from *Schor*. Whereas *Schor* uses waiver categorically – that is to say, a party waives its right to an Article III forum – modified appellate review theory uses the concept of voluntariness instrumentally. In other words, although a party's voluntary submission to an arbitral scheme may affect the degree of constitutionally required review, it does not affect the need for it. By contrast, as noted earlier, some courts relying on *Schor* to justify the constitutionality of arbitration have ended the argument with the waiver analysis.

Second, the structural analysis under modified appellate review theory differs from the "nonwaivable" aspect of *Schor*. With respect to this nonwaivable component of Article III, the Court evaluates a dispute resolution scheme's constitutionality using a multifactor balancing test. By contrast, modified appellate review theory tests the constitutionality of a scheme by reference to a single metric – the degree of Article III review – and calibrates the necessary degree of review along the axes of voluntariness and sovereign immunity.

Third, modified appellate review theory transforms the public rights doctrine. Some courts have relied on this doctrine to uphold certain arbitral schemes, and the Canadian government relied on it to defend NAFTA's arbitral scheme in *Coalition for Fair Lumber Exports*.[89] Traditionally, public rights were those claims where the government was a party or where the government had an actual interest in the dispute.[90] By contrast, claims exclusively between private individuals, even when the claims were of statutory creation, were ones of private right.[91] *Thomas* broke with that tradition when it classified certain claims as potentially public rights even where the claim arose between two private parties. Modified appellate review theory rejects this

[89] Brief of Respondents-Intervenors in *Coalition for Fair Lumber Imports Executive Committee v. United States*, No. 05-1366, at 27–33.

[90] *See* Granfinanciera, S.A. v. Nordberg, 492 U.S. 33, 65 (1989) (Scalia, J., concurring in part and concurring in the judgment) ("In my view a matter of public rights, whose adjudication Congress may assign to tribunals lacking the essential characteristics of Article III courts, must at a minimum arise between the government and others." (citation and internal quotations omitted)). For example, *Murray's Lessee v. Hoboken Land & Improvement Co.*, the case that spawned the public rights doctrine, concerned the government's effort to collect a debt owed by one of its customs agents. 59 U.S. 272, 275 (1855). *Ex Parte Bakelite Corp.* concerned a claim between the government and a private individual over a customs assessment imposed by the government. 279 U.S. 438, 447 (1929). In both cases, the Court held that the rights were "public rights." Bakelite, 279 U.S. at 452; *Murray's Lessee*, 59 U.S. 283–85. *Crowell v. Benson* sought to provide a non-exhaustive list of examples, including matters found in connection with the congressional power "as to interstate and foreign commerce, taxation, immigration, the public lands, public health, facilities of the post office, pensions and payments to veterans." 285 U.S. 22, 51 (1932). Perhaps the clearest statement came from the plurality in *Northern Pipeline Construction Co. v. Marathon Pipe Line Co.*: "[A] matter of public rights must at a minimum arise 'between the government and others.'" 458 U.S. 50, 71 (1982) (plurality opinion).

[91] For example, the Court in *Crowell* termed a worker's compensation claim by a longshoreman against his employer a private right, even though federal statutory law created that claim. 285 U.S. 22, 51. The plurality in *Northern Pipeline* classified a state law breach-of-contract claim as a private right, even where that claim was wrapped up in a governmentally created bankruptcy system for restructuring debtor–creditor relations. 458 U.S. 50, 71. Finally, the Court in *Granfinanciera* classified a bankruptcy trustee's right to recover for a fraudulent conveyance a "private right," even where the trustee's power to maintain the action derives from federally created bankruptcy law. 492 U.S. 33, 55–56. Again, the *Northern Pipeline* plurality stated the tradition clearly: "'The liability of one individual to another under the law as defined' is a matter of private rights." 458 U.S. 50, 69–70 (quoting *Crowell*, 285 U.S. 22, 51).

expansion of the public rights doctrine in *Thomas*. Instead, its emphasis on the presence or absence of a sovereign in the dispute more closely approximates the classic formulation of the public rights doctrine in cases such as *Murray's Lessee* and *Crowell*.

In sum, appellate review theory provides the most promising basis for reconciling the tension between Article III and arbitration. Such a theory vindicates the textual, historical, and policy concerns underpinning Article III while doing minimal violence to the existing precedent. The precise degree of review by an Article III court should not be a rigid, uniform standard, as the original expositor of appellate review theory proposed. Instead, it should reflect the distinct mix of values underpinning the dispute resolution system – a methodology that Fallon acknowledges is consistent with the underlying spirit of appellate review theory, but that he ultimately dismissed for debatable reasons. Once that aspect of Fallon's analysis is altered, the proper standard of review should account for both the voluntary nature of most arbitrations and the special legal status of an award under a judicial system. In the final part of this chapter, I sketch out how modified appellate review theory would apply to various arbitral schemes. Consistent with the book's overall scheme, I focus on private commercial arbitration but also consider trade and investment arbitration.

1. Private Commercial Arbitration

Commercial arbitration awards are subject to judicial review under one of two main frameworks. First, in some cases of confirmation (reducing a foreign or nondomestic award rendered in the United States to judgment) and enforcement (reducing an award rendered abroad to judgment), a multilateral treaty – typically the New York Convention – will set forth the standard of review.[92] Roughly speaking,

[92] Less frequently, other conventions may apply. These include the Inter-American Convention on International Commercial Arbitration (Panama Convention), *opened for signature* Jan. 30, 1975, 104 Stat. 448, 1438 U.N.T.S. 245 (governing awards in certain Latin American arbitrations) the Convention on the Settlement of Investment Disputes Between States and Nationals of Other States (Washington Convention, also known as the ICSID Convention), *opened for signature* Mar. 18, 1965, 17 U.S.T. 1270, 575 U.N.T.S. 159 (governing awards for certain investment arbitrations). The standards of judicial review under the Panama Convention are virtually identical to those under the

Article V of the New York Convention provides that an award may be denied recognition or enforcement where:

- The parties lacked capacity to enter it or the agreement was invalid.
- The losing party lacked adequate notice of the proceeding or an opportunity to be heard.
- The award concerns a matter beyond the parties' submission.
- The composition of the tribunal or the arbitral procedure deviated from the parties' agreement or, absent such agreement, the law of the arbitral forum.
- The award has been set aside.
- The dispute is non-arbitrable in the enforcement forum.
- The award violates the public policy of the enforcement forum.

Second, in cases of vacatur (setting aside an award rendered in the United States) and cases of confirmation and enforcement not falling under a treaty, the FAA sets forth the default framework for judicial review. Section 10 of the FAA provides as follows:

> [A district court] may make an order vacating the award upon the application of any party to the arbitration –
>
> 1. Where the award was procured by corruption, fraud or undue means;
> 2. Where there was evident partiality or corruption in the arbitrations, or either of them (sic);
> 3. Where the arbitrators were guilty of misconduct in refusing to postpone the hearing, upon sufficient cause shown, or in refusing to hear evidence pertinent and material to the controversy; or of any other misbehavior by which the rights of any party have been prejudiced;
> 4. Where the arbitrators exceeded their powers, or so imperfectly executed them that a mutual final and definite award upon the subject matter submitted was not made.[93]

New York Convention, so the analysis in the text applies equally in these specialized contexts.

93 9 U.S.C. § 10.

Neither Article V of the New York Convention nor Section 10 of the FAA expressly provides for any Article III review of the merits of the decision, whether on statutory or constitutional grounds.[94]

Despite the absence of any textual authorization for Article III review of legal questions, judicial decisions have partly filled the gap. Courts have constructed a doctrine that, at least arguably, attempts to mitigate this harsh conclusion. For several decades, the "manifest disregard of the law" doctrine has enabled federal courts to take a quick look at the merits of the award (even though that doctrine does not find any formal footing in the text of Section 10).[95] The formulations of the manifest disregard doctrine vary in slight terms, and its scope is not fully settled.[96] Under the generally accepted formulation of the doctrine, a federal court may vacate an award where the arbitrator was aware of the applicable law yet refused to apply it.[97] Putting to one side the legitimacy of the manifest disregard doctrine (a topic I have explored elsewhere),[98] the question then becomes whether the manifest disregard doctrine rescues the FAA from constitutional infirmity.

Although the issue is close, I ultimately conclude that ordinary private commercial arbitration survives Article III challenge under modified appellate review theory. Courts almost never review arbitral awards for factual errors, yet modified appellate review theory suggests that this does not present an Article III concern.[99] As to questions of constitutional law, the available review under the FAA and the New York Convention suffices. In some cases, courts can determine constitutional issues at the outset of the arbitration by ruling on a motion to

[94] BORN, *supra* note 12, at 81.

[95] Of course, manifest disregard need not be the standard governing the relationship between arbitration and the courts. Other systems use arbitrators more as referees or provide for de novo review of the arbitrator's decision. I am grateful to Roderick McDonald's response to my presentation at the McGill/University of Montreal matinee on this point.

[96] As I have explored elsewhere, a disagreement persists among the lower federal courts over whether the manifest disregard of the law doctrine is available in enforcement actions falling under the New York Convention. *See* Peter B. Rutledge, *On the Importance of Institutions – Review of Arbitral Awards for Legal Errors*, 19 J. Int'l Arb. 81 (2002).

[97] BORN, *supra* note 12, at 2641.

[98] Rutledge, *supra* note 96.

[99] BORN, *supra* note 12.

compel arbitration or stay litigation.[100] In other cases, courts can rule on constitutional issues when reviewing the arbitral award: several of the aforementioned standards under the New York Convention or the FAA incorporate constitutional norms. For example, both laws provide that an award can be denied enforcement (or vacated under the FAA) in cases where a party lacked proper notice of the arbitral proceedings. To evaluate these claims, courts applying these standards generally have imported due process norms.[101] Thus, under modified appellate review theory, the current regime provides Article III courts with sufficient oversight of constitutional questions.

The trickiest aspect of the analysis here is the limited role of Article III. This gap would be fatal to arbitration under the original conception of appellate review theory. Once one rejects consent as an escape hatch for the theory, federal courts are not conducting the de novo review of nonconstitutional questions that the theory requires. Nonetheless, under modified appellate review theory, the manifest disregard doctrine arguably supplies the necessary degree of federal appellate review. The voluntariness of the undertaking justifies a reduced role for federal courts. At the same time, the manifest disregard doctrine preserves a limited role for federal courts, thus vindicating the Article III values still present in an arbitration scheme.

Ironically, the origins of the manifest disregard doctrine strengthen this claim. The manifest disregard standard appears nowhere in the FAA (or, for that matter, in any other statute or treaty governing the enforcement of arbitral awards in the United States). Rather, it traces its origins entirely to the Supreme Court's decisions, almost as a type of federal common law governing the enforcement of awards.[102] This judicial pedigree affords a court greater flexibility to shape the doctrine's contours than if a statute constrained its interpretation. Although courts generally have been reluctant to vacate awards (or to decline enforcement) on this ground, some decisions involving federal

[100] *Id.*

[101] *Id.*

[102] *See* First Options of Chi., Inc. v. Kaplan, 514 U.S. 938, 942 (1995); Wilko v. Swan, 346 U.S. 427, 436–37 (1953) (holding that parties bound by arbitrator's decision were not in "manifest disregard" of the law), *overruled on other grounds by* Rodriguez de Quijas v. Shearson/Am. Express, Inc., 490 U.S. 477 (1989).

statutory claims have done so.[103] This jurisprudence suggests that the doctrine is malleable enough to vindicate the Article III values underpinning appellate review theory in this context. In this regard, it operates almost like a canon of constitutional avoidance to forestall inquiry into more nettlesome Article III questions.[104]

Although private commercial arbitration survives Article III challenge under the modified appellate review theory, the scheme in *Thomas* does not. Compared to the judicial review governing private commercial awards, judicial review under the FIFRA scheme in *Thomas* was more limited. FIFRA reserved absolutely no role for reviewing courts to evaluate the arbitrator's award, even where the arbitrator manifestly disregards the law. The total lack of judicial review over the merits of a dispute between two private parties cuts too deeply into the separation-of-powers values animating Article III review. Thus, like Fallon's original appellate review theory, the modified theory offered here would reject the holding in *Thomas*.

Modified appellate review theory also offers some insights into the debates about the enforceability of party-initiated efforts to modify the scope of judicial review contractually, a topic that the Supreme Court addressed in *Hall Street*.[105] In some cases, parties attempt to expand the grounds of judicial review (for example by providing that the arbitrator's factual findings shall be reviewed for clear error and the legal findings reviewed de novo).[106] Under the logic of the theory presented here, such clauses should be enforced, for they reinforce the separation-of-powers values justifying a role for the judiciary in reviewing an award. In this respect, *Hall Street* may have been wrongly decided.

In other cases, parties attempt to limit the grounds of judicial review (for example, by subjecting the award to review under state

103 *See, e.g.*, Patten v. Signator Ins. Agency, Inc., 441 F.3d 230, 237 (4th Cir. 2006) (vacating award in age discrimination case); Barclays Capital Inc., v. Shen, 857 N.Y.S.2d 873, 880 (Sup. Ct. 2008).

104 *See* Ashwander v. Tennessee Valley Authority, 297 U.S. 288, 345-48 (1936) (Brandeis, J., concurring).

105 Hall Street Assocs., L.L.C. v. Mattel, Inc., 552 U.S. 576, 582 n.2 (2008).

106 *See, e.g.*, Lapine Tech. Corp. v. Kyocera Corp., 130 F.3d 884, 889 (9th Cir. 1997), *overruled by* Kyocera Corp. v. Prudential-Bache Trade Servs., Inc., 341 F.3d 987 (9th Cir. 2003).

law grounds, which may be narrower than those under the FAA).[107] Modified appellate review theory suggests that these clauses should be unenforceable because they further erode the judiciary's residual role in policing awards before they are reduced to judgment.

The question is extremely close, but the manifest disregard doctrine, in my opinion, saves private commercial arbitration from constitutional defect. Its absence from the review scheme in *Thomas*, however, renders that scheme unconstitutional. Moreover, post-*Hall Street* jurisprudence has suffered from a lack of guidance from the Supreme Court regarding the status of the manifest disregard doctrine and its role in the constitutional order. Both the First and Fifth Circuits have held that the doctrine is null,[108] whereas several others have held that it still serves as a ground for appeal, although these circuits disagree whether it exists as a statutory or non-statutory ground for annulment.[109]

Although the Supreme Court has yet to confront this circuit split, its recent decision in *Stolt-Nielsen S.A. v. Animalfeeds International Corp.* raises another possible avenue of defense in place of the manifest disregard doctrine. There, the Court vacated the arbitration decision because the arbitrator had "exceeded [his] powers" under FAA §10(a)(4) when the panel "simply [] impose[d] its own view of sound policy regarding class arbitration."[110] This statutory ground for annulment would seem to be able to fill any gap the Supreme Court created by *Hall Street* when it placed the manifest disregard doctrine into open question. Although the Supreme Court cited its own decisions to support its broadening of §10(a)(4),[111] it has yet to be seen how the circuits will apply this rule, and if and to what extent it may serve as an alternative to the manifest disregard doctrine.

107 *See, e.g.*, Roadway Package Sys., Inc. v. Kayser, 257 F.3d 287, 293 (3d Cir. 2001).

108 Ramos-Santiago v. United Parcel Serv., 524 F.3d 120, 124 n.3 (1st Cir. 2008); Citigroup Global Mkts., Inc. v. Bacon, 562 F.3d 349, 354 (5th Cir. 2009).

109 Richard C. Reuben, *Personal Autonomy and Vacatur after* Hall Street, 113 PENN. ST. L. REV. 1103, 1145–46 (2009); Sims, *supra* note 64, at 425–26.

110 130 S. Ct. 1758, 1767–68 (2010).

111 Major League Baseball Players Ass'n v. Garvey, 532 U.S. 504, 509 (2001); Steelworkers v. Enterprise Wheel & Car Corp. 363, U.S. 593, 597 (1960).

2. NAFTA

Under Chapters 11 and 19 of NAFTA, the signatory countries agree to submit disputes over discriminatory treatment, expropriation, antidumping, and countervailing duties laws (following an initial agency determination) to a binational panel of arbitrators.[112] With respect to disputes over imports into the United States, NAFTA requires binational panels to choose U.S. law as the applicable substantive rule of decision. In the event that a party disagrees with the panel's determination, it may appeal the decision to an extraordinary challenge committee. Following that committee's review (or if no such committee is convened), the only recourse that a party has to a federal court is to file a constitutional challenge. The *Canadian Softwood Lumber* case, which settled following oral argument in the D.C. Circuit, involved such a challenge.[113] Thus, even though the interpretation of NAFTA is undoubtedly a federal question, a party may not seek review of the merits of a NAFTA tribunal's determinations in an Article III court, apart from the narrow exception for constitutional questions.

NAFTA arbitration also survives under appellate review theory.[114] With respect to two types of findings, the analysis is quite straightforward. A provision of the NAFTA–implementing legislation expressly grants the D.C. Circuit, an Article III Court, original jurisdiction over

[112] For discussions of NAFTA's dispute resolution procedure, see Curtis A. Bradley, *International Delegations, the Structural Constitution, and Non-Self-Execution*, 55 STAN. L. REV. 1557, 1575–77 (2003); Chen, *supra* note 1, at 1465–79; Susan L. Karamanian, *Dispute Resolution under NAFTA Chapter 11: A Response to the Critics*, *in* CESARE ROMANO, THE UNITED STATES AND INTERNATIONAL COURTS AND TRIBUNALS (2008); Monaghan, *supra* note 1, at 837–39; Pfander, *supra* note 33, at 766–68.

[113] *See* Coal. for Fair Lumber Imps. v. United States, 471 F.3d 1329, 1330 (D.C. Cir. 2006).

[114] Although not central to my thesis, I also believe that it would survive even under public rights theory as the Court has articulated it. Jim Chen has offered a forceful attack on NAFTA, arguing, among other things, that its dispute resolution system violates Article III. Chen, *supra* note 1, at 1463–79. Central to Chen's Article III argument is his contention that the claims under NAFTA constitute private rights. Although powerful, Chen's argument ultimately cannot overcome *Ex Parte Bakelite Corp.*'s clear holding that claims against the government arising out of customs determinations represent core public rights for which Congress can cut off Article III review altogether. 279 U.S. 438, 460–61 (1929). Indeed, until 1979, Article III Courts had no jurisdiction over customs determinations whatsoever. *See* Peter D. Ehrenhaft, *The "Judicialization" of Trade Law*, 56 NOTRE DAME L. REV. 595, 608 (1981).

facial constitutional challenges to NAFTA's binational panel review system.[115] Additionally, the Court of International Trade has jurisdiction over constitutional issues arising out of U.S. agency determinations that implement binational panel decisions in countervailing duty and antidumping cases.[116] Although neither NAFTA nor its implementing legislation authorizes Article III review of a binational panel's factual findings, such results are compatible with appellate review theory – both in its original form advanced by Fallon and in the modified form advanced here.

The more problematic aspect of NAFTA's system is the complete lack of federal judicial review of any legal findings made by binational panels. This would clearly be fatal to the NAFTA scheme under Fallon's original appellate review theory.[117] Under the modified appellate review theory offered here, however, this limit is not fatal. Evaluated by the flexible balance articulated in Part II, NAFTA claims implicate principles of sovereign immunity. The *Canadian Softwood Lumber* case, for example, technically involves an action by U.S. companies against the U.S. government (and Canadian intervenors). Barring a waiver, sovereign immunity principles would foreclose any action, a result entirely consistent with Article III.[118] Thus, a scheme foreclosing judicial review of binational panels' determinations of pure legal questions does not violate Article III.

3. Investment Arbitration

To facilitate the flow of capital to lesser-developed countries, the United States and other Western nations have entered into more than 2,800 BITs with capital-importing countries.[119] A critical feature of these treaties is that they protect the foreign investor against

[115] 19 U.S.C. § 1516a(g)(4)(A).
[116] *Id.* § 1516a(g)(4)(B).
[117] Pfander, *supra* note 33, at 767.
[118] Dep't of the Army v. Blue Fox, Inc., 525 U.S. 255, 260 (1999) ("Absent a waiver, sovereign immunity shields the Federal Government and its agencies from suit." (quoting FDIC v. Meyer, 510 U.S. 471 (1994))).
[119] Christopher M. Ryan, *Meeting Expectations: Assessing the Long-Term Legitimacy and Stability of International Investment Law*, 29 U. PA. J. INT'L L. 725, 736 (2008). For discussions of BIT arbitrations, see BORN, *supra* note 12, at 107–08; ALAN REDFERN

expropriation or other conduct. To substantiate this guarantee, many BITs include offers by the capital-importing country to arbitrate any expropriation claim, often administered under the auspices of the World Bank's International Center for the Settlement of Investment Dispute ("ICSID"). Unlike commercial arbitration, BIT arbitration does not require an underlying agreement to arbitrate. Rather, the capital-importing nation's treaty obligations suffice to subject the country to the jurisdiction of an arbitral tribunal. In an ICSID-administered arbitration, an annulment panel reviews the initial panel decision. Thereafter, judicial review is governed either by the New York Convention or by the Washington Convention of 1965. Under the latter, "awards are theoretically directly enforceable in signatory states without any method of review in national courts."[120]

Investment arbitration has some of the qualities of ordinary international commercial arbitration but with three salient differences. First, unlike international commercial arbitration, investment arbitration does not involve a voluntary agreement between the parties to submit their dispute to arbitration. Rather, the submission arises from the preexisting agreement of the capital-importing country or the state-owned entity with which the foreign investor is doing business.[121] Second, unlike private commercial arbitration, investment arbitration implicates concerns about how far the sovereign has waived immunity under its treaty obligations. As noted in the preceding section, both the voluntariness of the undertaking and the presence of sovereign immunity weigh in the value scale that determines the necessary degree of

ET AL., LAW AND PRACTICE OF INTERNATIONAL COMMERCIAL ARBITRATION 474–501 (4th ed. 2004); Andrea K. Bjorklund, *Reconciling State Sovereignty and Investor Protection in Denial of Justice Claims*, 45 VA. J. INT'L L. 809 (2005); Susan D. Franck, *The Legitimacy Crisis in Investment Treaty Arbitration: Privatizing Public International Law through Inconsistent Decisions*, 73 FORDHAM L. REV. 1521 (2005); Susan D. Franck, *The Nature and Enforcement of Investor Rights under Investment Treaties: Do Investment Treaties Have a Bright Future*, 12 U.C. DAVIS J. INT'L L. & POL'Y 47 (2005).

120 BORN, *supra* note 12.

121 For a discussion of the Washington Convention, see *id.* If one of the countries is not a signatory to the Washington Convention, then either another multilateral convention such as the New York Convention or, alternatively, the enforcement country's arbitration law supplies the relevant standard on enforcement. *See generally* Franck, *The Legitimacy Crisis supra* note 119, at 1545–57.

"adequately searching appellate review." Third, judicial review is far more circumscribed than in private international commercial arbitration.

With respect to questions of constitutional law and findings of fact, the analysis of bilateral investment treaties does not differ materially from the analysis of ordinary private commercial arbitration. With respect to legal questions, however, the analysis is markedly different. The absence of privity between the foreign sovereign and the investor suggests that greater scrutiny is required. On the other hand, the presence of sovereign immunity concerns reduces the need for plenary Article III review. Here, of course, it is not the immunity of the United States, but the immunity of the foreign sovereign, at issue. That immunity is the subject of legislative grace – one that Congress can strip if it so desires.[122] Here too, the question is close. Ultimately Congress's control over the foreign sovereign's immunity logically entails a power to decide the scope of any judicial action over the sovereign. Because Congress could restore the sovereign's immunity altogether, it proceeds logically that it should be able to regulate the degree to which the sovereign is amenable to suit in an Article III court. Given the dominance of the sovereign immunity values here, investment arbitrations, despite the limited review for legal errors, likewise pass constitutional muster.

CONCLUSION

Despite the salient differences between arbitration and other non-Article III schemes that the Supreme Court has approved, courts have mechanically rejected Article III attacks on arbitration. Although the sparse academic literature admits greater skepticism, those accounts also provide an inadequate explanation. In contrast to these efforts, appellate review theory – grounded in a careful balancing of values – provides the most useful tool for evaluating the constitutionality of arbitration. The theory is not flawless and, as originally designed,

[122] BORN, *supra* note 12.

yields conflicting answers to the question. Nonetheless, a more flexible approach, one entirely consistent with appellate review theory's underlying principles, is possible. Once refined to reflect a more flexible balancing of values, appellate review theory yields a more coherent system for evaluating arbitral schemes – one that adequately explains the constitutionality of both private and public international arbitration.

2 ARBITRATION AND EXECUTIVE POWER

"[The President] shall nominate, and by and with the Advice and Consent of the Senate, shall appoint . . . all other Officers of the United States, whose Appointments are not herein provided or, and which shall be established by Law, but the Congress may by Law vest the appointment of such inferior Officers, as they think proper, in the President alone, in the Courts of law, or in the Heads of Departments."[1]

"He shall take Care that the Laws be faithfully executed . . . "[2]

The preceding chapter introduced the idea that arbitration carries implications for the separation of powers. It focused on the relationship between arbitration and the judicial power. This chapter continues the focus on separation-of-powers principles but analyzes it from a different angle. Here, we consider the implications of arbitration for executive power. Unlike other chapters, this one focuses primarily on the areas of trade and investment arbitration; commercial arbitration, except in cases where the United States is a party to a contract (a topic I address at the end of this chapter), generally does not implicate these issues to the same extent that it does in the judicial power context.

An actual case, first introduced in the last chapter, provides the best frame for these issues. In 1989, the United States–Canada Free Trade Agreement went into effect; shortly thereafter, Congress ratified

[1] U.S. CONST., art. II, § 2. cl. 2.
[2] U.S. CONST., art. II, § 3.

the North American Free Trade Agreement, which added Mexico to the free trade zone.[3] A keystone of both agreements, as with many other free trade agreements and investment agreements, is the ability of an "interested party" in one signatory state to commence arbitration against another signatory state where it believes that the second state is acting in a manner inconsistent with its treaty obligations. In 2001, an association of U.S. lumber producers petitioned the U.S. Department of Commerce to impose antidumping and countervailing duties on Canadian softwood lumber imports.[4] Following an investigation, the Commerce Department found that the Canadian government had been subsidizing the softwood lumber industry, and the International Trade Commission determined that these subsidies threatened the U.S. lumber industry with material industry. After these two determinations, the Commerce Department imposed antidumping and countervailing duties on Canadian imports. In response, the Canadian government and other Canadian parties invoked provisions of the free trade agreements entitling them to review of the Commerce Department decision by a binational panel of arbitrators.[5] Pursuant to the treaties, a binational panel was assembled, consisting of appointees by the U.S. and Canadian governments. During the course of the arbitration, the tribunal issued several orders that, in effect, remanded the case to the U.S. International Trade Commission with express instructions to find that the record did not support a finding of injury to the American producers.[6] After the United States unsuccessfully appealed the decision of the binational panel to an extraordinary challenge committee (a type of appellate body composed of appointees by both countries), the American lumber associations then filed an action in the U.S. Court of Appeals for the District of Columbia Circuit arguing that these aspects of the treaties' dispute resolution scheme violated various provisions of the U.S. Constitution, including Article II.[7]

[3] *See* United States-Canada Free Trade Agreement Implementation Act of 1988, Pub. L. No. 100–449, 102 Stat. 1851 (1988): North American Free Trade Agreement Implementation Act of 1993, Pub. L. No. 103–182, 107 Stat. 2057 (1993).

[4] *See* Coalition for Fair Lumber Imports Executive Comm. v. United States, 471 F.3d 1329 (D.C. Cir. 2006).

[5] *Id.*

[6] *Id.*

[7] A provision of the implementing legislation permitted such a challenge to be filed in the D.C. Circuit *See* 19 U.S.C. § 1516a(g)(4)(A). In addition to the constitutional claims

The constitutional issues raised by this case include a host of important questions going to the scope of executive power. Did the tribunal's remand order – effectively requiring the Commerce Department to make certain findings – violate Article II's provision vesting the U.S. president with the power to "take care" that the laws of the United States are "faithfully executed?" Does an arbitrator constitute an "officer of the United States" such that the vesting of the appointment power in entities other than the president transgresses Article II's provision vesting in the president the power to appoint such officers? The stakes could not have been higher (and indeed perhaps explain why the parties were reluctant to risk a judicial ruling on these constitutional issues). At one point during oral argument in the case in the D.C. Circuit, the counsel for Canada explained that, if the Court found these provisions unconstitutional, It would be ripping the keystone out from the architecture upon which several decades of trade and investment treaties have been built.[8]

Ultimately, the *Canadian Softwood Lumber* case settled, enabling the parties and the court, at least temporarily, to avoid resolution of these high-stakes constitutional issues.[9] Yet the dispute has recently reopened, as the United States has commenced several arbitrations under the terms of the settlement agreement (known as the "Softwood Lumber Agreement").[10] Moreover, the issues have endured. Questions about the constitutionality of the dispute resolution architecture remain a ubiquitous issue whenever the United States enters into (or considers entering into) a trade or investment agreement. Consequently, it is essential to have a clearly theorized understanding of the boundaries of acceptable design, lest a commercially important treaty collapse under the weight of a constitutionally defective dispute resolution mechanism.

implicating executive power, the plaintiffs in the *Softwood Lumber* litigation raised claims under the Due Process Clause and Article III. *See* Brief for Petitioner in Coalition for Fair Lumber Imports Executive Committee v. United States (No. 05.1566).

8 Unofficial Transcript of Oral Argument in Coalition for Fair Lumber Imports Executive Committee v. United States (No. 05–1366) at 65 (Sept. 8, 2006) (on file with author).

9 *Coalition for Fair Lumber Imports*, 471 F.3d 1329.

10 *See* Press Release, Office of the United States Trade Representative, United States Requests Arbitration with Canada under Softwood Lumber Agreement (Jan. 2011); for the current claims, see Request for Arbitration in United States v. Canada (No. 111790) (Jan. 18, 2011).

This chapter develops an understanding of those boundaries. It begins by discussing the relationship between the appointments power and the manner in which arbitrators are appointed in trade and investment proceedings. It then considers the relationship between the "Take Care" and "Executive Power" Clauses and orders from arbitral tribunals such as those issues in the *Canadian Softwood Lumber* case. Finally, the chapter examines situations in commercial arbitration that might implicate these issues, such as where the U.S. government is a party to a contract containing an arbitration clause.

THE APPOINTMENTS ISSUE

The constitutionality of NAFTA's mechanism for the appointment of arbitrations to binational panels has been the subject of scholarly critique, legislative debate, and actual litigation. Scholars such as Jim Chen and Alan Morrison both have argued that the mechanism violates the Appointments Clause.[11] In the legislative debates surrounding the passage of implementing legislation for the United States–Canada Free Trade Agreement and, later, NAFTA, several witnesses and lawmakers questioned whether the mechanism for selecting members of NAFTA binational panels comported with the Appointments Clause.[12] Finally, on the litigation side, the petitioners in the *Canadian*

[11] Jim C. Chen, *Appointments with Disaster: The Unconstitutionality of Binational Arbitral Review under the United States-Canada Free Trade Agreement*, 49 WASHINGTON & LEE L. REV. 1455 (1992); Alan B. Morrison, *Appointments Clause Problems in the Dispute Resolution Provisions of the United States–Canada Free Trade Agreement*, 49 WASHINGTON & LEE L. REV. 1299 (1992).

[12] S. Rep. No. 100–509, Approving and Implementing the United States-Canada Free Trade Agreement, 100th Cong., 2 Sess. At 72 (additional views by Senators Orrin Hatch, Strom Thurmond and Gordon Humphrey); S. Hrg. 100–1007 pt. 3, United States–Canada Free Trade Agreement – 1988, Hearings Before the S. Comm. on Finance 233–34 (letter of Senators Hatch, Thurmond, and Humphrey); United States–Canada Free Trade Agreement, Hearings Before the Subcommittee on Trade of the Committee on Ways and Means, 100th Cong., 2d Sess. at 252–53 (prepared statement of Abercrombie Baker); United States–Canada Free Trade Agreement, Hearings Before the Subcomm. on Trade of the Committee on Ways and Means 540 (recommendations of the North Dakota Farmers Union); NAFTA: A Negative Impact on Blue Collar, Minority and Female Employment?, Hearing Before the Employment, Housing and Aviation Subcomm. of the H. Comm. on Government Operations at 41 (testimony of Ralph Nader); The Impact

Softwood Lumber dispute argued that the appointments mechanism violated the Constitution.[13]

The attack rests on two propositions. First, arbitrators on NAFTA binational panels are officers of the United States within the meaning of the Appointments Clause. Second, these arbitrators have not been chosen in the manner required by the Appointments Clause.

The second proposition of this argument is largely unassailable. Under NAFTA, binational panels consist of five arbitrators, at least two of whom are chosen by a foreign government. Moreover, none of the five members is confirmed by the U.S. Senate. Thus, if the first proposition is correct, the Appointments Clause challenge is certainly a plausible one.

To substantiate the first proposition, NAFTA's critics train on the power accorded to arbitrators on NAFTA binational panels. They stress that the arbitrators are reviewing determinations by Cabinet-level officials – namely Secretary of Commerce and ITC Commissioners. They also argue that the arbitrators are opining on issues of U.S. law, namely the compatibility of a determination under federal trade law with the U.S. obligations under NAFTA. NAFTA's critics also stress the lack of a structured mechanism for the removal of binational panel members. In the *Canadian Softwood Lumber* litigation, the Coalition for Fair Lumber Imports Executive Committee noted that, during the arbitration, allegations arose about the conflict and bias of one of panelist. When the coalition filed a recusal motion, the binational panel responded that it "lacked the authority to unseat one of its members."[14] Finally, critics stress the effective finality of a binational panel's decision. Although NAFTA provides for extraordinary challenge committees (ECC) to review the decisions of binational panels, those committees are required to show extreme deference to binational panels, reversing only if ruling "threatens the integrity of the

of the North American Free Trade Agreement on U.S. Jobs and Wages, Hearing Before the S. Comm. on Banking, Housing and Urban Affairs of the United States Senate 25 (testimony of H. Ross Perot).

13 Brief of Petitioner Coalition for Fair Lumber Imports Executive Committee, Coalition for Fair Lumber Imports Executive Committee v. United States (No. 05–1266) (D.C. Cir. Jan. 17, 2006).

14 *Id.* at 15.

binational panel review process."[15] At the time of the *Canadian Softwood Lumber* litigation, ECC review had been sought only six times, never successfully.[16]

To support their argument that individuals with this array of powers must be selected in accordance with the dictates of the Appointments Clause. Critics point to the Supreme Court's decision in *Buckley v. Valeo. Buckley* concerned an Appointments Clause challenge to the members of the Federal Election Commission, six of whom were appointed by Congress under the Federal Election Campaign Act. Rejecting the argument that Congress could appoint these commissioners without abiding by the requirements of the Appointments Clause, *Buckley* stated that all persons "exercising significant authority pursuant to the laws of the United States" function as officers of the United States.[17] This standard enables them to escape any claim that an Appointments Clause challenge requires proof that one branch of government is aggrandizing itself. For these reasons, according to NAFTA's critics, members of binational panels are properly treated as officers of the United States.

NAFTA's defenders offer a very different conception of the defining features of "officers of the United States."[18] First, they maintain that the Appointments Clause is not implicated because NAFTA arbitrators merely are acting pursuant to international law, not national law.[19] Second, they maintain that arbitrators are merely inferior officers, not officers of the United States and, thus, are not subject to the Appointments Clause. Rather than training on the arbitrators' power to review executive determination, this view stresses the limited duration of service, limited duties, and limited jurisdiction of NAFTA

[15] NAFTA art. 1904(13).

[16] Of course, depending on the constitutional analysis of binational panels, the ECC mechanism may raise its own issues. ECC members are neither appointed by the president nor confirmed by the Senate. Nor are ECC decisions subject to review in Article III court.

[17] 424 U.S 1, 126 (1976).

[18] For a good summary of these arguments, see Homer E. Moyer, *Chapter 19 of the NAFTA: Binational Panels as the Trade Courts of Last Resort*, 27 INT'L L. 707, 711–12 (1993).

[19] William J. Davey, *The Appointments Clause and International Dispute Settlement Mechanisms: A False Conflict*, 49 WASH. & LEE L. REV. 1315, 1316–17 (1992).

arbitrators.[20] Third, they point to the long history of arbitration as a mechanism for resolving interstate disputes without any concern about Appointments Clause difficulties. Because these mechanisms existed at the time of the founding,[21] NAFTA's defenders advance an originalist argument that the Framers believed such interstate dispute settlement mechanisms to be consistent with the Constitution.[22] Finally, they cite a general tradition of deference to the president on matters of foreign affairs.[23]

Several of these arguments do not do enough to allay the Appointments Clause concern. The last argument is simply question-begging. The mere fact that courts generally defer to the president on matters of foreign affairs does not imply that the president, in the exercise of that power, can cede away the Constitution's strictures. The third argument, although somewhat probative, is not entirely dispositive.[24] At best, the long history of arbitration as a mechanism for the United States to resolve interstate disputes (apparently dating back to the Jay Treaty)[25] does provide some support for the notion that the Framers believed arbitration to be compatible with the Appointments Clause.[26] But that argument only persuades to the extent a judge or commentator looks solely to history to inform his or her constitutional understanding. Moreover, the Court's Appointments Clause jurisprudence has never been rooted solely in history, so anchoring the argument solely on a historical proposition might be difficult to square with

[20] Brief of the Respondents//Intervenors Government of Canada in Coalition for Fair Lumber Imports Executive Committee v. United States at 37.

[21] *See* Alexander Hamilton, *The Defense* (No. 37) (Jan. 6, 1796) *reprinted in* 20 *The Papers of Alexander Hamilton* 13, 14 (H. Syrett, ed. 1974).

[22] In distinguishing the Jay Treaty model, NAFTA's critics observe that, prior to the United States–Canada and NAFTA agreements, the United States had never required private parties to submit rights under U.S. law to a foreign tribunal without the parties' consent.

[23] *See* Dames & Moore v. Regan, 453 U.S. 654, 686 (1981).

[24] *See* Bowsher v. Synar, 478 U.S. 714, 723–24 (1986).

[25] United States–Canada Free Trade Agreement Implementation Act of 1988, 100th Cong., 2d Sess. at 15 (Aug. 4, 1988); Zachary Jacobs, Note, *One of These Things Is Not Like the Other: U.S. Participation in International Tribunals and Why Chapter 19 of NAFTA Does Not Fit*, 45 COLUM. J. TRANSNAT'L L. 868 (2007).

[26] Indeed, several early opinions by the Attorney General did explain that the appointment of arbitrators to a state–state arbitration panel would not violate the Appointments Clause. *See* 22 Op. Att'y Gen. 184, 186 (1898); 22 Op. Att'y Gen 313, 315 (1900). The Court, however, does not appear ever formally to have endorsed those opinions.

intervening Appointments Clause precedent. Finally, the first argument is only partly accurate. Arbitrators on binational panels do apply international law insofar as they are interpreting the provisions of the treaty. However, as the foregoing description of the binational panels makes clear, they still are testing the compatibility of a determination under U.S. law with those treaty obligations. In particular, the third remand order in the *Canadian Softwood Lumber* decision – requiring the International Trade Commission to make a finding of no material injury (particularly with little opportunity for ECC review) – indicates that the binational panels are not confined solely to the interpretation of international law.

Thus, the issue boils down to measuring binational panel arbitrators against a standard differentiating "officers of the United States" from "inferior officers." On this central point, NAFTA'S defenders ultimately have the better of the argument as one more faithful to the complete chain of the Court's Appointments Clause precedents. Those precedents reveal that the core concern animating the Appointments Clause is the risk that one branch will exercise the appointments power in a manner to aggrandize itself at the expense of another, not simply a functional assessment of the powers exercised by the specific officer. The Court stressed this conception of the clause in its decision *Morrison v. Olson* when it wrote

> While the Constitution diffuses power the better to secure liberty, it also contemplates that practice will integrate the dispersed powers into a workable government. It enjoins upon its branches separateness but interdependence, autonomy but reciprocity.[27]

Nothing in NAFTA's scheme for naming arbitrators to binational panels runs afoul of this principle.[28] Unlike the scheme in *Buckley* (and like the scheme in *Morrison*), Congress is not attempting to arrogate power through the manner of appointing arbitrators to binational panels.[29]

[27] Morrison v. Olson, 487 U.S. 654, 694 (1988) (quoting Youngstown Sheet & Tube Co. v. Sawyer, 343 U.S. 579, 635 (1952) (Jackson, J., concurring).

[28] Yong K. Kim, *The Beginnings of the Rule of Law in the International Trade System despite U.S. Constitutional Constraints*, 17 MICH. J INT'L L. 967, 985–86 (1996).

[29] Davey, *supra* note 20, at 1322. Professor Davey takes *Morrison* one step further to argue that the manner of appointing arbitrators falls squarely within the criteria relied upon in *Morrison* for upholding the manner of appointment of the independent counsel.

Rather both the executive and legislative branches of government are operating in tandem to craft the dispute resolution mechanism – both are perhaps ceding a degree of power, but neither branch is ceding it to the benefit of another.

The quoted line from *Buckley* on which NAFTA's critics rely cannot bear the weight that they attempt to place upon it. Just as *Olson* did not rely upon this language; the Court's major pre-*Buckley* decisions also did not suggest the dispositiveness of this criterion.[30] To suggest otherwise would impute to the *Buckley* Court an intent to overrule *sub silentio* that long string of precedent. Yet the Court consistently has cautioned against interpreting its precedents to overrule prior decisions *sub silentio*.[31] Indeed, as noted earlier in this section, *Buckley* itself was an aggrandizement case – the appointment mechanism that the Court ultimately found constitutionally defective vested the power to appoint election commissioners in Congress (at the expense of the president's appointment power). Thus, the aggrandizement standard, rather than *Buckley*'s "significant authority" test, supplies the better rule for assessing the line between officers of the United States and inferior officers.[32] Consequently, because the mechanism for appointing arbitrators to binational panels does not aggrandize a coordinate branch of government, it does not run afoul of the Appointments Clause.

Even if the inferior officer argument in NAFTA is not airtight, the fallback mechanism should protect the treaty from any residual

Those criteria are (1) removability by a cabinet officer, (2) limited duties, (3) limited jurisdiction, and (4) temporary appointment. *Id.* at 1320–21. Unlike Professor Davey, I do not believe *Morrison* can be completely dispositive on the issue. Specifically, as noted above, arbitrators on binational panels cannot be removed by a Cabinet-level officer. Indeed, in the *Canadian Softwood Lumber* arbitration, the Extraordinary Challenge Committee suggested that the power to remove an arbitrator was quite limited. Thus, although I agree with Professor Davey that the principles underpinning *Morrison* do support a conclusion that NAFTA does not run afoul of the Appointments Clause, I do not believe the analogy to *Morrison* is airtight on "on all fours."

30 *See* Auffinordt v. Hedden, 137 U.S. 310, 326–27 (1890); United States v. Germaine, 99 U.S. 508, 512 (1879); United States v. Hartwell, 73 U.S. (6 Wall.) 385, 393 (1868).

31 *See, e.g.*, Hohn v United States, 524 U.S. 236, 252–53 (1998).

32 *See* Harold H. Bruff, *Public Programs, Private Deciders: The Constitutionality of Arbitration in Federal Programs*, 67 TEX. L. REV. 441 (1989).

Appointments Clause challenge.[33] The fallback mechanism obligates the president to accept the decisions of binational panels and extraordinary challenge committees. Designed in response to the constitutional concerns of the president and some legislators,[34] the fallback aimed to overcome any Appointments Clause concerns because, in the event the fallback kicks in, any action by Cabinet-level officials would be occurring at the behest of the president, rather than in response to a mandate issued directly by a binational panel.

This rationale behind the fallback mechanism offers an important insight into the relationship between arbitration law and constitutional law. Here, we see concerns about potential constitutional pitfalls influencing the level of systemic architecture of statutes. Even though no court ever affirmatively held that the Appointments Clause required such a system (or had invalidated a separate piece of legislation for its failure to include such a provision), nonetheless concerns over the constitutional dimensions of the NAFTA dispute resolution mechanism directly influences how arbitration law was shaped at the legislative level.

THE TAKE CARE/EXECUTIVE POWER CLAUSE

Even if the mechanism for selecting members of binational panels does not present a problem under the Appointments Clause, NAFTA's foes identified a second potential constitutional defect treading upon Article II of the Constitution. They asserted, in addition, that the mechanism for implementation of the decisions of binational panels violated the Take Care Clause, quoted at the beginning of this chapter which charges the president with the duty to take care that the laws of the United States be faithfully executed. The challenges under the

[33] Although the fallback mechanism may obviate any residual Appointments Clause problem, it arguably raises an independent problem under the Take Care Clause, discussed in the next section.

[34] H. Rep. No. 100–816, pt. 4, United States–Canada Free Trade Agreement Implementation Act of 1988 at 17–18 (Aug 4. 1988); S. Rep. No. 100–1007, pt. 3, United States–Canada Free Trade Agreement – 1988 at 233–24 (letter of Senators Hatch, Thurmond, and Humphrey).

"Take Care" Clause are manifold are, for the sake of analytical clarity, should be unpacked into three separate themes.[35]

One version of the argument essentially amounts to a facial attack on the design of NAFTA and its implementing legislation. This implementing legislation directs federal agencies to take action in a manner not inconsistent with the decisions of binational panels.[36] Although conceding that Congress could, if it desired, abolish the countervailing duty system altogether, NAFTA's opponents argued that this greater power did not necessarily include the lesser power to force the executive branch to administer the existing system in accordance with the dictates of a binational panel. They analogize this mechanism to the Supreme Court's decision in *Printz v. United States*, first introduced in Chapter 1, where the Court invalidated a scheme vesting local law enforcement officers with the power to carry out an executive function (background checks prior to handgun purchases).[37]

This argument does not carry much water. The weakness lies in the analogy to *Printz*. *Printz* rested on a concern that local law enforcement officials were being coerced into enforcing a federal law. That coercion was problematic both because the local law enforcement officials lacked any meaningful choice about whether they wished to undertake these duties and because the costs of carrying out the background checks would impose an involuntary burden on state fiscs. Implementation of awards by binational panels stands on a very different footing. For one thing, in the NAFTA context, the federal government voluntarily undertook this obligation when the president signed (and the Congress implemented) NAFTA. This stands in sharp contrast to the involuntary undertaking imposed on local law enforcement officials.

[35] Closely related is an argument that the NAFTA scheme violates the nondelegation doctrine. *See* A.L.A. Schechter Poultry Corp. v. United States, 295 U.S. 495 (1935); Carter v. Carter Coal Co., 298 U.S. 238 (1936). Under this argument, Congress has impermissibly delegated the power to make federal law to an entity (the binational panels) completely outside the control of the political branches. Neither the nondelegation clause nor its particular application in this context received much credence, so I have not independently explored it here. *See* Memo from Walter Dellinger, Assistant Attorney General, to John Schmidt, Associate Attorney General, *Constitutional Issues in Federal Arbitration* 13 (Sept. 7, 1995) (hereinafter "Dellinger Memorandum") (quickly dispensing with a challenge to binding arbitration by the United States under the nondelegation doctrine).

[36] 19 U.S.C. § 1516a(g)(7)(A).

[37] 521 U.S. 898 (1997).

For another thing, implementation of binational panel awards does not work a burden on the federal fisc in the same manner as the background check mandate. One might argue that the *Canadian Softwood Lumber* litigation demonstrates the burden on the federal fisc (when the panel essentially mandated that the U.S. government reverse its finding of material injury). Yet that burden, even if such characterization is proper, is one that the federal government has voluntarily undertaken by entering into the NAFTA regime. If the burden proves too weighty, the national government can simply withdraw from NAFTA or amend the implementing legislation. By comparison, the local law enforcement officials enjoyed no such comparable choice in *Printz*.

A second version of the argument represents an as-applied challenge based upon the particular conduct in the *Canadian Softwood Lumber* arbitration. After the binational panel remanded the case to the International Trade Commission, the Commission reaffirmed its finding that Canada's treatment of its softwood lumber exports caused material injury in the United States. Following a second proceeding, the binational panel again remanded the matter to the ITC, leaving it little time to respond and denying its request for an extension. The ITC reaffirmed its finding. Following a third proceeding, the binational panel remanded the matter again and affirmatively ordered the ITC "to make a determination consistent with the decision of this Panel that the evidence does not support a finding of threat of material injury." During review proceedings before an Extraordinary Challenge Committee, the ECC found that the binational panel had failed to apply the proper standard of review required under U.S. law but declined to find this error warranted vacatur of the binational panel's award, nothing that "it is not a fundamental determination necessary to be made."

This argument has a certain surface appeal but is also ultimately flawed. Certainly there is something unsettling about a politically unaccountable judge dictating to U.S. Cabinet officials what findings to make. Yet that is precisely the scheme into which the United States entered when the president signed NAFTA, and the Congress enacted implementing legislation. If anything, because NAFTA's implementing legislation is a "law of the United States," a system ensuring compliance with its dispute settlement mechanism carries out – rather than undermines – the president's duty to "take care" that the laws be faithfully executed. To suggest otherwise would undercut the stability of the treaty-making power embedded in the Constitution. Under the logic of NAFTA's opponents, the United States might (1) enter into a treaty committing itself to certain obligations and to a dispute settlement mechanism for fulfilling those obligations, (2) enact implementing legislation domesticating those obligations (or, in technical terms, executing the treaty as a matter of U.S. law),[38] but then (3) potentially be relieved from those obligations by arguing that compliance with them somehow undermines the president's "Take Care" power. The implications of this argument would have significant deleterious consequences for the ability of the United States to enter into international agreements. Fellow nation-states could have little confidence that any international obligation, even after its domestication, would remain secure under U.S. law. The treaty-making power could hardly have been designed to produce such an unstable result. For this reason, the "as applied" argument predicated on the "Take Care" clause must likewise fail.

A third version of the argument trains upon the fallback provision in the NAFTA implementing legislation. As noted earlier, under the provision, if the NAFTA dispute resolution mechanism is declared unconstitutional, the president is required to accept binational panel and ECC decisions "as a whole." Executive Orders 12662 and 12889, signed by Presidents Reagan and Clinton respectively, indicated their intent to pursue this course if necessary.[39] During the *Canadian Softwood Lumber* litigation, NAFTA's opponents argued that this mechanism created its own constitutional difficulties under

[38] *See, e.g.*, Sanchez-Llamas v. Oregon, 548 U.S. 331 (2006) (discussing relationship between self-executing and non–self-executing treaties); Peter B. Rutledge, *Delegation and (Conflicts of) Law*, 17 GEO. MASON L. REV. 191 (2009) (discussing delegation problems in international law).

[39] For a discussion of the executive orders, see Yong K. Kim, *The Beginnings of the Rule of Law in the International Trade System Despite U.S. Constitutional Constraints*, 17 MICH. J. INT'L L. 967, 982–83 (1996).

separation-of-powers principles. According to this argument, the "take it as a whole or not at all" condition enables the president to review a decision of an Article III court, in violation of the Supreme Court's decision in *Plaut v. Spendthrift Farm.*[40] In *Plaut*, the Supreme Court held that the political branches may not enact legislation in an effort to undo a final civil judgment; the underlying principle was rooted in separation of powers – that the political branches may not exercise their lawmaking powers to change retroactively the substantive legal regime governing the rights and remedies of parties whose dispute has already been tried to final judgment. To countenance such an exercise of legislative power would aggrandize the lawmaking branch at the expense of the judicial branch.

Unlike the situation in *Plaut*, NAFTA's fallback mechanism does not change the substantive rule upon which a civil judgment would rest. Any civil judgment would simply be holding that some aspect of the NAFTA implementing legislation did not comport with the Constitution. That holding, however, would not affect the substantive rule underpinning the decision or preclude other mechanisms for implementing the decisions of binational panels (such as through direct executive action). An executive order adopting the decisions of binational panels as a component of the president's "Take Care" power merely would be a means of implementing U.S. treaty obligations as a matter of international law.

Instead of *Plaut*, the closer analogy to the separation-of-powers question might be the Supreme Court's decision in the famous *Steel Seizure* case.[41] There, Justice Jackson's concurring opinion (later embraced by the Court) set forth the now-famous tripartite framework for assessing the dimensions of Executive Power.[42] Justice Jackson argued that the constitutionality of claims of Executive Power varied with the degree of congressional endorsement – when the executive is acting pursuant to congressional authorization, his power is at its zenith (Category I); when he is acting in the face of congressional

[40] 514 U.S. 211 (1995).

[41] Youngstown Sheet & Tube Co. v. Sawyer, 343 U.S. 579, 610–11 (1952).

[42] *Id.* at 637 (Jackson, J., concurring). For a decision in which a clear Supreme Court majority embraces the framework set forth in Justice Jackson's concurring opinion, see *Dames & Moore v. Regan*, 453 U.S. 654 (1981).

silence, his power lies at a midpoint (Category II); and when he is acting in the face of a congressional prohibition, his power is at its nadir (Category III).

Mapped onto the NAFTA's fallback mechanism, Justice Jackson's framework suggests that the president's power to implement the mechanism should not run afoul of separation-of-powers principles. If it proved necessary to invoke the fallback mechanism, the president would be doing so with express congressional approval – that is, Congress' instruction set forth in NAFTA's implementing legislation. Moreover, the president would be acting in a manner aiming to effectuate the intent of a coordinate branch of government, namely Congress. Thus, under the logic of the *Steel Seizure* framework, the fallback mechanism should not run afoul of separation-of-powers principles.

The Supreme Court's decision in *Dames & Moore v. Regan* reinforces this point.[43] There, the Supreme Court swept aside a constitutional challenge to the United States–Iran Claims Tribunal even though the Algiers Accord (setting up the tribunal) suspended claims pending in U.S. courts against Iran. In support of this conclusion, the Court highlighted the long-standing tradition of the executive branch entering into agreements setting up claims settlement mechanisms for resolving trade and other commercial disputes with foreign nations (such as the Jay Treaty).[44]

Compared to the Algiers Accord, NAFTA's fallback mechanism presents an even stronger claim to compatibility with separation-of-powers principles. Mapped onto Justice Jackson's framework, the United States–Iran Claims Tribunal was probably a Category II case – that is, one of executive action taken against congressional silence (or in action). By contrast in NAFTA, the fallback mechanism can claim to fall into Category I of Justice Jackson's tripartite framework – that is executive action backed by express congressional endorsement.[45] By implementing the decisions of NAFTA's binational panels, the president, acting pursuant to the fallback mechanism, would be giving effect

[43] 453 U.S. 654 (1981).

[44] *Id.* at 679–82.

[45] *See* Ethan Boyer, *Article III, The Foreign Relations Power, and the Binational Panel System of NAFTA*, 13 INT'L TAX & BUS. L. 101, 139–41 (1996).

to the views of a coordinate political branch. Such action would not tread upon separation-of-powers principles.[46]

In sum, the fallback mechanism does not present constitutional difficulties under *Plaut* or more general principles of separation of powers.

UNITED STATES AS PARTY

The preceding two sections have considered the relationship between arbitration and Article II in a specific context, namely arbitration pursuant to bilateral and multilateral trade agreements. This final section considers whether the issues explored above, namely the Appointments Clause and the Take Care Clause, carry implications beyond that setting for private arbitration more generally.

In most instances, the answer is no. Garden-variety arbitration between purely private parties does not implicate issues of executive power. By designating a private individual to resolve their contractual disputes, private parties are not appointing an "officer of the United States." Nor does that private individual's decision tread upon the duty of the president to "take care" that the laws be faithfully executed.

Notwithstanding the general irrelevance of these issues to commercial arbitration, they do potentially arise in one specific setting – that is commercial arbitration with the United States as a party. Indeed, on multiple occasions in the early 1990s (during the administration of President George H. W. Bush), President Bush's then-head of the Office of Legal Counsel, William Barr, testified repeatedly before

[46] The Supreme Court's decision in Medellin v. Texas, 552 *U.S.* 491 (2008), decided after conclusion of the *Canadian Softwood Lumber* litigation, does not alter this analysis. *Medellin* addressed the question whether the president could, pursuant to the U.S. obligations under a Protocol to the Convention on Consular Relations, require state governments to set aside their procedural default rules in state habeas cases challenging convictions on the ground that the foreign national had not been accorded his right to consult with consul under the Convention. The Court held that the executive's power did not extend so far, but it distinguished that case from cases involving the executive's power to settle claims with foreign countries (such as those at issue in *Dames & Moore*). Thus, even recognizing that *Medellin* trims an expansive view of executive power in the management of foreign affairs, cite, the decision does not alter the separation-of-powers analysis for NAFTA's fallback mechanism.

Congress that the Constitution forbade the United States from seeking or entering into binding arbitration unless the arbitration were appointed in a manner consistent with the Appointments Clause.[47] Shortly after Mr. Barr's testimony, President Bush issued Executive Order 12778, prohibiting government counsel from seeking or entering into binding arbitration.[48] Finally, in 1992, the Justice Department (by then under Barr's leadership as Attorney General) issued a manual announcing that "the Government cannot enter into agreements to participate in binding arbitration."[49]

Yet only a few years after these developments, the Justice Department (following a change in administration) took a very different approach. In a comprehensive memorandum, Barr's successor in the Office of Legal Counsel, Walter Dellinger, confidently declared that neither the Appointments Clause nor the Take Care Clause prevented the United States from entering into binding commercial arbitration.[50] It made express reference to Barr's prior testimony and the other legal authorities noted above. Yet it also essentially disavowed them, while noting that Executive Order 12778 remained in effect and therefore barred formation of commercial arbitration agreements by federal government officials on behalf of the United States.

So what explains the sudden change in view (apart from a change in administration)? NAFTA's implementing legislation supplies the likeliest explanation. The Dellinger Memorandum followed on the heels of earlier oral advice that the Office of Legal Counsel had given the Associate Attorney General about the matter,[51] and all of this occurred shortly after several members of Congress had raised concerns about NAFTA's implementing legislation. Moreover, although the Dellinger

[47] *See* Hearing Before the Subcomm. on Oversight of Government Management of the S. Comm. on Government Affairs Regarding the Use of Alternative Dispute Resolution by Federal Agencies (Sept. 19, 1989) (statement of William Barr); Hearing Before the Subcomm. on Administrative Law and Government Relations of the H. Comm. on the Judiciary Regarding the Use of Alternative Dispute Resolution by Federal Agencies (Jan. 31, 1990) (statement by William Barr).

[48] Executive Order 12778, 56 Fed. Reg. 55195 (1991).

[49] Guidance on the Use of Alternative Dispute Resolution for Litigation in the Federal Courts 4 (Aug. 1992).

[50] *See generally* Dellinger Memorandum, *supra* note 35.

[51] *Id.* at 1.

Memorandum purports to address contractual arbitration entered into by the United States, in several places it explicitly refers to the scholarship questioning the constitutionality of NAFTA's implementing legislation,[52] and it is reasonable to suspect that the Justice Department shortly anticipated constitutional challenges by NAFTA's skeptics. So although the memorandum itself discusses a form of arbitration quite distinct from that at issue in NAFTA, ultimately the NAFTA debate is looming in the background.

More importantly, between the Barr opinion and the Dellinger opinion, which has the stronger case on the merits? In my view, the Dellinger Memorandum appears to be on stronger footing than the prior testimony by Assistant Attorney General Barr. Ultimately, contractual arbitration between the United States and another party does not vary materially from arbitration before binational panels with the exception of two potentially salient differences. First, in private contractual arbitration unlike NAFTA arbitration, the U.S. government does not necessarily have Congress' imprimatur when it undertakes the arbitration obligation. Second, in private contractual arbitration, unlike NAFTA arbitration, the subject matter in dispute may cover a far wider range of topics (such as garden-variety breach of contract actions) as opposed to the limited domain of countervailing duty and antidumping disputes under NAFTA.

Neither distinction presents much of a worry under the Appointments Clause. The lack of a congressional imprimatur to enter into binding commercial arbitration does not bear on the question of whether the arbitrators are officers of the United States. As to the substance of the claims, that arguably weakens the Appointments Clause argument. Instead of opining on the compatibility of U.S. law with a treaty, the arbitrators in commercial arbitrations likelier would be offering opinions on garden-variety matters of contract and tort law where the national interests are not as great.

Precedent supports the view that the private contractual arbitration with the United States does not offend the Appointments Clause.[53] As the Dellinger Memorandum observes, in *Auffmordt v. Hecklen*, the

[52] *See, e.g., id.* at 4.
[53] *Id.* at 6.

Supreme Court rejected an Appointments Clause challenge to a statutory scheme under which importers dissatisfied with the government's valuation of a good could request determination by appraisers whose decision would be binding on the government and the importer.[54] Central to the Court's reasoning was the fact that the appraiser was appointed without "tenure, duration, continuing emolument or continuous duties."[55] Although the Dellinger Memorandum considers *Auffmordt* to resolve the question, that probably overreads the case. *Auffmordt* did not involve private contractual arbitration. Nonetheless, the reasoning underpinning the decision strongly supports the notion that the differences between trade arbitration and private contractual arbitration do not justify a different result on the Appointments Clause challenge.

Nor does the Take Care Clause present an impediment. Here, the entire analysis turns on the presence or absence of positive law governing the matter.[56] In most cases, positive law simply does not speak to whether the United States may (or may not) enter into binding arbitration. In those cases, the "Take Care" clause is not implicated for the simple reason that there is no law to "faithfully execute." In rarer cases, where positive law requires the United States to enter into binding arbitration (akin, although not identical, to NAFTA's scheme), then the decision to do so discharges, rather than undermines, the president's obligations under the Take Care Clause. Finally, in the hypothetical situation where U.S. law prohibits entering into binding arbitration agreements, the Take Care Clause issue never arises because an effort to enter into an arbitration agreement would be illegal and, thus, unenforceable. Thus, the contractual arbitration with the United States does not implicate any concerns under the Take Care Clause.

Despite the absence of a unique constitutional problem, it is worth emphasizing an interesting parallel between the shift in the position of the Office of Legal Counsel and the approach taken by Congress in drafting NAFTA's implementing legislation. Although the Dellinger Memorandum concludes that the participation of the United States

[54] 137 U.S. 310 (1890).

[55] *Id.* at 326–27.

[56] Dellinger Memorandum, *supra* note 35, at 9.

in commercial arbitration did not violate the Appointments Clause, it reaffirmed the continued applicability of Executive Order 12778. This allowed Executive Order 12778 to function as a type of constitutional avoidance mechanism – by strictly regulating the ability of U.S. officers to enter into binding arbitration, Executive Order 12778 ensured that no appointments challenge could effectively arise. Here too then constitutional law is not operating at the level of positive doctrine but, instead, is influencing sub-constitutional issues of systemic design, namely the U.S. policy on the extent to which its officers can (or cannot) enter into binding arbitration.

CONCLUSION

Arbitration raises potential issues involving the allocation of executive power under Article II. Ultimately, though, as with Article III, Article II does not present an impediment. Whether in the context of trade arbitration or other contexts, the manner of appointing arbitrators does not run afoul of the Appointments Clause. Nor does the rendering of a decision by an arbitrator tread upon the president's duty to "Take Care" that the laws of the United States be faithfully executed.

Although the Constitution does not present a direct impediment, it would be wrong to conclude that the document is entirely irrelevant. As in the Article III context, constitutional values here influence development at a sub-doctrinal level. Thus, for example, concerns about the risk of invalidity of NAFTA's dispute resolution mechanism influenced development of the implementing legislation's architecture, leading to the creation of the fallback mechanism. That mechanism enabled the United States to send a credible signal to its trading partners that it would honor its treaty obligations even if the binational panel system were struck down. Likewise, residual concerns about the possible (albeit slight) constitutional infirmities in the manner of appointing arbitrators in commercial relationships involving the United States prompted the government to issue a blanket order prohibiting government officials from entering into such agreements. Although a close analysis of the constitutional issues revealed that such concerns were slight at best, they were sufficiently palpable to prompt the president to adapt a risk-averse approach toward any questions of contracting by government officials on behalf of the United States.

Both of the first two chapters illustrated how the Constitution and its underlying values influenced arbitration law at a sub-doctrinal level but did not present an express doctrinal bar toward the development of arbitration law. The next section shows how a different area of intersection between arbitration law and constitutional law – namely federalism and vertical separation of powers – presents a more classic case of constitutional doctrine directly shaping the development of law in this area. To those topics, we now turn.

Part II ARBITRATION AND FEDERALISM

3 ARBITRATION AND STATE LAW

> This Constitution, and the Laws of the United States which shall be made in Pursuance thereof; and all Treaties made, or which shall be made, under the Authority of the United States, shall be the supreme Law of the Land; and the Judges in every State shall be bound thereby, any Thing in the Constitution or Laws of any State to the Contrary notwithstanding.
>
> – U.S. Constitution, Article VI

Systems of arbitration must coexist with the state systems in which they operate. This coexistence must work on several levels. One level concerns the regulation of the arbitration itself. Another level concerns the interaction between arbitration and the judiciary. The nature of this coexistence depends on the design of the state system.

In unitary systems (such as France or Austria), the interaction is relatively easy to manage.[1] A single national lawmaker (Parliament) sets forth a single law (or set of laws) regulating matters such as the enforceability of arbitration agreements, certain procedural matters in arbitration, and judicial review of arbitral awards. Those standards govern through the judicial systems in which the enforceability of the arbitration agreement will be challenged, judicial assistance in support of the proceedings will be sought, and post-award litigation will occur.

In federalist systems (such as the United States or Argentina), the interaction can be more complex.[2] Multiple lawmakers (both federal

[1] Federalism and Political Performance 192 (Ute Wachendorfer-Schmidt ed., 2000).

[2] *Id.*

and state) may regulate the foregoing topics (agreements, judicial assistance, and judicial review of awards). Moreover, questions will arise about which standard applies in a given court (particularly where more than one court may have jurisdiction over the matter). These increased complexities reflect the importance that these state systems place on the vertical distribution of power between sovereigns, both at the level of prescriptive jurisdiction and at the level of judicial jurisdiction.

It bears emphasis, however, that the added complexity does not necessarily follow from the design of a particular state system. A federalist system may nonetheless employ a unitary model for arbitration policy. It may do so where, for example, the state has concluded that the regulation of arbitration is solely the province of the national authority to the exclusion of state authorities.[3] A federalist system also may do so where, for example, the national sovereign channels arbitration-related disputes to a single set of courts or otherwise requires that the potentially competent tribunals apply a uniform standard to questions of arbitration law that may arise.

The United States has not followed this path. Instead, at both the level of prescriptive jurisdiction and judicial jurisdiction, the distribution of power between federal and state authorities is a complex one. Although Congress has enacted the Federal Arbitration Act, virtually all state legislatures have adopted some type of state arbitration action (often modeled on a uniform law),[4] and some have even adopted specialized acts for certain areas such as international arbitration.[5]

[3] For example in Switzerland, where arbitration is regulated at the federal level, except when parties explicitly agree to opt into canon rules. *See* Swiss Law on Private International Law, Art. 176. *See, e.g.*, Gary Born, International Arbitration 55–56 (2011).

[4] States that have adopted either the Uniform Arbitration Act (UAA) or Revised Uniform Arbitration Act (RUAA) include Alaska, Arizona, Arkansas, Colorado, Delaware, the District of Columbia, Florida, Georgia, Hawaii, Idaho, Illinois, Indiana, Iowa, Kansas, Kentucky, Louisiana, Maine, Maryland, Massachusetts, Michigan, Minnesota, Missouri, Montana, Nebraska, Nevada, New Jersey, New Mexico, North Carolina, North Dakota, Oklahoma, Oregon, and Pennsylvania.

States with laws similar to the UAA or RUAA include Mississippi, New Hampshire, New York, Ohio and Rhode Island.

States with laws most unlike the UAA and RUAA include Alabama and California.

[5] States that have international arbitration acts include California, Colorado, Connecticut, Florida, Georgia, Hawaii, Illinois, Louisiana, Maryland, North Carolina, Ohio, and Oregon.

In some respects, such as enforcement proceedings under the New York Convention or Panama Convention, federal law reigns supreme. Nonetheless, state law plays an important role, and state courts enjoy unique prerogatives in the area of arbitration law – prerogatives that they do not enjoy in other contexts and that, indeed, their legislative counterparts do not necessarily enjoy. This chapter unpacks those complex relationships and critiques them.

FEDERALISM AND THE ENFORCEMENT OF ARBITRATION AGREEMENTS

To begin to unpack the issues, let us start with the topic of arbitration agreements. Section 2 of the Federal Arbitration Act sets forth the following standard (applicable to arbitration agreements not falling under the New York Convention and, possibly, the Panama Convention):

> A written provision in any maritime transaction or a contract evidencing a transaction involving commerce to settle by arbitration a controversy thereafter arising out of such contract or transaction, or the refusal to perform the whole or any part thereof, or an agreement in writing to submit to arbitration an existing controversy arising out of such a contract, transaction, or refusal, shall be valid, irrevocable, and enforceable, save upon such grounds as exist at law or in equity for the revocation of any contract.[6]

As a matter of federalism, this language immediately raises two questions. First, where does this standard apply? Does it apply only in federal court, or does it also apply in state court? Second, regardless of where the standard applies, what precisely does the statute mean when it speaks of "such grounds as exist at law or in equity for the revocation of any contract"?

Let us begin with the first question, whose answer has important consequences for federalism. Applying Section 2 across both federal

[6] 9 U.S.C. § 2 (2006).

and state forums reduces the risks of forum shopping.[7] Under a uniform standard, a plaintiff cannot circumvent an arbitration clause by filing suit (and then challenging the agreement's enforceability) in the court of a state that is more skeptical of arbitration agreements. Also under a uniform standard, a defendant cannot attempt to enhance the enforceability of the arbitration clause by seeking to remove or transfer the case to a court or state that is more receptive to arbitration. In each of these cases, any court (in theory at least) would operate under the same standard.

That approach, however, undermines federalism values. Applying Section 2 across both federal and state forums cuts into the prerogative of states to regulate arbitration agreements. Depending on the nature of the agreement, the state may have especially powerful interests in regulating those agreements (whether by enhancing or limiting their enforceability).

Several examples illustrate the point. Consider first a state with an overburdened judicial system. Under those circumstances, the state may reasonably conclude that it wishes to maximize the enforceability of arbitration clauses in order to reduce those burdens. On the flip side, consider a state that has a particular concern about companies exploiting its vulnerable residents. To reduce those risks to its residents, the state may reasonably want to limit (or bar) the use of arbitration clauses. Universal application of Section 2 inhibits the power of states in both the arbitration-enhancing and the arbitration-restricting settings.

Despite its importance, the applicability of the FAA in state court lay largely unresolved for nearly sixty years following the statute's enactment. Finally, in *Southland Corp. v. Keating*, the Supreme Court confronted the question squarely.[8] *Southland* involved a group of actions by convenience store franchisees against a franchisor in which

[7] The FAA's requirement of an interstate nexus to the contract might have provided an independent basis restraint on the exercise of federal power in this area. *See* 9 U.S.C. §1 (2006). The Court, however, has chosen to stretch that nexus to the maximum extent permitted by the Constitution, thereby eroding the opportunity for advancing federalism-based values in this context. *See* Circuit City Stores, Inc. v. Adams, 532 U.S. 105 (2001); Allied-Bruce Terminix Cos., Inc. v. Dobson, 513 U.S. 265, 271 (1995).

[8] 465 U.S. 1 (1984).

the franchisees alleged claims under California common law and statutory law (namely California's Franchise Investment Law). All of the relevant franchise agreements contained arbitration clauses. Notwithstanding these clauses, the franchisees brought the claims in California state court, and cited a provision of the California franchise law declaring void any provision of a contract that purports to waive compliance with any of the franchise law's provisions (which the California Supreme Court interpreted to include jurisdiction over claims arising under the law). Most of the lower state court proceedings turned on the arbitrability of the statutory claims, and the courts also considered whether – if the franchise law's antiwaiver provisions applied – Section 2 of the FAA preempted them. The California Supreme Court held that the antiwaiver provisions did apply and were not preempted by Section 2.

When taken up by the Supreme Court, a majority of the Court held that the FAA preempted California's law (as interpreted by its state supreme court). For the Court to reach this conclusion, however, it was critical for the Court first to conclude that Section 2 applied in state court. It rested that logically anterior conclusion on three main grounds. First, the Court relied on prior precedent – *Prima Paint*[9] (which had applied Section 2 in a diversity case) and *Moses Cone*[10] (which had stated, albeit in dicta, that Section 2 created a body of substantive federal law applicable in both federal and state court). Second, the Court inferred from various snippets of the sparse legislative history surrounding the FAA's enactment an intent to apply the FAA in state court. Third, the Court rested on policy arguments – namely a federal policy favoring enforcement of arbitration agreements, which would be frustrated if Section 2 did not apply in state courts, where the lion's share of civil litigation is filed.

This majority opinion sparked a spirited dissent from the Court's newest member, Justice Sandra Day O'Connor (herself a product of state government, as both a former Speaker of the Arizona Assembly and, immediately prior to her ascent to the U.S. Supreme Court, a state judge). In relevant part, Justice O'Connor's dissent advanced the

[9] 388 U.S. 395, 404–05 (1967).
[10] 460 U.S. 1, 24 (1983).

proposition that the FAA applies only in federal court. To support this opposing viewpoint, she relied primarily on two grounds. First, she quoted extensively from the legislative history, which, in her view, unambiguously established conclusively that Congress intended the FAA to apply only in federal court. Second, she advanced a structural argument – based primarily on Sections 3 and 4 of the FAA (both of which expressly refer to "United States District Courts") – to support her claim that applying Section 2 in state court does not comport with the statutory scheme. After laying out the affirmative bases for her position, Justice O'Connor concluded by disputing the relevance on the precedents on which the majority had relied.

Criticism of the majority opinion did not stop with Justice O'Connor's dissent. Academic commentators largely pilloried it.[11] Moreover, in a series of subsequent cases, interested parties repeatedly urged the Court to overrule *Southland.*[12] After attracting the interests of a few justices, those efforts eventually fizzled, and the Court consistently reaffirmed *Southland*'s core holding. Eventually, one of *Southland*'s staunchest detractors, Justice Scalia, threw in the towel, claiming that the decision had achieved a degree of settled precedent such that, under principles of stare decisis, he felt bound to apply it even if he did not agree with it as an original matter.[13] Despite the pro-federalism proclivities of the Roberts' Court in other contexts, only one justice, Clarence Thomas, continues to hew to the position that *Southland* should be overruled.[14]

[11] For a good summary of the literature, see Christopher R. Drahozal, *In Defense of* Southland: *Reexamining the Legislative History of the Federal Arbitration Act*, 78 NOTRE DAME L. REV. 101 (2002).

[12] *See* Doctor's Associates, Inc. v. Casarotto, 517 U.S. 681, 681 (1996) (arguing to qualify Southland for limited preemptive force of FAA § 2); Allied-Bruce Terminix Cos., Inc. v. Dobson, 513 U.S. 265, 271 (1995) (recognizing counterarguments to the expansion of the scope of a statute stretching alongside the expansion of Commerce Clause power, but reaffirming the *Southland* holding).

[13] *Compare* Doctor's Associates, Inc. v. Casarotto, 517 U.S. 681, 681 (1996), *with* Allied-Bruce Terminix Cos., Inc., v. Dobson, 513 U.S. 265, 271 (1995).

[14] *See, e.g.*, Preston v. Ferrer, 552 U.S. 346 (2008) (Thomas, J. dissenting); Buckeye Check Cashing, Inc. v. Cardegna, 546 U.S. 440 (2006) (Thomas, J. dissenting); Doctor's Associates, Inc. v. Casarotto, 517 U.S. 681 (1996); Allied Bruce Terminix Cos. v. Dobson, 513 U.S. 265 (1995) (Thomas J., dissenting).

Southland thus can be understood as a decision that elevates the importance of uniformity over values of federalism. By subjecting arbitration agreements to a uniform standard, it reduces the risks of forum shopping. It does so, however, at the expense of state prerogatives to enhance (or contract) the enforceability of arbitration agreements.

The Court's anti-federalism jurisprudence on the first question ("where does it apply") has been counterbalanced, in part, by its more pro-federalist proclivities on the second question – namely, what does Section 2 mean when it talks about "such grounds as exist at law or in equity for the revocation of any contract"? Does this mean federal law or state law?

As with the first question, the stakes for federalism values are significant. If the quoted phrase means federal law, then uniformity values again trump federalism values. On other hand, if the quoted language means state law, then Section 2 serves as a potential counterbalance to the uniformity impulses that animated the majority decision in *Southland.*

Here, the Court has tipped its hand in favor of federalism, but not completely. The Court has made clear that federal law does not control the substantive standard (at least in the domestic context).[15] Instead, state law does so, albeit a particular type of state law: Specifically, according to the Court, arbitration agreements are subject to generally applicable contract defenses.[16] They are not, however, subject to state standards that single-out or discriminate against arbitration agreements (compared to other garden-variety contracts).

Several Supreme Court decisions exemplify application of this standard. For example, in *Southland,* the Court held that the FAA displaced a provision of California's franchise statute that required claims

[15] This principle at least holds true for domestic cases. By contrast, federal common law supplies the substantive standard with respect to the enforceability of international arbitration agreements falling under the New York or Panama Conventions. *See* BORN, *supra* note 3, at 246–60.

[16] *See* First Options of Chicago, Inc. v. Kaplan, 514 U.S. 938 (1995) (stating "courts generally . . . should apply ordinary state-law principles that govern the formation of contracts"). *See, e.g.* Mastrobuono v. Shearson Lehman Hutton, Inc., 514 U.S. 52, 62–63 (1995); Volt Info. Sci., Inc. v. Bd. of Trustees, 489 U.S. 468, 475–76, (1989); Perry v. Thomas, 482 U.S. 483, 492–93 (1987).

thereunder to be litigated in court.[17] Likewise in *Perry v. Thomas*, the Court overturned the California Supreme Court decision and held that Section 2 of the FAA preempted a provision of California Labor Law at issue, which stated that wage collection actions may be maintained, regardless of whether a private agreement to arbitrate exists.[18] In *Perry*, a former employee (Thomas) of a securities brokerage firm brought an action against his former employer and two of its employees, alleging breach of contract, conversion, civil conspiracy to commit conversion, and breach of fiduciary duty. Although Thomas had an agreement to arbitrate claims with his former employee, the California courts relied on California law to deny the defendants' motions to compel arbitration the Superior Court "further concluded that since Thomas' claims for conversion, civil conspiracy, and breach of fiduciary duty were ancillary to his claim for breach of contract and differed only in terms of the remedies sought, they should also be tried and not severed for arbitration."[19] However, the Supreme Court held that the California law was clearly preempted, as the congressional intent to enforce arbitration agreements fell within the ambit of congressional commerce authority.[20] Finally, in *Doctors Associates v. Casarotto*, the Court held that the FAA preempted a Montana statute imposing special notice requirements on arbitration clauses in contracts.[21]

These decisions suggest a possible divide between the Court's rhetoric and reality. Although the Court purports to preserve room for federalism principles through its standard that generally applicable state-law contract defenses govern the FAA, each of the foregoing holdings remains consistently anti-federalist.

All of this has prompted a serious academic debate over how to give meaning to the Court's standard. Two primary schools of thought

[17] Southland Corp. v. Keating, 465 U.S. 1, 6–8 (1984).

[18] *Perry*, 482 U.S. at 483.

[19] *Id.* at 487.

[20] *Id.* at 490 (stating "[b]y contrast, the present appeal addresses the pre-emptive effect of the Federal Arbitration Act, a statute that embodies Congress' intent to provide for the enforcement of arbitration agreements within the full reach of the Commerce Clause ... This clear federal policy places § 2 of the Act in unmistakable conflict with California's § 229 requirement that litigants be provided a judicial forum for resolving wage disputes. Therefore, under the Supremacy Clause, the state statute must give way.").

[21] 517 U.S. 681, 687 (1996).

have emerged. One school has taken the view that Section 2 requires arbitration to be put on an "equal footing" with other contracts.[22] In other words, courts are free to invalidate arbitration agreements, but they must rely on a ground applicable to contracts generally. According to the other school, the FAA embodies a nondiscrimination principle.

In my view, these debates overlook the importance of the government body articulating the standard. An alternative lens through which to view the doctrine is to consider the effort by the Court to reallocate horizontal separation of powers at the state level. Much of contract law develops through the common law rather than legislative enactment.[23] State courts are the primary expositors of that law.[24] Consequently, through the exercise of their common-law power, state courts enjoy a unique prerogative to regulate arbitration agreements under the guise of articulating generally applicable principles of contract law. State judges, as the primary expositors of general state-contract law, effectively assert greater regulatory authority over the enforceability of arbitration agreements than do state legislatures.[25]

Not only does the Court's doctrine expand the power of state courts, it limits the tools available to state legislatures. For example, when a state court (particularly a state supreme court) concludes that a type of arbitration clause is enforceable, the state legislature's options are relatively limited. The state legislature cannot directly overrule the state court on the clause's enforceability; that would run afoul of the nondiscrimination principle described earlier. The only option meaningfully available to the state legislature is to modify general principles

[22] For a helpful recent discussion of the debate, see Hiro Aragaki, *Equal Opportunity for Arbitration*, 58 U.C.L.A. L. REV. 1189 (2011).

[23] For a good summary of the scholarship on this issue, see Kevin Teeven, *A History of Legislative Reform of the Common Law of Contract*, 26 U. TOLEDO L. REV. 35 (1994).

[24] Even in situations where contract law has been codified, such as the Uniform Commercial Code, the antecedents to those codifications rest on judge-made law. JOSEPH M. PERILLO, CALAMARI AND PERILLO ON CONTRACTS (2009).

[25] *See id.*; LON L. FULLER & MELVIN ARON EISENBERG, BASIC CONTRACT LAW (2006); ROGER E. MEINERS, AL H. RINGLEB, & FRANCES L. EDWARDS, THE LEGAL ENVIRONMENT OF BUSINESS 243 (2006) (explaining "[c]ontract law is primarily state common law. It has developed through decades of judicial opinions that have resolved virtually every kind of contract dispute.").

of state contract law. Such a course inevitably has spillover effects on contracts other than arbitration agreements.

Moreover, the state legislature enjoys far more power to regulate an anti-arbitration judicial decision with which it disagrees than a pro-arbitration one. To illustrate the point, consider two cases. In the first case, the state supreme court interprets the state's generally applicable contract law to reach a conclusion that can be characterized as pro-arbitration. If the state legislature disagrees with that decision, Section 2 of the FAA (as interpreted by the Supreme Court) would prohibit the legislature from enacting a statute that sought to overturn this precise holding. At best, the state legislature could only enact a statute that altered general principles of state contract law in a manner that abrogates the state supreme court's decision. The risk, of course, to the state legislature in this context is that the alteration of generally applicable contract law principles may upend other areas of state commerce that the legislature does not wish to affect.

In the second case, imagine that the state supreme court decides a case in a manner that may be characterized as anti-arbitration, and with which the state legislature disagrees. Here, by contrast, the state legislature's hands are not tied as tightly. In this case, the legislature could, consistent with Section 2, overrule the state supreme court without running afoul of FAA preemption principles. Even though the state law "singles out" arbitration, it does so for purposes of according arbitration agreements more favorable treatment than they would be entitled to under state law. Nothing in Section 2 of the FAA prohibits a state legislative enactment from having that effect.

Taken to its logical conclusion, the foregoing doctrinal ingredients enable state courts to affect a degree of regulation not available to state legislatures under the Supreme Court's interpretation of FAA Section 2. To see this point, consider an example: Suppose that nursing homes in a state are routinely requiring incoming residents to sign arbitration agreements as a condition of admission. Suppose further that the state has reason to be concerned that nursing homes are using these clauses to reduce their liability risks (or, conversely, limit the recovery to patients who are somehow injured or otherwise mistreated under the home's care). So the legislature enacts a law that prohibits nursing homes from conditioning admission to the home on the prospective patient's consent to the arbitration clause. Such a law would run afoul of Section 2 on the ground that it singled out arbitration clauses for discriminatory treatment.

Now suppose that, instead of state legislative action, the state court acts. Despite signing an arbitration agreement, a nursing home resident commences litigation and argues that the arbitration agreement is unenforceable. The state court agrees. It concludes that the arbitration agreement violates "public policy" (which is a generally applicable defense under state contract law), and that preservation of the right of access to courts (or the jury) is a sufficiently weighty public policy as to require the voiding of any contract provision that attempts prospectively to waive such rights (whether contained in a jury clause or otherwise). Unless the Supreme Court stepped in and reviewed that decision (statistically an extremely unlikely proposition), the rule would bind courts throughout the state and, thereby, cause them to invalidate any subsequent arbitration agreements in nursing home contracts. Effectively, the state supreme court has accomplished exactly the same result that the legislature sought to accomplish but, under the Supreme Court's FAA jurisprudence, could not.

Consequently, judge-made state contract law becomes the primary vehicle by which to regulate arbitration agreements effectively. If this hypothesis is correct, then over time one would expect to see an increasing share of judicial decisions developing state contract law in the context of arbitration agreements. The available empirical literature on this point bears this out.[26]

This state of affairs should give us pause. Does it really make sense to design a patchwork system where state judges hold the reins to regulate this important right? This question becomes particularly stark when one considers that this vesting of power occurs irrespective of the manner of recruiting or retaining the state judge. The same rule applies regardless of whether the state judge is regularly elected, appointed by

[26] *See, e.g.*, Susan Randall, *Judicial Attitudes toward Arbitration and the Resurgence of Unconscionability*, 52 BUFF. L. REV. 185, 196 (2004) (documenting that in 2002–2003 courts were twice as likely to find arbitration agreements unconscionable as non-arbitration agreements).

the governor, or otherwise. Would it not make more sense to vest this power in democratically accountable state representatives?

Here, of course, two responses are possible. First, one might justify this reallocation of power as a type of rights-reinforcing jurisprudence. Much like the famous Footnote Four in *Carolene Products* envisioned a special role for courts in buttressing the rights of discrete and insular minorities, the approach taken to Section 2 ensures that courts likewise will play a primary role in ensuring that parties lacking much political power are protected from oppressive arbitration clauses.[27] This hypothesis rests on the premise that state legislatures otherwise could not be trusted to protect the interest of such powerless classes in the arbitral process, a dubious presumption in light of the numerous examples of state enactments designed to protect consumers, employees, or other groups subject to arbitration clauses.

Second, one might justify the *Southland* line of reasoning not in terms of a horizontal reallocation at the state level but, instead, a vertical reallocation between state and federal authorities. In other words, the design wrought by *Southland* does not render the system of arbitration regulation wholly immune from the democratic process. Rather, it simply shifts the mechanisms of democratic accountability to Congress. Nothing precludes Congress from amending Section 2 and declaring certain times of pre-dispute agreements (such as those in nursing home contracts) non-arbitrable, or imposing greater procedural requirements on arbitration agreements before they will be enforced.

This latter account, even if correct, remains problematic for at least two reasons. First, it is notoriously difficult to get Congress to do anything.[28] Second, the model that focuses democratic accountability

[27] United States v. Carolene Prods. Co., 304 U.S. 144, 153 (1938); ALEXANDER BICKEL, THE LEAST DANGEROUS BRANCH: THE SUPREME COURT AT THE BAR OF POLITICS (1962); JOHN HART ELY, DEMOCRACY AND DISTRUST (1980); Bruce Ackerman, *Beyond* Carolene Products, 98 HARV. L. REV. 713 (1985); Lea Brilmayer, Carolene, *Conflicts and the Fate of the "Insider-Outsider"*, 134 U. PA. L. REV. 1291 (1986); Felix Gilman, *The Famous Footnote Four: A History of the* Carolene Products *Footnote*, 46 S. TEX. L. REV. 163 (2004); Louis Lusky, *Footnote Redux: A* Carolene Products *Reminiscence*, 82 COLUM. L. REV. 1093 (1982); Lewis F. Powell, Jr., Carolene Products *Revisited*, 82 COLUM. L. REV. 1087 (1982).

[28] *See* Michael E. O'Neill, *A Legislative Scorecard for the United States Senate: Evaluating Legislative Productivity*, 36 J. LEGIS. 297 (2010).

mechanisms at the national level overlooks the need for regionally based solutions. Going back to our original example, consider two states. One has an extensive history of nursing home abuse, but also relatively modest jury awards. The other has virtually no history of nursing home abuse and a history of runaway jury verdicts. As a policy matter, the former state presents a much stronger candidate for a law banning pre-dispute arbitration agreements than the latter state, yet the design of the FAA preemption doctrine means that such a ban could only be enacted (legislatively at least) on a nationwide basis. This consequence may be justified by the national policy favoring arbitration, but it certainly is not costless.

The Supreme Court's recent decision on *AT&T Mobility v. Concepcion* significantly alters the landscape governing Section 2 analysis and perhaps suggests the Court's discomfort with this reallocation of horizontal power at the state level.[29] That case involved a challenge to a judicially created rule of California law under which an arbitration clause coupled with a class action waiver was unconscionable. Because unconscionability was a generally applicable contract defense under California law, this rule represented nothing more than an unremarkable application of what cases such as *Prima Paint* contemplated.

Not so, said a bare majority of the Supreme Court. It held that Section 2 preempted the California rule notwithstanding the fact that the rule was cloaked in the mantle of unconscionability. In the Court's view, the California rule effectively confronted the parties with an unreasonable choice – they could arbitrate, but only if they agreed to the possibility of class arbitration (a mechanism that the Court had highly criticized in a decision from the previous term).[30]

Although *Concepcion* formally was limited to the California rule and the class action waiver, its implications are far more significant. The

[29] 131 S. Ct. 1740 (2011). Thomas J. Stipanowich, *The Third Arbitration Trilogy: Stolt-Nielsen, Rent-A-Center, Concepcion and the Future of American Arbitration*, 23 AM. REV. INT'L ARB. (forthcoming 2012) (manuscript at 110–11), *available at* http://papers.ssrn.com/sol3/papers.cfm?abstract_id=1919936; Peter B. Rutledge, *Common Ground in the Arbitration Debate*, 1 Y.B. ARB. & MEDIATION 1 (2009); Ronald W. Novotny, *Drafting Class Action Waivers after* AT&T Mobility v. Concepcion, 66 DISP. RESOL. J. 40 (Jan. 2012); Hans Smit, AT&T Mobility v. Concepcion*: Can Class Actions Be Brought in Arbitration*? 20 AM. REV. INT'L ARB. 469 (2009).

[30] *See* Stolt-Nielsen S.A. v. AnimalFeeds Int'l Corp., 130 S. Ct. 1758 (2010).

sweeping language in the Court's opinion betrays a general skepticism about reliance on certain generally applicable state-law contract doctrines, especially unconscionability and public policy, as grounds for invalidating arbitration agreements. Indeed, at one point in the Court's opinion, the Court went out of its way to criticize reliance on the public policy defense even though the issue technically was not before the Court.[31]

Viewed through the federalism lens developed in this chapter, *Concepcion* can be understood as an opinion that fundamentally restructured the federal/state balance governing the regulation of arbitration agreements. Prior to *Concepcion*, state contract law could be understood to provide a safe harbor for state regulation.[32] Provided that a state rule fit within one of the generally applicable doctrines, federal law did not intrude. After *Concepcion*, the harbor is no longer safe. Instead, the mere fact that an anti-arbitration rule falls within a generally applicable state contract doctrine supplies merely a necessary – *but no longer a sufficient* – condition for that rule to survive Section 2 preemption. Instead, the rule must undergo a second level of federal review.

What precisely is the nature of that review? *Concepcion* leaves the matter rather unclear. The decision may be understood to require a court to ask whether application of the state rule would result in an arbitration under terms other than those the parties agreed upon. If that is the approach, the sweep of the Court's rule is hard to predict. Virtually any state-law rule that calls into doubt the enforceability of a term of arbitration (such as a cost-shifting provision or a discovery limitation), if applied, would effectively impose on the parties arbitration under terms other than those on which they agreed. On the other hand, if instead the Court means to ask simply whether the generally applicable contract doctrine is really an anti-arbitration rule in disguise,

[31] 131 S. Ct. at 1747. Subsequently, the Court extended *Concepcion* and reversed a state Supreme Court's reliance on the public policy doctrine to invalidate an arbitration agreement. *See* Marmet Health Care Center, Inc. v. Brown, 132 S. Ct. 1201 (2012).

[32] A possible exception is the Supreme Court's decision in Perry v. Thomas, 482 U.S. 483 (1987). That decision built upon *Southland* and could be understood to hold that state courts may not read state statutes as embodying a "public policy" that, under the general public policy defense to contract enforcement, may supply a basis for invalidating an arbitration clause.

then maybe the sweep of the Court's decision will not be as great. Yet in that case, the Court's decision leaves much to be desired in terms of providing courts, state judges, and parties much guidance on the defining characteristics of such a rule.

Although the Court's Section 2 jurisprudence can be viewed in these terms – that is, a delicate balance between the unitary values underpinning Section 2's application in state court and the federalism values (before *Concepcion* at least) underpinning the substantive law governing the Section 2 defense – it bears emphasis that neither the Court nor Congress has expressly articulated this balance. This parallels the lack of deep reflection of the Court on the underlying constitutional values that we first encountered in Chapter 1's discussion of vertical separation of powers. Despite the lack of deep reflection, however, the Court's decisions continue to work important and, at times, inconsistent effects on the balance of power between the federal and state governments.

FEDERALISM AND ARBITRAL PROCEDURE

Although the Court's views on the enforceability of arbitration agreements reflect a mixed attitude toward federalism principles, its views on arbitral procedures, again with limited exceptions, tilt more strongly in favor of federalism. Indeed, apart from agreement enforceability, the FAA provides states an outlet to regulate arbitration.

Let me briefly define arbitral procedures. Specifically, this refers to the procedural law governing the arbitration, typically as set forth in the law of the arbitral forum. These may include matters such as the nomination of arbitrators, designation of the forum, discovery and evidence taking, and rendering of the award. Although arbitral rules often regulate such matters and leave them, subject to broad constraints, to the arbitrator's discretion, national arbitration law plays a residual, sometimes gap-filling role. For example, provisions of the FAA govern matters such as the appointment of arbitrators,[33] designation of the

[33] 9 U.S.C. §§ 5, 206 (2006).

forum,[34] and subpoenaing of witnesses.[35] In many respects, though, the FAA is silent.

This creates the conditions for state law to play a role in arbitral procedures. The opportunity traces to a structural feature of the FAA central to Justice O'Connor's dissent in *Southland:* Namely, many sections of the FAA, apart from Section 2, speak explicitly in terms of commands to or the power of U.S. District Courts. For example, consider Section 4 ("[a] party aggrieved by the alleged failure, neglect, or refusal of another to arbitrate under a written agreement for arbitration may petition any United States district court")[36] or Section 7 ("any [subpoenaed] person or persons so summoned to testify shall refuse or neglect to obey said summons, upon petition the United States district court . . . may compel the attendance of such person or persons before said arbitrator or arbitrators, or punish said person or persons for contempt").[37] To interpret such statutory language to control the activities of state courts would simply be an implausible reading. Thus, the FAA's design leaves significant breathing room for state law to govern arbitration proceedings, at least where the matter arises in state court.

Limitations on removal enhance the possibilities for state arbitration law to play an important role in matters of arbitration procedure. The Court has repeatedly made clear that cases involving arbitration, whether concerning the enforceability of an agreement or a request for judicial assistance, do not arise under federal law merely because they might potentially implicate some provision of the Federal Arbitration Act.[38] Rather, for the case to wind up in federal court, there must be some other basis for subject matter jurisdiction. These might be cases arising under the New York or Panama Conventions,[39] cases arising

[34] 9 U.S.C. §§ 4, 206, 303 (2006).

[35] 9 U.S.C. § 7 (2006).

[36] 9 U.S.C. § 4 (2006).

[37] 9 U.S.C. § 7 (2006).

[38] Vaden v. Discover Bank, 556 U.S. 49, 59 (2009); Hall Street Assocs., L.L.C. v. Mattel, Inc., 552 U.S. 576, 582 (2008); Allied-Bruce Terminix Cos. v. Dobson, 513 U.S. 265, 271–72 (1995); Volt Info. Sci., Inc. v. Bd. of Trustees, 489 U.S. 468, 476–77 (1989); Moses H. Cone Mem. Hosp. v. Mercury Constr. Corp., 460 U.S. 1, 24–27 (1983).

[39] 9 U.S.C. §§ 2–3 (2006).

under the court's diversity or alienage jurisdiction,[40] or cases where the underlying arbitration involves a federal cause of action.[41] If an arbitration falls outside these three categories, any proceedings related to the arbitration remain squarely in state court. This residual jurisdiction has given states an incentive to develop a variety of procedural mechanisms in aid of an arbitration such as asset freezes, discovery and subpoena authority, use of temporary injunctions, ability to appoint arbitrators, and issuance of protective orders.

In some cases, the procedural rights available under state law are superior to those under federal law. State law may significantly alter the role for judicial assistance with third-party discovery issues, as well as provide more advantageous avenues for discovery and interim measures available to parties under state law. Under the Uniform Arbitration Act as enacted by several state legislatures, arbitrators have the power to permit depositions to be taken under full backing of the power of the state of any witnesses unable to testify at the arbitration hearing.[42] Further, in Colorado, arbitrators have the power to issue provisional remedies such as interim orders "as the arbitrator finds necessary to protect the effectiveness of the arbitration proceeding and to promote the fair and expeditious resolution of the controversy."[43]

In some cases, these tools are not available only in cases where federal jurisdiction is excluded. Parties may rely on these devices through parallel state proceedings even where they might have the option of bringing the action in federal court. The tale of New York's asset freeze statute supplies a good example. Federal law does not explicitly authorize federal courts to issue asset freezes in support of arbitration,

[40] *See* Republic Fin. v. Cauthen, 343 F. Supp. 2d 529, 532 (N.D. Miss. 2004) (holding "[t]his action is based upon diversity jurisdiction and there is no argument that diversity and the requisite amount in controversy is lacking."); Rio Grande Underwriters, Inc. v. Pitts Farms, Inc., 276 F.3d 683, 685 (5th Cir. 2001) (reasoning "[t]he FAA is not an independent source of jurisdiction. A party may obtain relief in federal court under the FAA only when the underlying civil action would otherwise be subject to the court's federal question or diversity jurisdiction."); Jumara v. State Farm Ins. Co., 55 F.3d 873, 877 (3d Cir. 1995) (stating "the Jumaras established the complete diversity required by § 1332(a)" and the court compelled arbitration).

[41] Vaden v. Discover Bank, 556 U.S. 49 (2009).

[42] *See* A.R.S. § 12–507; MCA 27–5-215.

[43] C.R.S.A. § 13–2-208.

and decisions of the Supreme Court[44] further constrained the federal courts' authority. State law began to fill the gap, but initially some state courts such as New York took the view that their own state arbitration laws did not permit such freezes.[45] The New York legislature amended its law in 1985 to authorize such freezes, but even then New York courts construed the law narrowly to be limited to arbitrations sited in New York. Thereafter, the New York legislature again amended the law in 2005, this time to make clear that it applied to international arbitrations subject to the New York Convention irrespective of where the arbitration is sited.[46] Following this enactment, New York's appellate courts confirmed that this new law authorized its courts to freeze assets located in the state in support of an arbitration sited elsewhere (and even when that arbitration arose between two foreign parties). The availability of such remedies, and their compatibility with a significantly different federal regime, exemplifies how U.S. arbitration law advances federalism values.

What explains the Court's comparatively greater tolerance of federalism principles in the context of arbitration procedures as opposed to arbitration awards? Obviously, the stakes are quite different. A nonuniform standard governing the enforceability of arbitration agreements threatens to scuttle the entire undertaking before the arbitration has even commenced; parties resisting arbitration agreements will seek to challenge them in the most arbitration-unfriendly forum whereas parties seeking to enforce them will seek refuge in arbitration-friendly forums. By contrast, once the arbitration agreement is enforced (and the arbitration commenced), the need for uniformity declines, and the conditions emerge for the growth of a "law market" for different arbitral procedures. This diversity can actually benefit arbitration, for it

[44] Grupo Mexicano de Desarrollo S.A. v. Alliance Bond Fund, Inc., 527 U.S. 308 (1999).

[45] Cooper v. Ateliers de la Montobecane, SA, 442 N.E.2d 1239 (1982).

[46] *See* N.Y. C.P.L.R. § 7502(c) (McKinney 2005) (amending the statute to read in relevant part "[t]he supreme court . . . may entertain an application for an order of attachment or for a preliminary injunction in connection with an arbitration that is pending or that is to be commenced inside or outside this state, whether or not it is subject to the United Nations convention on the recognition and enforcement of foreign arbitral awards. . . . "); Sojitz Corp. v. Prithvi Info. Solutions Ltd., 921 N.Y.S.2d 14 (1st Dep't 2011) (affirming the proposition that pre-attachment awards in international arbitration cases are proper).

encourages parties to site their disputes in jurisdictions whose mix of procedural devices best serves the parties' interests. Thus, the Court's greater tolerance for federalism principles in the context of arbitration procedures can be understood as an effort actually to support arbitration as an institution.

FEDERALISM AND THE ENFORCEMENT OF ARBITRATION AWARDS

U.S. law governing the enforceability of arbitral awards displays a solicitude for federalism similar to that shown in the context of arbitral procedure. In contrast to the rules governing arbitral procedures, the law here actually leaves space for states that adopt anti-arbitration positions (again with limited exceptions).

The starting point for the analysis is Section 10 of the Federal Arbitration Act. Like the provisions on arbitral procedures, Section 10 speaks explicitly in terms of the U.S. district courts. Again, therefore, it would be incoherent to read the statute as setting forth a standard applicable in state court.[47] Coupled with the limits on the removability of arbitration actions to federal court, this reserved power for the states again enables state courts (and state law) an opportunity to play an important role in enforcement proceedings.

The critical difference between award enforcement and arbitration procedure comes in the opportunity for state law to undermine arbitration. Unlike rules at the procedural stage of a case, anti-arbitration standards governing the enforceability of an award have more bite. In the case of procedures, if a party does not like the procedural tools made available in one state, it can always seek to avail itself of procedural rights in other jurisdictions. By contrast, in the case of awards, the losing party naturally has the incentive to seek vacatur[48] in the most

[47] Although the Court has not expressly ruled on the applicability of Section 10 in state courts, most courts have concluded that it does not apply, leaving vacatur actions in state court subject to state law. *See* Nafta Traders, Inc. v. Quinn, 339 S.W.3d 84 (Tex. 2011); Cable Connection, Inc. v. DIRECTV, Inc., 44 Cal. 4th 1334 (2008).

[48] By vacatur, I mean an action by the award debtor to deprive the award of legal effect. Some commentators utilize the term "annulment" or "set aside" to describe this phenomenon.

arbitration-unfriendly forum possible. To the extent state law supplies that forum, the losing party can exploit the rules of that forum through a prompt vacatur action. Removal restrictions may preclude the prevailing party in the arbitration from removing the case to federal court (insofar as the federal standard might be more favorable). If a state court vacates the award, full faith and credit principles enhance the importance of a state standard. Vacatur of the award by the state court would be given preclusive effect in sister states and federal courts (subject to ordinary limits on claim and issue preclusion).[49] Consequently, the law governing award enforcement leaves greater room for state courts and, indeed, state legislatures, to promote an agenda skeptical of arbitration, through the development of broad standards permitting vacatur of the award.[50] We return to these themes in the next chapter.

What I have set forth so far is the standard account. This is, however, subject to two important qualifications, which allow federal interests to override competing state interests. First, parties can circumvent state courts (and legal regimes) unfavorable to arbitration by designating the forum in the arbitration clause. Generally, vacatur actions are only going to be brought in the arbitral forum[51] except in the rare case

[49] *See* Blumberg v. Berland, 678 F.2d 1068 (C.A. Ga. 1982) (holding that New York Supreme Court's judgment to confirm arbitration award was res judicata and entitled to full faith and credit). *See, e.g.*, CHARLES ALAN WRIGHT et. al., 18B FED. PRAC. & PROC. JURIS. § 4469 (2d ed. 2011).

[50] Although not central to the argument here, it is worth comparing the treatment of these principles in a system such as the United States with the treatment of similar principles on the international stage. Depending on the jurisdiction, vacatur in the arbitral forum does not guarantee a refusal to enforce the award elsewhere. *See* TermoRio SA v. Electranta SA E.S.P., 487 F.3d 928 (D.C. Cir. 2007); Baker Marine Ltd. v. Chevron Ltd., 191 F.3d 194 (2d Cir. 1999); Omnium De Traitement et de Valorisation S.A. v. Hilmarton Ltd., XXII Y.B. Comm. Arb. 696 (French Cour de cassation 1997); Chromalloy Gas Turbine Corp. v. Arab Republic of Egypt, 939 F. Supp. 907 (D.D.C. 1996). For commentary on the subject, see Christopher R. Drahozal, *Enforcing Vacated International Arbitration Awards: An Economic Approach*, 11 AM. REV. INT'L ARB. 451, 462 (2000); Jan Paulsson, *The Case for Disregarding LSAs (Local Standard Annulments) under the New York Convention*, 7 AM. REV. INT'L ARB. 99 (1996); Albert Jan van den Berg, *Enforcement of Annulled Awards?*, ICC INT'L CT. ARB. BULL. 15 (Nov. 1998); ALBERT JAN VAN DEN BERG, THE NEW YORK ARBITRATION CONVENTION OF 1958: TOWARDS A UNIFORM JUDICIAL INTERPRETATION (1981); Jan Paulsson, *Arbitration Unbound: Award Detached from the Law of Its Country of Origin*, 30 INT'L & COMP. L. Q. 358, 373 (1981) (stating a "country might allow enforcement of an award even though it has been set aside in its country of origin").

[51] BORN, *supra* note 3, at 1040–45.

when, perhaps, parties subject the arbitration to a procedural law other than that of the arbitral forum.[52]

Second, an entirely different analysis applies in cases arising under the New York and Panama Conventions. Those actions are far easier to remove, reducing the opportunities for state court (and thus state law) to influence vacatur. Moreover, those treaties set forth a common enforceability standard for all awards. Thus, even when the case remains in state court, opportunities for variation are diminished.[53] Furthermore, even where the enforcement standards do not specify the applicable law, the lower courts' construction of those standards (implicitly endorsed by the Supreme Court in *Mitsubishi Motors Corp. v. Soler Chrysler-Plymouth, Inc.*, stresses the relevance of federal policy (and the corollary irrelevance of state policy) in their enforcement.[54]

CONCLUSION

Arbitration law implicates federalism at all three stages of a dispute – agreement enforcement, procedural law, and award enforcement. The doctrine has developed most fully in the agreement-enforcement context and displayed crosscutting impulses. Although the applicability of FAA Section 2 in state court erodes federalism principles, the influence of state contract law on the standard provides a counterbalance, albeit one that the Supreme Court has begun to erode through decisions such as *Concepcion*. Though less fully developed, federalism plays an important role in both procedural law and award enforcement. In the area of procedural law, the coexistence of federal and procedural rights such as asset freezes and discovery enable states to play a distinct role, albeit one primarily focused on support for arbitration. In the area of award enforcement, states likewise enjoy even greater latitude, able to develop standards both more favorable and less favorable to those available under Section 10 of the FAA. Tellingly, this

[52] *Id.*

[53] Jack M. Graves, *Arbitration as Contract: The Need for a Fully Developed and Comprehensive Set of Statutory Default Legal Rules*, 2 Wm. & Mary Bus. L. Rev. 227, 257–59 (2011).

[54] 473 U.S. 614 (1985).

jurisprudence has developed without extensive consideration of either its broader implications or its relationship with other doctrines that advance (or undermine) federalism values. The product has been an inconsistent patchwork of federalism jurisprudence devoid of a deep theoretical grounding. The next chapter continues this examination into the relationship between arbitration and federalism, focusing on the significance of party choice.

4 ARBITRATION AND THE CHOICE OF LAW

> In recognition of Congress' principal purpose of ensuring that private arbitration agreements are enforced according to their terms, we have held that the FAA preempts state laws that require a judicial forum for the resolution of claims that the contracting parties agreed to resolve by arbitration. But it does not follow that the FAA prevents the enforcement of agreements to arbitrate under different rules than those set forth in the Act itself. Indeed, such a result would be quite inimical to the FAA's primary purpose of ensuring that private agreements to arbitrate are enforced according to their terms. Arbitration under the Act is a matter of consent, not coercion, and parties are generally free to structure their arbitration agreements as they see fit. Just as they may limit by contract the issues that they will arbitrate, so too may they specify by contract the rules under which that arbitration will be conducted.[1]

The preceding chapter considered the relationship between arbitration and vertical separation-of-power principles. We saw how the relationship between the Supremacy Clause, the Federal Arbitration Act, and state law created an odd arrangement under which federal law initially displaced state law that "singled-out" arbitration, but state law might still creep back into the analysis through the application of judicially crafted rules of generally applicable contract law. That entire discussion operated on the assumption that parties were bound by that vertical choice-of-law system. This chapter relaxes that assumption and considers the extent to which parties can (and should be able to) contract around those rules.

1 Volt Inf. Sci., Inc. v. Bd. of Trustees, 489 U.S. 468, 478–79 (1989) (citations omitted).

To lay the groundwork for the discussion, consider the following two hypotheticals:

> Hypothetical 1: Acme and Widget enter into a contract with an arbitration clause designating Los Angeles, California, as the arbitral forum. The contract also contains a choice-of-law clause specifying that the contract will be governed by California law. Despite the arbitration clause, Acme commences litigation against Widget in California state court, bringing various breach-of-contract claims and alleging that the arbitration clause is unenforceable. Under California law (but not federal law), an arbitration is automatically stayed in cases where one party commences litigation in the state courts and challenges the enforceability of the arbitration agreement.
>
> Hypothetical 2: Beta and Delta enter into a contract with an arbitration clause designating Los Angeles, California, as the arbitral forum. The arbitration clause also specifies that a court reviewing the arbitral award may conduct a de novo review of the award for legal error. The contract contains a choice-of-law clause specifying that the contract will be governed by California law. Delta commences arbitration against Beta and wins. Beta then files an action to vacate the award in California state court and argues that the arbitrator committed an error of law. Under California law (but not federal law), contractual provisions that expand the grounds for judicial review are enforceable.

Read against the backdrop of the preceding chapter, both hypotheticals bring the issue of party autonomy into stark relief. In the first hypothetical, if the parties are allowed to derogate from Section 2's standard, they can (on the margins at least) alter the distribution of power between federal and state authorities over the enforceability of arbitration agreements. In the second hypothetical, if the parties are allowed to derogate from Section 10's standard, they can alter the distribution of power over the enforceability of arbitral awards.

Before we delve into the theoretical framework, it is worth noting that issues of choice are operating at three levels here. The first level is the choice-of-law clause itself. This raises a host of subsidiary issues, many of which concern the scope of the clause. Does the clause merely designate the applicable law for the parties' contractual obligations? Does it also govern any noncontractual claims (such as tort claims)? Finally, does the choice-of-law clause also bear on the arbitration clause? Under the principle of separability, the arbitration clause is deemed to be a contract within the contract.[2] A corollary of this principle is that the arbitration clause may be subject to a different applicable law than the parties' substantive agreement.[3] Yet parties rarely, if ever, take this step.[4] Where they do not, does the law chosen to govern the parties' substantive obligations also represent an implied choice by the parties to subject issues about the arbitration clause (such as scope, validity, interpretation, etc.) to the same law?[5]

The second level is the choice of forum by the party challenging or enforcing the agreement (or award). Invocation of that forum subjects the dispute to a particular set of conflicts principles.[6] Even in cases where parties have designated the law applicable to the contract (or the arbitration clause), the enforceability and interpretation of that choice is a matter of conflicts of law (or private international law).[7] Although many jurisdictions coalesce around a common standard such as that set forth in Section 187 of the Restatement (Second) or the Rome I Regulation, variations remain.[8] Those variations can create

[2] Buckeye Check Cashing, Inc. v. Cardegna, 546 U.S. 440, 447 (2006); Prima Paint Corp. v. Flood & Conklin Mfg. Co., 388 U.S. 395, 402–05 (1967).

[3] GARY B. BORN, INTERNATIONAL COMMERCIAL ARBITRATION 411–24, 2208–10 (2009).

[4] *Id.* at 454–59.

[5] Telenor Mobile Commc'ns AS v. Storm LLC, 584 F.3d 396, 411 n.11 (2d Cir. 2009); Motorola Credit Corp. v. Uzan, 388 F.3d 39, 50 (2d Cir. 2004) ("[A] choice-of-law clause in a contract will apply to disputes about the existence or validity of that contract."); BORN, *supra* note 3, at 454–59; RESTATEMENT (SECOND) OF CONFLICT OF LAWS § 218 (1971) ("Frequently, the arbitration agreement will refer only to disputes arising under a certain contract and will be one of the provisions of that contract. If so, the state whose local law governs the arbitration agreement will ... usually be the same as the state whose local law would be applied to determine other issues relating to the contract.").

[6] RESTATEMENT (SECOND) OF CONFLICT OF LAWS § 218 cmt. b (1971); A. EHRENZWEIG, CONFLICT OF LAWS 540 (1962).

[7] Klaxon Co. v. Stentor Electric Mfg. Co., 313 U.S. 487, 495 (1941); Mann v. GTCR Golder Rauner, L.L.C., 351 B.R. 685, 695 (D. Ariz. 2006) ("A federal court sitting in diversity must apply the forum state's choice of law rules ... even in the face of contractual choice of law provisions, as the one expressed here, which purport to preclude the courts from engaging in such analysis.").

[8] RESTATEMENT (SECOND) OF CONFLICT OF LAWS § 187 (1971); Parliament and Council Regulation 593/2008, Law Applicable to Contractual Obligations (Rome I), 2008 O.J.

opportunities for a party to behave strategically by bringing challenge and enforcement actions in forums whose conflicts principles are most advantageous for that party.

The third level is the parties' choice of the arbitral forum. That designation may itself influence (or constrain) the second-level choice about where to bring the action challenging the agreement or award. This designation also bears a relationship to the first level of analysis. The designation of the arbitral forum, like the choice of substantive law, may influence a decision maker's view about the parties' implied choice to subject the arbitration clause to a particular law.[9] For example, where parties have entered into a contract containing an arbitration clause specifying London as the arbitral forum and French law as the applicable substantive law, does English law, French law, or some other law govern matters pertaining to the arbitration clause?

As the remainder of this chapter will show, all three levels of that choice – the choice-of-law clause, the choice of forum for any challenges, and the choice of arbitral forum – bear on the vertical allocation of power between federal and state authorities.

To begin to unpack these relationships, it is important to develop an analytic framework. Scholarship on mandatory and default rules provides a useful framework by which to analyze these hypotheticals and broader questions about the degree of party autonomy to manipulate by contract the relative distribution of power between federal and state authorities to regulate arbitration agreements and arbitral awards.[10] For readers unfamiliar with the literature, mandatory rules are those

(L 177) 10; Symeon C. Symeonides, *Choice of Law in the American Courts in 2011: Twenty-Fifth Annual Survey*, 60 AM. J. OF COMP. L.___ (forthcoming 2012); BORN, *supra* note 3, at 432–34, 479–82, 2112–14; Jason Webb Yackee, *Choice of Law Considerations in the Validity and Enforcement of International Forum Selection Agreements: Whose Law Applies?*, 9 U.C.L.A. J. INT'L L. & FOREIGN AFF. 43 (2004).

9 UNCITRAL Model Law on International Commercial Arbitration, G.A. Res. 40/72, at Art. 34(2)(a)(i), U.N. Doc. A/40/17 (July 7, 2006); Convention on the Recognition and Enforcement of Foreign Arbitral Awards New York Convention Art. V(1)(a), June 10, 1958, 330 U.N.T.S. 38; BORN, *supra* note 3, at 2122–23; RESTATEMENT (SECOND) OF CONFLICT OF LAWS § 218 cmt. b (1971) ("Provision by the parties in a contract that arbitration shall take place in a certain state may provide some evidence of an intention on their part that the local law of this state should govern the contract as a whole.").

10 Christopher R. Drahozal, *Contracting Around RUAA: Default Rules, Mandatory Rules, and Judicial Review of Arbitral Awards*, 3 PEPP. DISP. RESOL. L.J. 419, 420–22 (2003); Stephen J. Ware, *Default Rules from Mandatory Rules: Privatizing Law through Arbitration*,

around which parties may not contract. An example of a mandatory rule might be minimum wage laws, under which parties (generally) cannot contract for a wage lower than that set by statute.

Default rules are those around which parties may contract. An example of a default rule might be the 1980 United Nations Convention on the International Sale of Goods.[11] That Convention sets forth various rules governing the formation, performance, and remedies in international sales contracts. It applies in situations where parties to a contract have their place of business in signatory states. But the parties can exclude the Convention's application by inserting a clause to that effect in their agreement.[12]

As we move from the descriptive to the normative, scholarship on mandatory rules and default rules teach us when each form of rule may be desirable. Default rules facilitate contracting by relieving parties of the need to contract completely; default terms fill the gap in the parties' agreement.[13] Thus, default rules make sense when the costs of contracting are high and the social gain from contracting is substantial.[14]

Mandatory rules typically are explained as justifiable restraints on contractual freedom. Such mandatory rules may be appropriate where, for example, parties within the contract are unable to protect themselves.[15] This may result from unequal bargaining positions. Mandatory rules may also be appropriate when necessary to

83 MINN. L. REV. 703, 744–53 (1999); Randy E. Barnett, *The Sound of Silence: Default Rules and Contractual Consent*, 78 VA. L. REV. 821 (1992).

[11] United Nations Convention on Contracts for the International Sale of Goods, Apr. 10, 1980, S. Treaty Doc. No. 98–9 (1983), U.N. Doc. A/CONF 97/19, *available at* http://www.uncitral.org/pdf/english/texts/sales/cisg/V1056997-CISG-e-book.pdf [hereinafter CISG].

[12] *Id.* at Art. II, part 2, B.

[13] Drahozal, *supra* note 10, at 420; Barnett, *supra* note 10, at 825.

[14] Ian Ayres & Robert Gertner, *Filling Gaps in Incomplete Contracts: An Economic Theory of Default Rules*, 99 YALE L.J. 87, 93 (1989).

[15] Michael Galanis, *Vicious Spirals in Corporate Governance: Mandatory Rules for Systemic (Re)Balancing?*, 31 OXFORD J. LEGAL STUD. 327, 355–61 (2011) (discussing the need for mandatory rules to protect against power differentials in corporate governance structures); PETRI MANTYSAARI, THE LAW OF CORPORATE FINANCE: GENERAL PRINCIPLES AND EU LAW: VOLUME II, at 121–22 (2009); Stephen J. Ware, *Consumer Arbitration as Exceptional Consumer Law (with a Contractualist Replay to Carrington & Haagen)*, 29 MCGEORGE L. REV. 195, 214 n.97 (1998) ("[M]andatory disclosure laws are "paternalist" restrictions on autonomy"); Ayres & Gertner, *supra* note 14, at 88 ("Immutability

protect third parties. This may result where the contract results in externalities to the third party's interest that cannot (or should not) otherwise be bargained around.[16] Mandatory rules generally rest on some underlying normative account justifying a restraint on contractual freedom.[17]

Resort to this analytic framework is appropriate in this context in light of the basic issue. The entire analysis set forth in Chapter 3 proceeded on the assumption that the parties were bound by the rules governing the relationship of federal and state law as set forth in the FAA and as interpreted by the Supreme Court. If those rules were rigid and unbending, they would operate in a fashion not unlike mandatory rules. Readers familiar with this area of law know, however, that the Court has not been entirely inflexible in its views about the distribution of power to regulate arbitration between federal and state authorities. To a degree, the Court has allowed parties to redefine that allocation through the affirmative use of choice-of-law clauses. That re-definitional power exemplifies the degree to which the federalism principles set forth in Chapter 3 operate more like "default rules."

FEDERALISM, AUTONOMY, AND ARBITRATION AGREEMENTS

Since its *Southland* holding that Section 2 of the Federal Arbitration Act applies in state court proceedings and displaces contrary state law, the Supreme Court has grappled with the extent to which parties can reinvigorate state law through the use of choice-of-law clauses designating the application of state law. Three cases – *Volt, Mastrobuono, and Preston* – set forth the broad parameters of its work.[18]

is justified only if unregulated contracting would be socially deleterious because parties internal or external to the contract cannot adequately protect themselves.").

16 MANTYSAARI, *supra* note 15, at 121–22; Richard C. Buxbaum, *Facilitative and Mandatory Rules in the Corporation Law(s) of the United States*, 50 AM. J. COMP. L. 249, 250–55 (2002) (providing in the Corporation Codes of mandatory rules protecting third parties).

17 Alan Schwartz & Robert E. Scott, *Contract Theory and the Limits of Contract Law*, 113 YALE L. J. 541, 609–18 (2003); Ayres & Gertner, *supra* note 14, at 88.

18 *See* Archis Parashami & Kevin Ranlett, *Supreme Court's Addresses Volt's Choice of Law Trap: Is the End of the Problem in Sight?*, 64 J. DISP. RESOL. 22 (2009).

In *Volt Information Sciences, Inc. v. Stanford University*, the notion that private choice could reinvigorate federalism reached its high watermark in the Supreme Court's doctrine.[19] *Volt* involved an unusual set of facts. Volt, a construction company, entered into a contract with Stanford University. The contract contained a standard arbitration clause and a choice-of-law clause. The choice-of-law clause provided that the contract "shall be governed by the law of the place where the Project is located" (which in this case was California).

A dispute arose between the parties, and Volt demanded arbitration. Stanford responded by commencing litigation in California state court against Volt and seeking indemnification from two other companies that were involved in the project but were not parties to an arbitration agreement with Stanford. After Volt moved to compel arbitration, Stanford invoked a provision of California's arbitration law authorizing the court to stay arbitration pending parallel litigation when that litigation could result in "conflicting rulings on a common issue of law or fact."[20]

The California appellate court construed the contractual choice-of-law clause to mean that the parties intended to invoke California's arbitration law. In other words, drawing on the tripartite framework described earlier, the court relied on its answer to the first-order question about the scope of the choice-of-law clause to inform its treatment of the third-order question, the conflicts analysis governing the "separate" arbitration clause. This enabled the state appellate court to apply the stay provisions and uphold the trial court's stay of the arbitration proceedings.

The Supreme Court affirmed the decision in an opinion by Chief Justice Rehnquist unfolding in two stages.[21] In the first stage, the Court refused to revisit the California appellate court's construction of the arbitration clause, ruling it a question of state law on which the Supreme Court could not pass. In the second stage, the Court held that the FAA did not preempt application of California's stay rule. The Court declined to hold that Sections 3 and 4 of the Federal Arbitration Act

[19] 489 U.S. 468 (1989).

[20] CAL. CIV. PROC. CODE §1281.2(c) (1989).

[21] Volt Info, Sci., Inc. v. Bd. of Trustees, 489 U.S. 468, 476–77 (1989).

do not apply in state court. Instead, the Court reframed the "federal policy favoring arbitration" that was so critical to *Southland*'s application of Section 2 in state court. Rather than construe this policy to favor generalized enforcement of arbitration agreements, *Volt* instead cast this policy in terms of enforcing arbitration agreements "according to their terms."[22] Under this conception (and in light of the construction of the choice-of-law clause engrafted by the state appellate court), the FAA did not preempt the stay provision of California's arbitration act.

Volt is curious on at least three levels. Perhaps most curious was the Court's refusal to find that the FAA simply did not cover the issue. As the Court recognized, the provisions of the FAA addressing what a court should do when confronted with a challenge to the arbitration – namely Sections 3 and 4 – arguably do not apply in state court at all. Both of those provisions explicitly refer to U.S. district courts in the text, lending strong evidence that Congress did not intend to give those sections effect in state court. Moreover, such an approach would have been most consistent with Justice Rehnquist's vote in *Southland*, joining Justice O'Connor's dissenting view that the FAA simply did not apply in state court.[23] So holding in *Volt* would have weakened the anti-federalist foundations of *Southland*: It would have created the odd state of affairs in which certain provisions of the FAA applied in state court even though other provisions of the same law, enacted at the same time as part of the same statutory scheme, did not. Perhaps precisely due to the uncomfortable tension such an opinion would have created with *Southland*, Chief Justice Rehnquist could not go down this path and still have held a majority (particularly considering Justice O'Connor recused herself from the case).

The second oddity in *Volt*, and the one attracting the greatest attention in the literature, is the Court's treatment of the choice-of-law clause. The Court's reasoning rested on a re-characterization of the FAA's pro-arbitration policy – one that moved away from promoting arbitration under all circumstances to one enforcing the terms of the parties' agreement. This reasoning implied that the Court might have

22 489 U.S. at 478.
23 Chapter 3, p. 84.

reached a different result if the parties had not included the California choice-of-law clause in their contract. In that scenario, the Court likely would have had to confront the preemption question on which it passed. If Sections 3 and 4 did apply, that would undercut federalism values (but with an escape hatch through a choice-of-law clause). But if Sections 3 and 4 did not apply, that would have greatly advanced federalism values (and reduced the importance of the choice-of-law clause).

The third oddity in *Volt*, and arguably the most important one, yet the least explored in the literature, is the treatment of the state court's construction of the choice-of-law clause. Such a move was hardly necessary or obvious. As noted previously, party choice in arbitration can operate at several levels. The Court might well have concluded that a generalized choice-of-law clause merely operates to set forth the law governing the parties' substantive rights and obligations: It leaves untouched the law governing the arbitration agreement (or the procedural law arbitration itself). Under the principle of separability, the law governing the arbitration agreement might well be different from that governing the parties' substantive obligations.[24] Moreover, the procedural law governing the arbitration might be entirely different from either of the former two (that is, the substantive law or the law governing the arbitration agreement). Under this tripartite division, the Court might well have concluded, as a matter of federal common law, that a general choice-of-law clause merely governs the substantive rights while leaving the other two issues untouched.

The Court's refusal to follow this alternative course in the context of the state appellate court's construction of the choice-of-law clause is significant. Its analysis supplies a new pathway by which state courts, in cooperation with private parties, can promote federalism values. State courts can do so by liberally construing general choice-of-law clauses to encompass an implied choice to subject the arbitration clause to state law. To the extent those state-law determinations are immune from federal review (as *Volt* suggests), that strengthens state power to regulate arbitration. And because the FAA does not displace these choices, the net effect is to dampen the FAA's reach.

[24] BORN, *supra* note 3, at 411–24, 2208–10.

Viewing *Volt* through this lens, one can understand the Court's subsequent decision in *Mastrobuono* as part of an effort to trim back the state power granted by *Volt*.[25] *Mastrobuono* similarly involved a contract with an arbitration clause and a choice-of-law clause (in this case New York law). The sweep of that clause was important in light of New York's *Garrity* rule that precluded arbitrators (but not courts) from awarding punitive damages.[26] Despite the choice-of-law clause, a panel of arbitrators, convened pursuant to the contract, awarded punitive damages, relying on arbitral rules that authorized them to award "damages and other relief." Federal courts reviewing the award found that the arbitrators had exceeded their powers and, citing the choice-of-law clause and the *Garrity* rule, vacated the award of punitive damages.

The Supreme Court reversed and rejected the lower courts' view on the enforceability of the arbitral award. In an apparent effort to cabin the reach of the *Volt* rule, the Court construed the New York choice-of-law clause merely "to encompass the substantive principles that New York courts would apply, but not to include [New York's] special rules limiting the authority of arbitrators."[27] This meant that the New York choice-of-law clause did not incorporate the *Garrity* rule even though, like the stay provision at issue in *Volt*, it formed part of New York's arbitration law.

Obviously the contrast with *Volt* was sharp. In one case, the Court construed a substantive choice-of-law clause narrowly (in order to prevent the importation of state arbitration law); in the other case, the Court declined to revisit a state court's contrary determination of the issue. This commonality between the clauses in *Volt* and *Mastrobuono* prompted a dissent by Justice Thomas, who saw the two cases as indistinguishable.[28] In response, the majority explained away *Volt* on the ground that it involved deference to a state court's construction of a choice-of-law clause, as opposed to *Mastrobuono*, which emerged through the federal court system.

25 Mastrobuono v. Shearson Lehman Hutton, Inc., 514 U.S. 52 (1995).
26 Garrity v. Lyle Stuart, Inc., 40 N.Y.2d 354, 357–58 (N.Y. 1976).
27 Mastrobuono, 514 U.S. at 64.
28 *Id.* at 64–72.

As a factual matter, the distinction was valid, but it created an even more perplexing state of affairs for the relationship between private choice and federalism. Now, the *exact* same clause could have very different consequences depending solely on the court through which it percolated. State courts could interpret a choice-of-law clause to incorporate the state arbitration law (as in *Volt*), and that determination would be immune from federal review. State courts would have a selfish incentive to accord clauses such interpretations in order to give effect to their own arbitration laws. By contrast, under *Mastrobuono*, a federal court could *not* construe the exact same general choice-of-law clause to have this effect. Moreover, a federal court would not have the same incentive to give effect to the state arbitration law.

As we return to the matrix developed at the outset of this chapter, *Volt* and *Mastrobuono* demonstrate the interplay of the first and second levels of "choice" analysis. Private choice about the applicable law (the first-level issue) can influence the law governing the arbitration clause (and thus the result). But the nature of that influence depends critically on where those issues are being litigated (the second- level issue) in light of the differing federal and state approaches to construction of the choice-of-law clause.

The Court finally sought to untangle this web in *Preston v. Ferrer.*[29] *Preston* concerned a contract between an actor and a California attorney. The contract, which envisioned the attorney representing the actor's interests (not unlike a talent agent), contained an arbitration clause. The trouble was that the attorney was performing the services of a talent agent without a license, which triggered a provision of California's Talent Agencies Act. That Act authorized California's Labor Commissioner to make the preliminary decision whether the attorney was acting in violation of the Act's provisions, and the question arose whether the pending proceeding before the Labor Commissioner necessitated an injunction of the arbitration. The California courts issued the injunction, prompting Supreme Court review.

Ordinarily, the Court might easily have held that the divestment of the arbitrator's jurisdiction was inconsistent with the FAA. What complicated the case was that the parties' agreement also contained a

[29] Preston v. Ferrer, 552 U.S. 346 (2008).

California choice-of-law clause, resurrecting the debate between *Volt* and *Mastrobuono*. Unlike *Mastrobuono*, the case did not arise from a federal forum, thus preventing the Court from relying on the distinction it used to respond to Justice Thomas's dissent. Without overruling *Volt*, the Court held that the FAA preempted the provision of the Talent Agencies Act lodging primary jurisdiction of the arbitrable dispute with California's Labor Commissioner.[30]

The Court's holding rested on a re-characterization of *Volt*. Instead of grappling with *Volt*'s language about enforcing arbitration agreements according to their terms, the Court re-characterized *Volt* as a case about statutory silence. According to the *Preston* Court, *Volt* involved parallel litigation against nonsignatories – a topic that the FAA did not explicitly address – so it was appropriate for the Court "to recognize state law as the gap filler."[31] Moreover, the *Preston* majority stressed that the arbitration clause (a standard AAA clause) vested the arbitrators with the power to determine their own jurisdiction (including the validity of the arbitration clause), much like the clause in *Mastrobuono* incorporated rules granting the arbitrators power to order any relief. Nothing in *Volt* suggested the case turned on the meaning of gap fillers; far from it, the Court's purpose was to give effect to the parties' affirmative choices. Moreover, as to the arbitral rules, the clause in *Volt* also designated an applicable set of rules – a fact overlooked by the *Preston* Court – but the decision did not suggest that they somehow reduced the appropriateness of relying on the state choice-of-law clause to incorporate application of the state arbitration law.

The Court also re-characterized *Mastrobuono*, and facts salient to *Mastrobuono*'s treatment of *Volt* suddenly became irrelevant to the *Preston* Court's analysis. As noted earlier, *Mastrobuono* greatly emphasized the fact that the construction of the clause in that case rested on a state court's interpretation. That distinction was given short shrift in *Preston*, which did not pause to consider the importance of the state court's interpretation that the choice-of-law clause invoked California's rules on the primary jurisdiction of the Labor Commissioner.

[30] Preston, 552 U.S. at 356; CAL. LAB. CODE §§ 1700.44(a), 1700.45 (West 1986).
[31] *Preston*, 552 U.S. at 360–62.

As the Supreme Court's last word on the relationship between FAA preemption and choice-of-law, *Preston* is remarkably unsatisfying. It leaves the reader wondering why the Court refused to take a side in the *Volt/Mastrobuono* debate instead of simply interring *Volt*, as one speculates Justice Ginsburg would have liked to have done.

Perhaps *Preston* is better understood as an attempt to trim the "default" nature of the Court's FAA preemption jurisprudence and, thereby, shift that jurisprudence more in the direction of mandatory rules favoring the application of uniform federal law. *Preston* trims the ability of parties, whether through state choice-of-law clauses or choice-of-forum decisions (favoring state court) to reinvigorate state regulation of arbitration agreements. Tellingly, though, *Volt* has not been overruled and remains, at least theoretically, a viable avenue for buttressing states' rights.

To echo a theme that has permeated each of the chapters to this point (and presages future chapters), this evolution of these federalism principles from a "default" system to an increasingly "mandatory" one have occurred without much systematic examination or input from the political branches. Although the federalism values underpinning preemption debates largely involve construction about the sweep of enactments by federal and state legislatures, those branches have been largely absent from the debate over the proper allocation of values. Moreover, the lens through which those debates occur judicially, namely particular cases presenting the Court with particular factual settings, are not especially conducive to a systematic examination of the first principles underlying the proper allocation of power between federal and state officials.

FEDERALISM, AUTONOMY, AND ARBITRATION PROCEEDINGS

The law governing arbitration proceedings has followed a very different course from the *Volt-Preston* line. Whereas that line of cases has focused principally on the meaning of a choice-of-law clause in the contract, the relationship among federalism, choice, and arbitral procedure has focused principally on the choices about forums, whether arbitral or judicial. By that, I mean the parties' choice about where to arbitrate and where to seek judicial assistance plays a more significant role in the design of the arbitration proceedings and the role of state law in the development of arbitration.

Before I explain why this is the case, it is worth noting that this *need* not be the case. Parties might rely on contractual choices to influence the role of state law in arbitration. They could do so, for example, by specifying in the arbitration clause that a particular state's procedural rules will apply.[32] Alternatively, arbitral institutions might influence this choice by setting forth more detailed procedural guidelines in their arbitral rules that the parties incorporate by reference.[33] Neither parties nor arbitral institutions have pursued this option, meaning that other choices will influence the role of state law in arbitration procedures.[34]

The primary device used by parties has been the choice of arbitral forum. At the beginning of this chapter, we noted how the choice of arbitral forum could be read to imply a choice by the parties about the law governing the validity or interpretation of the arbitration agreement. By the same logic, the designation of the arbitral forum might be understood to imply a choice about the law governing the *procedures*

[32] *See* Dr. Kenneth Ford v. NYLCare Health Plans of Gulf Coast, Inc., 141 F.3d 243, 249 (5th Cir. 1998) (holding that the parties intended through a choice-of-law clause to have Texas law and the Texas General Arbitration Act (TGAA) govern the scope of arbitration clause in the medical services agreement between the surgeon and HMO).

[33] The IBA Rules represent a step in this direction. *See* IBA Rules on the Taking of Evidence in International Commercial Arbitration (2010); 1999 IBA Working Party and 2010 IBA Rules of Evidence Review Subcommittee, *Commentary on the Revised Text of the 2010 IBA Rules on the Taking of Evidence in International Arbitration*, 5 DISP. RESOL. INT'L 45 (2011); Peter Ashford, *Rule Changes Affecting the International Arbitration Community*, 22 AM. REV. INT'L ARB. 87 (2011) (stating "[p]arties to arbitrations, as well as arbitral tribunals, are free (subject to any contractual provision to the contrary) to adopt the Revised Rules (in whole or in part) to govern arbitration proceedings, or they may vary them or use them as guidelines in developing their own procedures. The Revised Rules are not intended to limit the flexibility that is inherent in, and an advantage of, international arbitration and parties and arbitral tribunals are generally free to adapt the Rules/Revised Rules to suit the particular circumstances of each arbitration."). Direct application of the IBA Rules requires, however, an affirmative choice by the parties either in the arbitration agreement or in a post-submission agreement. Parties rarely make this choice. GARY B. BORN, INTERNATIONAL ARBITRATION 562 (2011). Otherwise, at most, the IBA Rules supply a relevant, though ultimately non-binding, guidepost on the applicable procedures.

[34] Gary B. Born, INTERNATIONAL ARBITRATION 562 (2011).

of the arbitration. This has often been the case in international arbitration, where arbitrators look to the law of the arbitral forum to supply the governing procedural law.[35]

When we move from the international analogy, the question arises whether, in the United States, arbitrators consult the law of the state in which they sit to make the relevant procedural determinations. Both courts and arbitrators have made clear that siting an arbitration in a particular jurisdiction does not entitle a party to utilize that jurisdiction's rules of civil procedure.[36] To what extent, however, does the choice of forum influence the arbitrator's resort to the forum state's arbitral law?

State law can have this influence in at least two different ways. First, the arbitrator might look to state law to determine what procedures he or she may follow. Second, state law grounds for award vacatur can influence the arbitrator's procedural decisions. As numerous commentators have observed, arbitrators have a natural incentive to render an enforceable award, and this incentive prompts them to avoid any decision that would run afoul of the vacatur standards of the arbitral forum. Many arbitration laws include, among their vacatur grounds, procedural irregularities (the meaning of which has been subsequently interpreted by the state courts). To reduce the risks of vacatur, therefore, arbitrators attempt to render decisions that ensure compliance with the procedural requirements of the law of the arbitral forum, as interpreted by that state's courts.

Class arbitration supplies a good example. In *Bazzle*, the Court when interpreting the construction of the parties' arbitration clause acknowledged that one of the main goals of the arbitrators was to render an enforceable award under South Carolina law with respect to the permissibility of multi-party arbitration.[37] The Court specifically acknowledged that the arbitrators' decision to follow the state court's

35 Gary B. Born, International Arbitration 715–16 (2011).

36 Lessin v. Merrill Lynch, Pierce, Fenner & Smith, Inc., 481 F.3d 813, 817 (D.C. Cir. 2007); Bowles Fin. Group, Inc. v. Stifel, Nicolaus & Co., Inc., 22 F.3d 1010, 1013 (10th Cir. 1994) ("This court has no power to judicially impose our rules of evidence on an arbitral proceeding"); Yasuda Fire & Marine Ins. Co. v. Continental Cas. Co., 37 F.3d 345 (7th Cir. 1994) ("That does not mean, however, that the parties before an arbitration panel are entitled to all of the process that accompanies a judical proceeding.").

37 Green Tree Fin. Corp. v. Bazzle, 539 U.S. 444, 453 (2003).

reasoning in *Bazzle* (though not a persuasive argument on appeal in *Bazzle* itself) indicated that an arbitrator wanted to construe state law in the same manner as the state courts in order to secure an enforceable arbitral award.[38]

Apart from the designation of the arbitral forum, party choice can intersect with federalism in another respect. Parties can invoke the assistance of a state's procedural law even where the arbitration is not sited in that state. New York's asset freeze statute, discussed in the preceding chapter, supplies a good example. Even though New York has utterly no interest in the dispute apart from the presence of property in the jurisdiction, its courts become available to support arbitration sited outside the state. Further as previously discussed in Chapter 3, parties can avail themselves in limited circumstances of state procedural rules in aid of discovery, even when the arbitration is sited elsewhere.[39]

FEDERALISM, AUTONOMY, AND ARBITRATION AWARDS

Although the Court has followed an inconsistent path with respect to parties' prerogative to promote federalism values through the exercise of contractual choice regarding arbitration agreements, it has followed a more consistent path with respect to arbitration awards. Much like in Chapter 3, we see the Court more tolerant of state variation in the law governing the enforcement of arbitral awards, including in cases where parties have sought to manipulate the applicable legal rules by contract.

The seminal case here, which supplies the springboard for our discussion, is thc Supreme Court's decision in *Hall Street v. Mattel*.[40] As discussed in Chapter 1, *Hall Street* emerged from an unusual dispute involving a commercial lease agreement. In the first phase of the dispute, a court held that the lessee (Mattel) had the right to terminate the lease. At that point, the parties agreed to arbitrate the question whether

[38] *Id.*

[39] *See* Gary B. Born, INTERNATIONAL ARBITRATION 53 (2011).

[40] *Hall Street Associates, L.L.C. v. Mattel, Inc.*, 552 U.S. 576 (2008).

the lessor (Hall Street) could seek indemnification for cleanup of the commercial site. That agreement, drawn up under court supervision, provided in relevant part:

> The United States District Court for the District of Oregon may enter judgment upon any award, either by confirming the award or by vacating, modifying or correcting the award. The court shall vacate, modify or correct any award where (i) the arbitrator's findings of facts are not supported by substantial evidence, or (ii) where the arbitrator's conclusions of law are erroneous.[41]

Effectively, the agreement expanded the grounds for judicial review of the award beyond those specified in Section 10 of the FAA (which does not explicitly authorize review either for factual or legal error).

The Court, however, held that the FAA's grounds for judicial review of arbitral awards were exclusive and, therefore, contractual modification by the parties were not enforceable, at least in federal court.[42] Central to the Court's reasoning was the strong federal policy favoring arbitration. Moreover, the Court contrasted the seemingly mandatory language of Sections 9–11 (specifying that a court "shall" enforce an award unless one of the Section 10 grounds is present) with other sections of the Act (such as Section 5) that more explicitly give effect to party choice. Yet the Court in *Hall Street* stopped short of declaring such contractual modifications of the standards of review wholly unenforceable. Instead, the Court reserved the possibility that such modifications might be enforceable either under state law or as a matter of contract law.[43]

Hall Street can be understood to reflect two separate, perhaps conflicting, regulatory concerns about the investment of judicial resources. One concern is preventing the overinvestment of resources. The narrow review of arbitral awards contemplated by Section 10 of the FAA can be understood to reflect an implicit determination by Congress that courts should invest relatively few resources in scrutinizing arbitral awards. The grounds set forth in Section 10 of the FAA generally concern matters external to the arbitration such as the

[41] *Id.* at 2.
[42] *Hall Street*, 552 U.S. at 586.
[43] *Id.* at 590.

relationship between the arbitrator and the parties or whether the arbitrator exceeded his or her mandate. Even when Section 10 addresses the arbitration itself (such as the failure to postpone the hearing), the relevant factual premise upon which the issue turns does not require the reviewing court to delve very deeply into the record.

Review along the lines set forth by the clause in *Hall Street* entails a significantly greater investment of judicial resources. If parties could contractually expand those standards, it would increase, relatively speaking, the workload on the federal courts. This would be particularly true if parties could authorize courts to scrutinize awards for legal or factual errors. Such review would entail a much more extensive inquiry into the record of the arbitration and the legal rationale for the arbitrator's decision.

The second concern is regulating the enforcement of arbitral awards. The act of enforcement invokes the coercive power of the state to seize the award-debtor's property in satisfaction of the award. As discussed in Chapter 1, the degree of judicial review preserved by Section 10 of the FAA can be understood to reflect an implicit determination by Congress about the minimum levels of fairness that an award must satisfy before that coercive power can be invoked. If parties could contractually modify the grounds for judicial review of an award, then it might logically follow that those modifications need not be limited to expansions of judicial review, but might also entail contractions as well. Narrowing judicial review (or eliminating it altogether) would gut Congress' interest in controlling the invocation of the state's coercive power.[44]

Although either of the foregoing reasons might explain *Hall Street*'s conclusion that contractually expanded judicial review of arbitral

[44] Like the grounds set forth in Section 10 of the FAA, nearly all national arbitration legislation provides for limited judicial review. *See* GARY B. BORN, INTERNATIONAL ARBITRATION 1094 (2011). However compare Belgian law, which allows for non-Belgian national parties to expressly contract provisions that shield their award from judicial review by Belgian courts. Belgian Judicial Code, Art. 1717(4) (1999) (stating "[t]he parties may, through an express declaration in the arbitration agreement or through a later agreement, exclude any action for the annulment of an arbitrator's award when neither of them is either a natural person with a Belgian citizenship or a residence in Belgium, or a legal person having its main establishment or having a branch there.") (*translation available at* GARY B. BORN, INTERNATIONAL ARBITRATION 1071 (2011).).

awards is incompatible with Section 10, what explains the Court's willingness to preserve the possibility to enforce such rights outside federal court? Federalism supplies the best lens through which to view this limitation on the Court's opinion. If we recall the ideas explored in Chapter 3, such an opportunity *only* is possible if Section 10, unlike Section 2, does not apply directly in state court proceedings.[45] (Thus *Hall Street* might be understood to resolve implicitly an issue that technically has been left open since *Southland*.)

If the foregoing premise is correct, then *Hall Street* created new opportunities to promote federalism values through the application of state arbitration law. *Hall Street* leaves open the opportunity for state law to play an important residual role by enforcing such contractual modifications of review standards. Although Congress struck one balance of regulatory interests in the FAA, states could strike a different one.

Like *Volt*, the Court appears to be motivated by an effort to promote federalism principles when coupled with an affirmative choice by the parties, but the dynamics differ in several important respects. First, the two cases differ in terms of the precise method by which private parties promote federalism. In *Volt*, the parties advanced federalism values through a combination of a choice-of-law clause and an effort to enforce that clause in a state forum (recall *Mastrobuono*'s distinction between state and federal forums in terms of the rules of construction for that choice-of-law clause). In *Hall Street*, the parties advance federalism values through a slightly different form – a contractual modification of the judicial review standards coupled with a choice to enforce those standards in the state forum (in other words, the first and second levels of choice, discussed at the outset of this chapter, are operating in tandem).

Second, the two federalism-promoting models of *Volt* and *Hall Street* differ in terms of the institutions that can affect the enforcement standards. As discussed in Chapter 3 state courts play the primary role in the law governing arbitration agreements. They do so both with respect to their construction of generally applicable state law contract defenses (excepting *Concepcion*) and with respect to their construction

45 Chapter 3, p. 83.

of choice-of-law clauses (as evident in *Volt*). By contrast, in the area of award enforcement, the doctrine leaves room for both state legislatures and state courts to advance federalism values. State legislatures can do so through amendments to the state's arbitration law explicitly allowing for expanded review. State courts can do so either through their common-law making power or through their interpretation of the state's arbitration statute.

Actual practice has borne out both models.[46] Even before *Hall Street*, at least one state (New Jersey) embedded within its state arbitration law the possibility of "opting in" to expanded judicial review.[47] Although adopting the Uniform Arbitration Act in large part, New Jersey included the following exceptional language: "nothing in this act shall preclude the parties from expanding the scope of judicial review of an award by expressly providing for such expansion." The legislation followed an earlier debate over whether a prior version of New Jersey's arbitration law allowed (similar to the FAA's "exceed powers" ground) courts to vacate awards for egregious legal errors.[48]

Several state supreme courts, particularly since *Hall Street*, have upheld, as a matter of state law, contractual modifications of the standards of review of arbitral awards, including modifications allowing

[46] For commentary, see Leigh F. Gill, *Manifest Disregard after* Hall Street: *Back from the Dead – The Surprising Resilience of a Non-Statutory Ground for Vacatur*, 15 LEWIS & CLARK L. REV. 265 (2011); Christopher R. Drahozal, *Contracting around* Hall Street, 14 LEWIS & CLARK L. REV. 905 (2010); John James Barceló III, *Expanded Judicial Review of Awards after* Hall Street *and in Comparative Perspective*, *in* RESOLVING INTERNATIONAL CONFLICTS – LIBOR AMICORUM, TIBOR VÁRADY 1 (Peter Hay et al. eds., 2009); Stephen K. Huber, *State Regulation of Arbitration Proceedings: Judicial Review of Arbitration Awards by State Courts*, 10 CARDOZO J. CONFLICT RES. 509 (2009).

[47] N.J. STAT. ANN. § 2A: 23B-4(c) (West 2003) ("[N]othing in this act shall preclude the parties from expanding the scope of judicial review of an award by expressly providing for such expansion in a record"). California does not have a statute but in Cable Connection, Inc. v. DIRECTV, Inc., 44 Cal. 4th 1334, 1353–55 (Cal. 2008) it states that *Hall Street*'s holding is confined to reviews under the FAA. *See* Barceló, *supra* note 46. Alabama – Raymond James Fin. Servs, Inc. v. Honea, 55 So. 3d 1161, 1169 (Ala. 2010) ("We are accordingly at liberty to decide whether to apply § 10 in state court proceedings on motions to vacate or to confirm an arbitration award."); Texas – Nafta Traders, Inc. v. Quinn, 339 S.W. 3d 84, 101 (Tex. 2011) ("The only reasonable reading of the opinions in *Hall Street*, in our view, is that the FAA does not preempt state law that allows parties to agree to greater review of arbitration awards.").

[48] *See* Tretina Printing, Inc. v. Fitzpatrick & Assocs., Inc., 640 A.2d 788 (N.J. 1994); Perini v. Greate Bay Hotel & Casino, 610 A.2d 364 (N.J. 1992).

the court to review the award for legal or factual errors. For example, the high courts of both Texas and California have held, as a matter of common law, that party-initiated expansions of judicial review are enforceable in their courts. In other cases, states such as Maine and Tennessee have joined this dialogue by construing their state arbitration laws to track the Supreme Court's interpretation of the FAA in *Hall Street*.[49]

Such developments have promoted federalism values within the arbitral sphere beyond those available under Section 2. Relative to federal forums, state forums become more hospitable to such contractual modifications of judicial review and give parties seeking to utilize such modifications an incentive to bring their vacatur actions in state court (as opposed to federal court) and to rely on state law (as opposed to federal law) to test the award's enforceability. The upshot has been to wed federalism to party choice in the award enforcement context, much like *Volt* did in the agreement context.

Is this a salutary development? For one thing, from the perspective of federalism values, the answer would seem to be an unequivocal *yes*. It enables parties, through their affirmative choice, to give effect to state regulatory decisions designed to give even greater effect than the federal standard. To be sure, the greater diversity of state practice – and the variation from federal practice – tolerated by these rules dampens the uniformity goals that animated decisions such as *Southland*. Yet perhaps this is a sensible price – at least in cases where the federalism values are wedded with freedom-of-contract values (that is, giving effect to the parties' choices about the scope of judicial review of the award).

For another thing, the enforceability of party-initiated modifications of judicial review reinforce federalism values in a second, important respect. Namely, they facilitate jurisdictional competition among states that offer differing regimes for the enforcement of such party-initiated modifications of the standards of judicial review. For a variety of reasons, mostly jurisdictional, parties naturally will be inclined to bring vacatur actions in the arbitral forum. Consequently, parties valuing

[49] HL 1, LLC v. Riverwalk, LLC, 2011 ME 29 (2011); Pugh's Lawn Landscape Co. v. Jaycon Dev. Corp., 320 S.W.3d 252 (Tenn. 2010).

the "safety valve" of judicial review of the merits of an award have a natural incentive to favor forums providing that review.

This type of interjurisdictional competition exemplified by the New Jersey statute and decisions such as those of the California and Texas high courts exemplify the "law market" described in a recent book by Erin O'Hara and Larry Ribstein.[50] In the book, the authors examine the extent to which parties can (and do) exploit the diversity of potential legal rules regulating their conduct in order to organize their affairs around the set of rules most favorable to them. Familiar examples include the decision to organize corporations under Delaware law (given the simplicity of doing so, the predictability of Delaware's well-developed corporate law, and the reputation of Delaware judges for understanding issues of corporate governance) or the decision by many credit card issuers to organize their operations in states such as South Dakota (where usury laws are relatively weak, enabling the banks to charge higher rates of interest).

O'Hara and Ribstein's model has important implications for the issues of choice and federalism that this chapter has explored. A party who has strong reasons to favor arbitration may attempt to maximize the enforceability of any agreement by specifying that the arbitration clause will be governed by a substantive law that is especially favorable to arbitration. Alternatively, the party may insist that any arbitration take place in a forum whose courts (or whose substantive law) is especially predisposed to enforcing arbitration agreements. Conversely, a party who wishes to preserve, to the maximum extent possible, its right to challenge an arbitration agreement or award can opt into a system designed to give effect to such private choice. Much like Delaware has attracted corporate business or South Dakota has attracted credit card business, a forum might attract "dispute" business by creating conditions particularly conducive to a party (or parties) favoring arbitration.

Although it is too soon to tell whether such interjurisdictional competition will take place among states, evidence at the international level suggests that such jurisdictional competition facilitated by private choice is possible. Much like states, nations can compete for arbitral

[50] O'HARA & RIBSTEIN, THE LAW MARKET (2009).

business within the "law market."[51] One way in which they might differentiate themselves from "competing" states is to design the arbitral laws to give greater (or lesser) effect to such party choice. Belgium employed precisely this strategy when it enacted a law allowing parties who were not Belgian citizens to specify the Belgian arbitral forum and then affirmatively opt out of any judicial review of the award.[52] Sweden likewise has recently amended its arbitration act to allow for this possibility. Both examples illustrate how, at least on the international stage, countries are engaging in interjurisdictional competition to attract arbitration business through creating "default rules" about vacatur standards around which parties can contract.

Of course, the European experience differs from the state anecdotes in an important respect. Whereas the state anecdotes all involve party-initiated expansions of judicial review, the Belgian and Swedish models involve party-initiated contractions of judicial review. At first blush, the latter model would appear to be more likely to enhance a jurisdiction's appeal in the law market. Excluding grounds for vacatur enhances the predictability that the arbitral award will be enforced, whereas expanding the grounds undermines that predictability.

This distinction is, though, subject to two responses. First, the "value" of a particular jurisdiction's legal regime (as it interacts with party choice) depends critically on the party's utility curve. If the party favors a regime for award enforcement that assures maximum enforceability, then the state models do not offer much comparative advantage. On the other hand, to the extent a party favors the "safety valve" of judicial review, then models such as those in New Jersey actually give parties a greater incentive to site their arbitration there.

The second point is that the logic of *Hall Street* has not been fully tested judicially. Given its facts, *Hall Street* merely had to hold that the

51 Christopher R. Drahozal, *Commercial Norms, Commercial Codes, and International Commercial Arbitration*, 33 VAND. J. TRANSNAT'L L. 79 (2000); Philip J. McConnaughay, *The Risks and Virtues of Lawlessness: A "Second Look" at International Commercial Arbitration*, 93 N.W. U. L. REV. 453 (1999); William W. Park, *National Law and Commercial Justice: Safeguarding Procedural Integrity in International Arbitration*, 63 TUL. L. REV. 647, 680 (1989) ("[T]here has been a scramble among Western European nations to accommodate their arbitration laws to what they perceive to be the consumers' tastes, thereby attracting a greater share of the fees to go to lawyers and arbitrators at the place of the proceedings.").

52 Code Judiciare de belgique art. 1717 (1986) or Belgian Judicial Code, art. 1717, reprinted in m11 W.B. Commercial Arb. 369 (1986).

FAA did not permit party-initiated expansions of judicial review. The Court did not address how it would treat party-initiated *contractions* of judicial review. The issue has risen rarely in the case law, and the dominant (prevailing) view is that such contractions are not enforceable under the FAA.[53] *Hall Street* strongly supports this result, for it rests on the proposition that parties cannot contractually manipulate the FAA's grounds for judicial review of arbitral awards.

Nonetheless, to the extent that *Hall Street* implicitly rests on the pro-federalism premise that state law may go in another direction, and this premise logically suggests that states might also follow the lead of Belgium and allow parties to contract the standards for judicial review of an award. In principle, a state might choose to follow a similar lead with respect to domestic arbitration and, thereby, "attract" arbitral business much like Delaware has done with respect to corporate law or South Dakota with respect to credit card law (as O'Hara and Ribstein have explained).

CONCLUSION

Building on Chapter 3, this chapter has delved deeper into the relationship between arbitration law and federalism. Its central premise is that, through the principle of party autonomy, notions of federalism have had a powerful effect on the development of arbitration law. With respect to arbitration agreements, the Supreme Court's view has evolved from an approach defined by default rules (thereby allowing parties to favor federalism principles through the incorporation of state law) to one characterized by something approaching mandatory rules (narrowing the importance of such state choice-of-law clauses to the enforcement of the arbitration agreement). By contrast, in the areas of arbitral procedure and award enforcement, the Court has been more solicitous of party-initiated efforts to invoke state law. The *Hall Street* decision and subsequent state-court jurisprudence suggest that the area of award enforcement will continue to be an especially ripe area for experimentation in state arbitration law safe from federal preemption.

[53] Bowen v. Amoco Pipeline Co., 254 F.3d 925, 937 (10th Cir. 2001).

Part III ARBITRATION AND INDIVIDUAL RIGHTS

5 ARBITRATION, STATE ACTION, AND DUE PROCESS

"Nor shall any person . . . be deprived of life, liberty or property, without due process of law . . . "

– Fifth Amendment to the U.S. Constitution

"[N]or shall any State deprive any person of life, liberty, or property, without due process of law . . . "

– Fourteenth Amendment to the U.S. Constitution

Prior chapters have examined the relationship between arbitration and principles of government structure. This chapter and the next one shift the focus to the relationship between arbitration and civil liberties. That topic has taken on renewed importance ever since the Supreme Court permitted arbitration of statutory claims between companies and individuals (whether in the employment, consumer, or securities setting). Since then, various constituencies have called for greater procedural protections in arbitration. These arguments have taken various forms, ranging from calls to declare arbitration to be state action (and thereby impose due process norms on arbitration directly) to attempts to develop private "due process protocols."

Calls in Congress for arbitration reform have given renewed attention to these proposals. Bills introduced in recent years would impose these protections by statute. One bill, introduced by Senator Jeff Sessions, would require arbitrations to observe certain procedural protections. Another bill would add a new Chapter 4 to the Federal

Arbitration Act and require any arbitration to observe the principles of certain private protocols developed in the 1990s.

Although these debates have prompted a great deal of discussion about *whether* due process principles should be embedded into arbitration, far too little attention has been paid to corollary questions about the proper *mode* through which these procedural protections might develop and evolve. At least four modes are possible – constitutional rules, statutory change, judicial interpretation of existing statutory schemes without further congressional action, and private norms such as the due process protocols. In this chapter, I focus on that under-explored question about *mode*.

Jurisprudential theory helps to inform the analysis. As the classic debates between Austin, Hart, and others make clear, law can operate in various ways. It can be understood as a set of dictates by the state, which private individuals must obey.[1] Alternatively, it can operate as a moral command, which private individuals observe.[2] Seen in this latter perspective, the line between law, as a positivist act of the state, and other sets of rules developed by private organizations can begin to blur. Sometimes, the private rules can operate even more powerfully than the public one.

Just as rules (whether in the form of law, norms, or some other private arrangement) can take various forms, so too can they be articulated by various institutions. Thus, law may take the form of a constitutional command announced by a court interpreting a general provision in a constitutional document or, alternatively, a private contractual norm developed by private parties and heeded by them without any need for public enforcement.

MODES OF LEGAL DEVELOPMENT

To begin to unpack how legal rules take shape – and the institutions that shape them – take a simple example such as a rule prohibiting

1 John Austin, The Province of Jurisprudence Determined (W. Rumble ed., 1832).

2 H.L.A. Hart, The Concept of Law (2d ed. 1994).

the execution of individuals for crimes committed before they turned eighteen. Such a rule might come about as a Supreme Court decision interpreting the Eighth Amendment, which would be instantly applicable to the states by virtue of the incorporation doctrine.[3] It also might come about as a result of a statutory prohibition enacted by legislative bodies. A court might interpret an existing statute – that does not explicitly proscribe the death penalty in those circumstances – nonetheless to have that effect. Finally, the "rule" might come about as a result of private behavior if, for example, prosecutors simply stopped seeking the death penalty in those circumstances (or juries stopped convicting capital defendants in them).

Although the result in each case is the same, the four forms differ in several material respects. First, they differ in terms of their stickiness. For example, legal rules that develop by means of Supreme Court interpretation of the Constitution are especially sticky. This is because there are relatively few pathways for undoing them – only a constitutional amendment or a revisitation of the decision (whether narrowing or overruling) by the Supreme Court can do so. By contrast, legislatively crafted rules provide additional outlets for change (that is, judicial interpretation or reform by the legislative process), although the number of veto points in the legislative system may complicate legislative change.[4] Finally, the development of private legal norms can be relatively less sticky, depending on the identity and number of parties involved in the rule-articulation process as well as the decision-making methods employed by those entities.

Second, legal rules differ in terms of the inputs that can shape the rule. For example, judicially created rules often are bound by the evidence in the "record" of the case as well as whatever information of which a court may properly take judicial notice.[5] By contrast, legislatively and privately developed rules do not operate under such strict constraints. Decision makers may consult a variety of sources in determining the optimal legal rule to govern a situation.[6]

[3] *See* Roper v. Simmons, 543 U.S. 551 (2005).

[4] John W. Kingdon, Agendas, Alternatives and Public Policy (1984).

[5] *See* Sherrer v. Sherrer, 334 U.S. 343, 365–66 (1948) (Frankfurter, J., dissenting).

[6] *See* Edward McWhinney, *The Supreme Court and the Dilemma of Judicial Policy-Making*, 39 Minn. L. Rev. 837, 844 (1955) (*quoting Sherrer*, 334 U.S. at 365–66); *see also* Michael

Third, modes of rulemaking differ in terms of the method by which the decision maker comes to a conclusion. For example, judicial decision making simply requires a judge to articulate an opinion (or a panel of judges to agree upon a judgment and perhaps a common opinion in support of that judgment). By contrast, legislative decisions generally require some sort of consensus on the language of a bill.

Efforts to incorporate due process principles into arbitration have taken the form of several of these modes. Litigants in some early casesargued that arbitration constituted a form of state action[7] and, thus, principles of procedural due process applied automatically by operation of the Fourteenth Amendment. Although most courts rejected this view,[8] it attracted a great deal of attention in the arbitration scholarship.[9]

A. Rebell, *"Judicial Activism" and Public Policy*, 50 JUDGES' J. 9, 10 (2011); Michael Grynberg, *The Judicial Role in Trademark Law*, 52 B.C. L. REV. 1283, 1301 (2011). This proposition, though, is not without controversy. *See, e.g.*, K. Davis, *Facts in Lawmaking*, 80 COLUM. L. REV. 931, 934 (1980) ("[T]he [Supreme] Court is quite capable of casually going beyond the record for facts that are crucial to the decision . . . and casually remaining silent about the possibility that fair procedure might require that the losing party be given a pre-decision chance to respond to the Court's extrarecord facts.").

7 On the origins of the state action requirement, *see, e.g.*, Erwin Chemerinsky, *Rethinking State Action*, 80 Nw. U.L. Rev. 503 (1985).

8 *See, e.g.*, Perpetual Securities, Inc. v. Tang, 290 F.3d 132, 138 (2d Cir. 2002); D.L. Cromwell Invs. v. NASD Regulation, 279 F.3d 155, 161–63 (2d Cir. 2002); Desiderio v. NASD, 191 F.3d 198, 206 (2d Cir. 1999); Koveleskie v. SBC Capital Markets, Inc., 167 F. 3d 361, 368 (7th Cir. 1999); Duffield v. Robertson Stephens & Co., 144 F.3d 1182, 1202 (9th Cir.1998)., *overruled on other grounds*, E.E.O.C. v. Luce, Forward, Hamilton & Scripps, 345 F.3d 742 (9th Cir. 2003); Gallus Investments, L.P. v. Pudgie's Famous Chicken, Ltd., 134 F.3d 231, 234 (4th Cir. 1998); Davis v. Prudential Sec. Inc., 59 F.3d 1186, 1190–92 (11th Cir.1995); FDIC v. Air Florida Sys., Inc., 822 F.2d 833, 842 (9th Cir. 1987); InterChem Asia 2000 Pte. Ltd. v. Oceana Petrochemicals AG, 373 F. Supp.2d 340, 359 n.16 (S.D.N.Y. 2005); Lawrence v. Wilder Richman Sec. Corp., 359 F. Supp.2d 161, 166 (D. Conn. 2005); Mesdag v. MBNA Am. Bank, N.A., No. CV 04–1321-MO, 2005 WL 418549 (D. Or. Feb. 17, 2005); Yonir Tech., Inc. v. Duration Sys. (1992) Ltd., 244 F. Supp.2d 195, 208 (S.D.N.Y. 2002); Century Aluminum of West Virginia, Inc. v. United Steelworkers of Am., 82 F. Supp. 2d 580, 583 n. 4 (S.D. W. Va. 2000); Martens v. Smith Barney, Inc., 190 F.R.D. 134, 140 (S.D.N.Y. 1999); Porush v. Lemire, 6 F. Supp. 2d 178, 186 (E.D.N.Y. 1998); Sanders v. Gardner, 7 F. Supp. 2d 151 (E.D.N.Y. 1998); Cremin v. Merrill Lynch, Pierce, Fenner & Smith, Inc., 957 F. Supp. 1460, 1466 (N.D. Ill. 1997); Illyes v. John Nuveen & Co., Inc., 949 F. Supp. 580, 584 (N.D. Ill. 1997). *But see* R.J. O'Brien & Assoc., Inc. v. Pipkin, 64 F.3d 257, 262 (7th Cir. 1995) (holding that National Futures Association was a state actor when it performed registration function delegated by federal government).

9 *See* Sarah R. Cole, *Arbitration and State Action*, 2005 B.Y.U. L. REV. 1; Richard C. Reuben, *Constitutional Gravity: A Unitary Theory of Alternative Dispute Resolution and Public Civil*

IS ARBITRATION STATE ACTION?

The state action question deserves close consideration, for the stakes are enormous. If arbitration does constitute state action, various consequences might follow. Procedural due process rules could apply to arbitrations. The Seventh Amendment jury right could be implicated. Challenges to arbitrators could be subject to *Batson* review.[10] Finally, arbitrators could be subject to Section 1983 liability (unless they qualify for official immunity).[11]

In my view, arbitration generally does not constitute state action. Although typologies may vary slightly, the Supreme Court has held that a private entity may be considered a state actor in two main situations: (1) where the private actor is performing a power traditionally reserved exclusively to the state; and (2) where the state has provided "significant encouragement" for the private actor's conduct.[12] This portion of the chapter addresses each theory in turn.

Traditional State Function: In prior decisions, the Court has recognized that a private actor can engage in state action where the state has delegated to a private party "powers traditionally exclusively reserved to the state."[13] For example, in *Marsh v. Alabama*, the Court held

Justice, 47 U.C.L.A. L. REV. 949 (2000); Jean R. Sternlight, *Rethinking the Constitutionality of the Supreme Court's Preference for Binding Arbitration: A Fresh Assessment of Jury Trial, Separation of Powers, and Due Process Concerns*, 72 TUL. L. REV. 1 (1997).

10 *See* Sarah R. Cole & E. Gary Spitko, *Arbitration and the Batson Principle*, 38 GA. L. REV. 1145 (2004) (considering whether challenges to arbitrators motivated by a discriminatory purpose violate *Batson* principles); Smith v. Am. Arbitration Assoc., Inc., 233 F.3d 502 (7th Cir. 2000) (rejecting *Batson* challenge to arbitral tribunal).

11 *See, e.g*, Weinraub v. Glen Rauch Sec., Inc., 399 F. Supp.2d 454 (S.D.N.Y. 2005) (relying on lack of state action to reject Section 1983 claim against arbitrator premised on alleged deprivations of procedural due process). On the scope of arbitrator liability and immunity, see Peter B. Rutledge, *Toward a Contractual Approach for Arbitral Immunity*, 39 GA. L. REV. 151 (2004); Maureen A. Weston, *Reexamining Arbitral Immunity in an Age of Mandatory and Professional Arbitration*, 88 MINN. L. REV. 449 (2004); Susan D. Franck, *The Liability of International Arbitrators: A Comparative Analysis and Proposal for Qualified Immunity*, 20 N.Y.L. SCH. J. INT'L & COMP. L. 1 (2000); Andrew T. Guzman, *Arbitrator Liability: Reconciling Arbitration and Mandatory Rules*, 49 DUKE L.J. 1279 (2000).

12 *See* ERWIN CHEMERINSKY, CONSTITUTIONAL LAW: PRINCIPLES AND POLICIES §6.4.4 (2d ed. 2002); 2 Ronald D. ROTUNDA & JOHN E. NOVAK, TREATISE ON CONSTITUTIONAL LAW: SUBSTANCE AND PROCEDURE § 16 (3d ed. 1999).

13 *See, e.g.*, Am. Mfrs. Mut. Ins. Co. v. Sullivan, 526 U.S. 40, 55 (1999); Jackson v. Metropolitan Edison Co., 419 U.S., a345, 352 (1974).

a private company's complete provision of municipal services in a "company town" constituted state action and, therefore, subjected the company's regulations on the distribution of religious literature to the First Amendment's constraints.[14] Likewise, in *Terry v. Adams*, the Court held that the privately held preprimary election, which effectively determined the winner of a primary and the general election, constituted state action and, thus, subjected a privately organized political party to the Fifteenth Amendment's restrictions.[15]

Building on this line of precedent, some scholars, most notably Richard Reuben, have constructed an elegant argument that arbitration constitutes state action. The first premise of Reuben's argument is that dispute resolution is a "power traditionally exclusively reserved to the state." The second premise is that the state, by upholding arbitration agreements, has effectively delegated this power to private actors. Under Reuben's syllogism, these two premises support the conclusion that private arbitration constitutes state action.[16] By permitting arbitration, the State has delegated its traditional power to resolve disputes to purely private entities, much like the State in *Marsh* delegated the management of the town or the State in *Terry* delegated the elections to private groups.

Analyzed at this level of generality, as Professor Sarah Cole has explained, this argument is problematic.[17] The Court has repeatedly stressed that the delegation theory requires the private entity to exercise an *exclusive* public function.[18] In *Flagg Brothers v. Lefkowitz*, for example, the Court stated that "the settlement of disputes between debtors and creditors is not traditionally an *exclusive* public function."[19] Of course, *Flagg Brothers* need not be read as broadly as Cole suggests. The case could easily be read more narrowly to apply to "lien" systems,

[14] 326 U.S. 501 (1946).

[15] 345 U.S. 461 (1953).

[16] Reuben, *supra* note 9, at 994–99.

[17] Cole, *supra* note 9, at 48.

[18] *See* San Francisco Arts & Athletics, Inc. v. U.S. Olympic Comm., 483 U.S. 522, 544 (1987); Rendell-Baker v. Kohn, 457 U.S. 830, 842 (1982).

[19] 436 U.S. 149, 161 (1978) (emphasis added). *See also id.* at 173 ("There are a number of state and municipal functions not covered by our election cases or governed by the reasoning of *Marsh* which have been administered with a greater degree of exclusivity by States and municipalities than has the function of so-called 'dispute resolution,'").

such as the ones at issue in *Flagg Brothers*, rather than all forms of dispute resolution. Such a narrow reading of *Flagg Brothers* would leave open the broader question whether resolution of an entire commercial dispute (rather than invocation of a more limited lien remedy) constitutes a traditionally exclusive public function.

Even assuming though that *Flagg Brothers* cannot be read so narrowly, Cole analyzes the question at the wrong level of generality. Cole's argument assumes that "dispute resolution" covers a broad array of activities, ranging from two neighbors who resolve a fence dispute with a handshake to two companies whoo battle out a commercial case in scorched-earth litigation. Analyzed at that level of generality, of course the resolution of disputes is not a traditional prerogative exclusively exercised by the State, for the State plays no role in the handshake between neighbors.

A better portrayal of the issue might be to ask whether the resolution of disputes – *where the resolution is backed by lawful use of force if necessary to enforce result* – is a traditional function exclusively exercised by the State. Analyzed at that level of generality, dispute resolution could be seen as more akin to a traditional prerogative exclusively exercised by the State. As any student of civil procedure will recognize, that was at bottom the traditional effect of a judgment – to resolve a dispute in a manner that, if not voluntarily complied with, would be subject to enforcement through coercive State acts. The power to render such a judgment was one traditionally exercised only by the State. Arbitration laws, so the argument would continue, extend this exceptional power to arbitrators. Arbitration awards, like judgments (and also like handshakes) can be used to resolve disputes. Unlike the handshakes, though, arbitration awards enjoy a special status. Through the recognition and enforcement process, exemplified by Section 10 of the Federal Arbitration Act, arbitral awards can be placed on an equal footing with a judgment.[20] That is, once recognized, they can be backed with the full coercive power of the State if necessary to give effect to the award's commands.

The jurisdictional ouster cases also support the argument that arbitration – as a form of dispute resolution potentially backed by State

[20] *See* 9 U.S.C. § 10.

coercion – qualifies as private performance of a traditional public function. As noted in the Introduction in the nineteenth century courts refused to enforce arbitration agreements, on the ground that they illegally ousted the courts of jurisdiction.[21] Those cases only make sense if one accepts the notion that arbitrators are performing a function traditionally performed by courts. Eventually, courts and legislatures backed away from the jurisdictional-ouster argument. Indeed, one of the primary purposes of the FAA was to overcome the decades-long hostility that courts have displayed toward arbitration.[22] As these reforms took effect, therefore, arguably a portion of that traditional public function of resolving disputes with the potential for coercive enforcement was delegated to arbitration.

Ultimately, though, this argument, even when analyzed at this level of generality, does not support the conclusion that arbitration constitutes state action under the "traditional public function" theory. This is because, in most cases, the state does not delegate its *entire* dispute resolution function to arbitrators. Instead, it reserves some residual, albeit limited, power of review. Under domestic arbitration, therefore, courts still review arbitral awards under Section 10 of the FAA and various non-statutory grounds such as manifest disregard of the law.[23] Similarly, in international arbitration falling under the multilateral conventions to which the United States is a party, courts still reserve a limited role for judicial review.[24] Arguably, in a system where the State had ceded entirely any role of judicial review (as Belgium did for certain forms of arbitration not involving Belgian residents), then the state action argument would be more persuasive.[25] So long as the State

[21] *See supra* pages 3–4.

[22] *See, e.g.*, Circuit City Stores, Inc. v. Adams, 532 U.S. 105 (2001); Allied-Bruce Terminix Cos., Inc. v. Dobson, 513 U.S. 265, 272 (1995); Gilmer v. Interstate/Johnson Lane Corp., 500 U.S. 20, 24, 111 S. Ct. 1647, 114 L. Ed. 2d 26 (1991); Mitsubishi Motors Corp. v. Soler Chrysler-Plymouth, Inc., 473 U.S. 614, 625 n.14 (1985); Dean Witter Reynolds Inc. v. Byrd, 470 U.S. 219–21 & n.6 (1985); Scherk v. Alberto-Culver Co., 417 U.S. 506, 510 & n.4 (1974).

[23] *See* 9 U.S.C. § 10; First Options, Inc v. Kaplan, 514 U.S. 938 (1995); Wilko v. Swan, 346 U.S. 427, 436–37 (1953), *overruled on other grounds*, Rodriguez de Quijas v. Shearson/Am. Express, Inc., 490 U.S. 477 (1989).

[24] *See, e.g.*, Convention on the Recognition and Enforcement of Foreign Arbitral Awards Art. V; Interamerican Convention Art. V.

[25] For an English translation of the Belgian law, see *Belgium: Statute on the Setting Aside of Arbitral Awards*, Mar. 27, 1985, 25 I.L.M. 725 (1986). For discussion of the Belgian law,

reserves for itself some residual power to decide whether to recognize and enforce the award, though, it has not delegated away the public function. For that reason, arbitration should not be considered state action under the public function theory of *Marsh* and *Terry*.[26]

Significant Encouragement: A second ground on which private conduct may qualify as state action is where the State has provided "significant encouragement" of the private activity. In *American Manufacturer's Mutual Insurance Co. v. Sullivan*, the Court characterized this line of doctrine:

> In cases involving extensive state regulation of private activity, we have consistently held that the mere fact that a business is subject to state regulation does not itself convert its action into that of the State for purposes of the Fourteenth Amendment. . . . [Thus, there must be] a sufficiently close nexus between the State and the challenged action of the regulated entity so that the action of the latter may be fairly treated as that of the State itself. What such a close nexus exists . . . *depends on whether the State has exercised coercive power or has provided such significant encouragement, either over or covert, that the choice must in law be deemed to be that of the State.*[27] (emphasis added)

More so than the "public function" test, this "significant encouragement" test has been the major battleground over which most recent state action debates have been fought. Under this test, for example, in *Edmonson v. Leesville Concrete Co., Inc.*, the Court held that a private litigant's use of statutorily authorized peremptory challenges constitutes state action and, thus, is subject to the limitations set forth in the Equal Protection Clause.[28] By contrast, in *Sullivan*, the Court held

see H. Van Houtte, *La Loi Belge du 27 mars 1985 sur l'Arbitrage International*, 595 Revue De L'Arbitrage 29 (1986); Edward Chukwuemeke Okeke, *Judicial Review of Foreign Arbitral Awards: Bane, Boon or Boondoggle?*, 10 N.Y. INT'L L. REV. 29, 44–46 (1997).

26 One might criticize this argument on the ground that it elevates form over substance. Why should the residual reserve of state power to review an arbitral award relieve arbitration from the "state action" doctrine if courts, in the exercise of that power, routinely uphold arbitral awards? The short answer is that the Court has consistently employed a formalist approach in applying this strand of the state action doctrine. Functionalist approaches are reserved for other strands, discussed below. Thanks to Nic Howell for pushing me on this point.

27 526 U.S. 40, 52 (1999) (citations and internal quotations omitted).

28 500 U.S. 614, 622–25 (1991).

that a state's decision allowing private insurers to defer workers' compensation payments during a review period did not constitute the type of "significant encouragement" giving rise to state action and, therefore, did not subject the private insurer's review mechanisms to the strictures of the Due Process Clause.[29]

Richard Reuben grounds in this line of cases a second argument that arbitration constitutes state action. Reuben posits that, notwithstanding everyday conceptions about arbitration as removed from judicial process, courts are intimately involved in arbitration. Among other things, they decide whether to compel arbitration; whether to stay litigation pending arbitration; and whether to enforce, modify or vacate an arbitral award.[30] In some arbitrations, courts play additional roles – sometimes nominating arbitrators where parties cannot agree, resolving disputes over the arbitral situs, and deciding whether to enforce subpoenas issued by the arbitrators.[31] The law also ordinarily accords arbitrations absolute immunity from civil liability.[32] The net sum of this involvement, Reuben argues, arguably "establish[es] an inseverable and indispensable nexus between seemingly private actors and their governmental partners."[33]

Reuben's argument finds support in the Supreme Court's decision in *Shelley v. Kramer*.[34] *Shelley* involved a pair of cases in which real property owners executed contracts containing restrictive covenants that prohibited non-Caucasians from occupying the property. In both cases, African-Americans purchased the property in question, and neighbors filed suit to enforce the restrictive covenants. The Supreme Court held that judicial enforcement of the restrictive covenants constituted state action and, thus, denied the African-American purchasers equal protection.[35] Under the logic of *Shelley*, the argument runs, a State "significantly encourages" private conduct when it enforces

[29] 526 U.S. at 53–55.

[30] *See* 9 U.S.C. §§ 3, 4, 9–11.

[31] 9 U.S.C. §§ 5, 7. *See generally* CHRISTOPHER R. DRAHOZAL, COMMERCIAL ARBITRATION 367–93, 418–32 (2d ed. 2006); BORN, INTERNATIONAL COMMERCIAL ARBITRATION 469–514, 573–643 (2009).

[32] *See* Rutledge, *supra* note 9, at 151.

[33] *See* Reuben, *supra* note 9, at 1006.

[34] 334 U.S. 1 (1948).

[35] *Id.* at 20.

an arbitration agreement or an award, much in the same way that it encouraged private conduct when it enforced the racially restrictive covenant.

As Professor Erwin Chemerinsky and others have recognized, precedents such as *Shelley* "taken to their logical conclusion, demonstrate that under a positivist analysis, state action is present in all private violations of constitutional rights."[36] *Shelley* potentially amounts to a sweeping expansion of the meaning of state action, largely reversing the tradition of narrow interpretation dating back to the *Civil Rights Cases*.[37] In the context of arbitration, the implications of *Shelley* are equally profound. Consistent with the general judicial reluctance to expand *Shelley*, no court has embraced Reuben's theory in the context of arbitration, but at least one court has acknowledged its plausibility.[38]

Sarah Cole tries to avoid the force of the argument rooted in *Shelley v. Kramer* by confining the case's logic to race-based exclusions. Although that argument finds support in the scholarship, the case is not so easily limited. Of course, as a textual matter, the state action requirement does not distinguish between "race-based" and "non–race-based" exclusions. Nor as a matter of precedent has the Court held that the contours of the state action doctrine vary with the constitutional right at stake. This distinction, moreover, ignores the fact that the state action limitation traces its roots all the way back to Bill of Rights, not just the Fourteenth Amendment. Thus, the obvious historical underpinnings to that doctrine lay not in race but, instead, in other values such as liberty, federalism, and separation of powers.[39] Indeed, if Cole were correct that the state action requirement was broadest in race-based cases, one would have expected certain cases such as the *Civil Rights Cases* to come out the other way.

36 Chemerinsky, *supra* note 7, at 524. *See also* Steven Siegel, *The Constitution and Private Government: Toward the Recognition of Constitutional Rights in Private Residential Communities Fifty Years after Marsh v. Alabama*, 6 WM. & MARY BILL RTS. J. 461 (1998); Shelley Ross Saxer, Shelley v. Kramer*'s Fiftieth Anniversary: "A Time for Keeping; A Time for Throwing Away?*," 47 U. Kan. L. Rev. 61 (1998); Louis Henkin, Shelley v. Kramer: *Notes for a Revised Opinion*, 110 U. Pa. L. Rev. 473 (1962).

37 109 U.S. 3 (1883).

38 *See* Commonwealth Associates v. Letsos, 40 F. Supp. 2d 170, 177 n.37 (S.D.N.Y. 1999).

39 *The Civil Rights Cases*, 109 U.S. 3, 11, 23 (1883).

Rather, Reuben's argument fails to appreciate the salient distinctions between the judicial enforcement in *Shelley* and judicial enforcement in arbitration. In *Shelley*, when the lower courts enforced the restrictive covenants, they were giving effect to legal relationships between private individuals (the Caucasian homeowners) *that affected third parties* (the African-American home buyers). By contrast, when a lower court enforces an arbitral agreement (or award), it generally is only giving effect to legal relationships between the parties themselves *without any effect (at least directly) on third parties.*[40] This distinction is more than happenstance. Recall that the critical component of this strand of the state action doctrine is "significant encouragement" of the private activity. Viewed in this light, giving legal effect to private relationships affecting third parties reinforces a private norm in a manner absent when a court is merely rendering a decision whose import does not extend beyond the parties themselves.

Admittedly, this argument is not airtight in at least two respects. First, it downplays a type of "encouragement" present in both cases. In both cases, judicial enforcement – whether of the restrictive covenant or the arbitral agreement (or award) – encourages the private conduct by ensuring that it will be given legal effect against an *unwilling* party (the African-American purchasers in *Shelley*, the party resisting arbitration). Second, the distinction presupposes that both parties in the arbitration setting are willing participants. As defenders of the adhesion-contract model of arbitration have noted, typically one party has a significantly inferior bargaining position and, thus, arguably does not have a choice whether to enter into the agreement.[41]

[40] In some cases, courts will enforce arbitration agreements against parties that are not signatories to the arbitration agreements (such as guarantors, assignees and third-party beneficiaries). *See* BORN, *supra* note 31, at 668–72. Under the distinction proposed here, those cases would seem more closely aligned with *Shelley*, and judicial enforcement of an obligation against such parties would constitute state action. They may, however, be reconciled with the customary model of arbitration among signatories on the ground that third parties such as guarantors are best understood as "agents" or "representatives" of the parties themselves and, thus, parties to the arbitral arrangement.

[41] *See, e.g.*, Lucy T. France & Timothy C. Kelly, *Mandatory Arbitration of Civil Rights Claims in the Workplace: No Enforceability without Equivalency*, 64 MONT. L. REV. 449 (2003); Kenneth R. Davis, *Arbitration Claws: Unconscionability in the Securities Industry*, 78 B.U. L. REV. 255 (1998); Richard E. Speidel, *Contract Theory and Securities Arbitration: Whither Consent?*, 62 BROOK. L. REV. 1335, 1349 (1996).

Accepting the validity of that account, then, the party in the arbitration with the inferior bargaining position begins to resemble the third-party African-American purchaser in *Shelley*. Nonetheless, accepting these limitations, the "third-party" distinction supplies a more coherent and principled means of distinguishing judicial enforcement of arbitral agreements from *Shelley* than the race-based/non–race-based distinction offered by Cole.

Apart from arguments grounded in *Shelley*, a second argument for the alleged "significant encouragement" of arbitration finds its roots in the Supreme Court's alleged pro-arbitration bias in its decisions. This line of argumentation, advanced most forcefully by Professor Jean Sternlight, assumes that neutral judicial enforcement of contractual remedies does not constitute state action but nonetheless claims that the Supreme Court has been far from neutral.[42] Instead, Sternlight argues that a number of doctrines and canons announced by the Supreme Court reflect a bias in favor of arbitration, thereby giving rise to state action. These doctrines include (1) construing ambiguous arbitration clauses in favor of arbitrability,[43] (2) narrowly construing defenses to the enforcement of arbitration agreements,[44] (3) interpreting Section 2's defenses to the enforcement of an arbitration agreement to extend only to generally applicable contract defenses,[45] (4) allowing the arbitrator to decide defenses to the contract's enforceability,[46] (5) narrowly interpreting Section 1's exclusion for workers engaged in interstate commerce,[47] and (6) holding that the FAA preempts state laws that do not place arbitration agreements on an equal footing with other contracts.[48] Under Sternlight's argument, these indicia of a judicial pro-arbitration bias, singularly and collectively, constitute the type of "significant state encouragement" converting arbitration into state action.

[42] Sternlight, *supra* note 9, at 44–47.
[43] *See, e.g.*, Mastrobuono v. Shearson Lehman Hutton, Inc., 514 U.S. 52 (1995).
[44] *See, e.g.*, Moses H. Cone Mem'l Hosp. v. Mercury Constr. Corp., 460 U.S. 1, 24–25 (1983).
[45] *See, e.g.*, Doctor's Associates, Inc. v. Casarotto, 517 U.S. 681 (1996).
[46] *See, e.g.*, Buckeye Check Cashing, Inc. v. Cardegna, 126 S.Ct. 1204 (2006); Prima Paint Corp. v. Flood & Conklin Mfg. Co., 388 U.S. 395 (1967).
[47] *See, e.g*, Circuit City Stores, Inc. v. Adams, 532 U.S. 105 (2001).
[48] *See, e.g.*, Doctor's Assocs., Inc. v. Casarotto, 517 U.S. 681 (1996).

This argument, although forceful, has several flaws. First, to the extent it depends on the premise that a judicial decision can constitute state action, it collapses for the same reasons as Reuben's argument rooted in *Shelley*.[49] Second, Sternlight mischaracterizes several of these doctrines. For example, Sternlight claims that the Court has allowed arbitrators to decide whether arbitration agreements are void under Section 2's generally applicable contract defenses.[50] In fact, the Court has said exactly the opposite – it has repeatedly stressed that courts, not arbitrators, must decide challenges to the arbitration agreement unless the parties have employed clear and unmistakable language delegating that decision to the arbitrator.[51] Likewise, the Supreme Court's limitation of enforcement defenses to ones generally applicable to contracts does nothing more than apply the plain terms of Section 2, which states that "an agreement in writing to submit to arbitration . . . shall be . . . enforceable, save upon such grounds as exist at law or in equity for the revocation *of any contract*."

Even putting those inaccuracies to one side, though, Sternlight's argument founders for the simple reason that it fails to establish that the alleged "bias" in the Supreme Court's jurisprudence constitutes the type of "significant encouragement" such that a private actor's conduct may be "fairly attributable" to the state. Sternlight's argument elides this critical point entirely. She cites no authority for this implicit proposition, and that is hardly surprising for its logical conclusions would be preposterous. If Sternlight were correct, then every private actor who relied on a judicial interpretation of an arguably ambiguous statute would suddenly transform into a state actor by virtue of that reliance. That position, if valid, would swallow all limits on the state action doctrine. Rather, the Court's interpretation of the Federal Arbitration Act – and consequent reluctance to intervene in arbitrable disputes – is better understood as "inaction," as the Court has explained in analogous

[49] *See supra* at pp. 136–37.

[50] Sternlight, *supra* note 10, at 45–46.

[51] *See, e.g., Buckeye Check Cashing*, 126 S.Ct. at 1209 (reading several of the Court's prior precedents to establish the proposition that "*unless the challenge is to the arbitration clause itself*, the issue of the contract's validity is considered by the arbitrator in the first instance.") (emphasis added).

contexts.[52] For example, the Court's decision in *Sullivan* to enforce the statute resulted in insurers having the option to withhold payments under review. Permitting a party to exercise its own discretion does not rise to the level of "significant encouragement" so as to convert this undeniable private action into state action.[53] Similarly, in *Flagg Brothers*, the Court properly construed its refusal to intervene in a private transaction as inaction. The Court argued that characterizing this inaction as state action would convert a State's refusal to provide a remedy through a statute of limitations into a positive act by the State.[54] In light of that inaction, the conduct of the private parties – those engaging in the arbitration – cannot therefore be fairly said to be "fairly attributable" to the State.[55]

A third and more subtle argument treats arbitration as state action based on the relationships between the arbitrating parties and certain public or quasi-public agencies involved in the regulation of those parties. This argument, advanced by Sarah Cole, divides arbitration into three types: court-ordered, agency-initiated, and contractual.[56] Court-ordered arbitration involves some of the types of involuntary arbitrations noted in the definitional paragraph in the introduction.[57] Agency-initiated arbitration involve situations where a regulator, such as the Securities and Exchange Commission ("SEC"), approves the rules of an entity that, among other things provides arbitration services, such as the NASD, whose members must arbitrate their disputes. Contractual arbitration involves the most straightforward transaction – two parties enter into a contract containing an arbitration clause, which a court subsequently enforces. Under this typology, Cole argues, both

52 *See* Am. Mfrs. Mut. Ins. Co. v. Sullivan, 526 U.S. 40, 53–54 (1999); Flagg Brothers, Inc. v. Brooks, 436 U.S. 149, 164–65 (1978).

53 *Sullivan*, 526 U.S. at 54.

54 *Flagg Brothers*, 436 U.S. at 166.

55 Here, one should acknowledge a conceptual tension between the "public function" and "significant encouragement" strands of the doctrine. Whereas the limits on the "public function" doctrine depend on the state's *reservation* of some residual role in policing arbitration agreements and awards, the limits on the "significant encouragement" depend on the state not playing *too great* a role. This tension illustrates one of the difficulties of maintaining a principled line between public and private conduct in the state action realm.

56 Cole, *supra* note 9.

57 *See supra* at 6–7.

court-ordered and agency-initiated arbitration constitute state action whereas contractual arbitration does not. I agree with Cole (and others) that pure court-ordered (i.e., involuntary) arbitration constitutes state action,[58] so I focus instead on her claim that agency-initiated arbitration does so as well.

Cole's original argument, although initially quite appealing, does not withstand close scrutiny. At the outset, Cole's proposed differentiation between agency-initiated and contractual arbitration imports some biases that should be made explicit. For one thing, the term "agency-initiated" is a misnomer in a number of respects. Does the term "agency" mean the SEC or the NASD? Whatever the meaning, in neither case is the "agency" "initiating" anything. The garden-variety arbitration between a brokerage house and a broker or between a broker and an investor involves a contract between two private parties that contains an arbitration clause. Seen in this light, the treatment of these arbitrations should be no different from other contractual arbitrations, which Cole herself acknowledges do not trigger state action requirements.

Here, of course, one might respond that agency-initiated arbitrations differ from contractual arbitrations in an important respect. Agency-initiated arbitrations, the response would go, involve terms that are imposed on the employee or the investor whereas contractual arbitrations involve voluntary choice. This response, though, would be inaccurate. In many industries, standard-form employment contracts contain arbitration clauses as a matter of course. Moreover, in the agency-initiated context, much like in the contractual context, the contracting parties maintain a voluntary choice. They are free to withdraw from the transaction – whether it be employment, investment, or otherwise – in order to avoid the arbitration obligation altogether. The results, to be sure, may be harsh, particularly in the securities industry, which is unquestionably heavily dominated by the use of arbitration. But if monopolistic arrangements do not constitute state action,[59] then adoption of standardized norms across a more competitive industry logically cannot. The theoretical opportunity

[58] *See supra* at 6–7.
[59] *See Jackson*, 419 U.S. at 351–52; *Moose Lodge*, 407 U.S. at 462.

to withdraw in both types of arbitrations demonstrates that Cole's effort to differentiate contractual and agency-initiated arbitration is too facile.

For another thing, to the extent Cole's argument hinges on the nature of self-regulatory organizations such as the NASD, this argument misapprehends the nature of such entities. The NASD and other SROs are not agencies. They are private corporations set up to oversee the exchanges.[60] Although it is true they are subject to the oversight of the SEC, which, among other things, approves the SROs' rules, the Court has made clear that public regulation of a private entity – even a monopolistic one such as a utility – does not give rise to the type of "significant encouragement" necessary to constitute state action.[61]

If it is to work at all, therefore, Cole's argument that agency-initiated arbitration constitutes state action depends on three interrelated facts: (1) the SEC's approval of SRO arbitral rules, (2) its requirement that parties register with an SRO, and (3) the SEC's knowledge that the SRO itself mandates arbitration. Even in its strongest form, though, this argument ignores *Jackson, Sullivan*, and *Blum*. Recall that *Jackson* made clear that subjecting a customer to a private utility's dispute resolution mechanism did not constitute state action. *Jackson* involved the provision of a basic utility, electricity. So it was reasonable to expect that virtually every Pennsylvania resident would need to make use of the utility. Moreover public officials were undoubtedly aware of the utility's dispute resolution mechanism when they granted the utility the monopoly to provide electricity. Despite this awareness, though, the Court held that the state did not overtly or covertly encourage participation in the utility's dispute resolution program and, thus, that program could not be fairly attributable to the state. By analogy, therefore, the requirement of registration with an SRO, coupled with the SEC's awareness that investors and brokers in the SRO will make use of the SRO's arbitral program, cannot be considered conduct fairly attributable to the state.

[60] For a good history of self-regulatory organizations such as the NASD and the NYSE, see David A. Lipton, *A Primer on Broker-Dealer Registration*, 36 CATH. U. L. REV. 899 (1987).

[61] *See Jackson*, 419 U.S. at 351–52.

Both *Sullivan* and *Blum* involved private actors making decisions by applying criteria either promulgated by or approved by state regulators. Indeed, in *Sullivan*, the insurance companies used a utilization review system that received state approval. Yet the Court held that the utilization decision did not constitute state action. This determination tracked a long line of decisions in which the Court had made clear that "even extensive regulation by the government does not transform the actions of the regulated entity into those of the government."[62] Although it is true that *Sullivan* held that the state's creation of the utilization review mechanism constituted state action, the Court distinguished *creation* of the mechanism (which constituted state action) from *utilization* of the mechanism (which did not).[63] That distinction is critical in the context of agency-initiated arbitration. By analogy, even if the SEC's *approval* of the dispute resolution rules itself constituted state action, *Sullivan* instructs that *utilization* of that state-approved system by private parties does not. For purposes of the state action doctrine, it constitutes a distinct act.

At this point, it is worth recapping how far the argument has come. Arbitration, in the form of a voluntary agreement between two or more parties, does not constitute state action. By enforcing arbitration agreements and arbitration awards, the state has not delegated to private actors a traditional public function – whether described as "dispute resolution" or "dispute resolution backed by coercive sanction." This is because the state has preserved the ability to engage in judicial review, albeit limited, of the arbitration agreement and the arbitration award. Nor does the state "significantly encourage" arbitration as that term is understood in the state action doctrine. It follows, therefore, that arbitration is not subject to a variety of constitutional norms such as procedural due process. Despite the lack of any requirement as a matter of constitutional law, as the next part explains, private arbitration organizations have undertaken many of the same obligations voluntarily.

62 *See, e.g.*, San Francisco Arts & Athletics, Inc. v. U.S. Olympic Comm., 483 U.S. 522, 544 (1987); Rendell-Baker v. Kohn, 457 U.S. 830, 841 (1982).

63 Am. Mfrs. Mut. Ins. Co. v. Sullivan, 526 U.S. 40, 53 (1999).

DOES IT MATTER?

The foregoing section demonstrated why arbitration, as a formal matter, is generally not required to observe the dictates of procedural due process. That conclusion, however, does not end the analysis. Instead, as with other topics analyzed throughout this book, constitutional principles have seeped into arbitration through other mechanisms. This section of the chapter examines three such mechanisms by which principles of due process have entered the arbitration jurisprudence – (1) the development of private protocols (of particular importance in domestic arbitration in the United States), (2) judicial interpretation (of particular importance in both domestic and international arbitration), and (3) treaty design (of particular importance in the current debates over the development of "transparency" protocols for use in investment treaty arbitration).

1. Private Protocols

In some cases, private protocols have supplied the form by which due process norms have seeped into arbitration. These protocols trace their roots to the Commission on the Future of Worker-Management Relations ("Dunlop Commission"). In 1993, the Clinton administration established the Commission, headed by John Dunlop, the former Labor Secretary, to investigate the current state of worker–management relations in the United States.[64] Part of its mandate required the Commission to consider "[w]hat (if anything) should be done to increase the extent to which work-place problems are directly resolved by the parties themselves, rather than through recourse to state and federal courts and government regulatory bodies."[65] The timing of the Commission's creation was no coincidence – it came on the heels of the Supreme Court's decision in *Gilmer v. Interstate./Johnson Lane Corp.* Nominally, *Gilmer* held simply that claims under the Age Discrimination in Employment Act were arbitrable. More generally

[64] Commission on the Future of Worker-Management Relations, Fact-Finding Report xi (May 1994).

[65] *Id.*

though, as several have noted, *Gilmer* sounded one of the final notes in the death knell of the non-arbitrability doctrine – the doctrine for decades had precluded arbitration of federal statutory claims (including employment claims) and, as noted in the Introduction, was one of the primary doctrines that maintained the wall between arbitration and the Constitution.[66] *Gilmer* contained sweeping language rejecting broadside attacks on the procedural unfairness of arbitration.[67] After *Gilmer*, the new fault lines were clear. No longer would the arbitrability of a dispute turn on a substantive question – whether Congress intended for a particular claim to be subject to arbitration. Instead, it would turn on a procedural one – whether a particular arbitration had the rudimentary features of procedure and fundamental fairness.

In the wake of *Gilmer*, therefore, the Dunlop Commission's focus on arbitration was perhaps inevitable.[68] Calls for enhanced procedural protections in arbitration soon followed. At the request of Chairman Dunlop, a coalition of labor, management, and arbitration representatives turned to employment arbitration – the area at issue in *Gilmer*.[69] The primary vehicle for their reform efforts came in the form of a "due process" protocol – that is, a set of rules governing certain arbitrations falling under the protocols.[70] As Paul Verkuil has observed the choice of terminology is an "odd" one in light of the widely accepted view that

[66] For discussions of *Gilmer*'s impact, *see, e.g.*, Margaret M. Harding, *The Redefinition of Arbitration by those with Superior Bargaining Power*, 1999 UTAH L. REV. 857; Martin H. Malin, *Arbitrating Statutory Employment Claims in the Aftermath of* Gilmer, 40 *St. Louis U. L. J.* 77 (1996); Lewis L. Maltby, *Paradise Lost – How The* Gilmer *Court Lost the Opportunity for Alternative Dispute Resolution to Improve Civil Rights*, 12 N.Y.L. SCH. J. HUM. RTS. 1 (1994).

[67] *See* Gilmer v. Interstate/Johnson Lane Corp., 500 U.S. 20, 30–32 (1991).

[68] *See* Margaret M. Harding, *The Limits of the Due Process Protocols*, 19 OHIO ST. J. DISP. RES. 369, 373–74 (2004).

[69] On the history behind the drafting of the employment protocol, including a rich history of the industry participants, see Richard J. Bales, *The Employment Due Process Protocol at Ten: Twenty Unresolved Issues and a Focus on Conflicts of Interest*, 21 OHIO ST. J. DISP. RES. 165 (2005); Harding, *supra* note 69, at 371, 390–91.

[70] See Nat'l Academy of Arbitrators, Due Process Protocol for Mediation and Arbitration of Statutory Disputes Arising Out of the Employment Relationship (May 9, 1995); Nat'l Consumer Disputes Advisory Cmte., Due Process Protocol for Mediation and Arbitration of Consumer Disputes (Apr. 17, 1998); Nat'l Consumer Disputes Advisory Cmte., Due Process Protocol for Mediation and Arbitration of Health Care Disputes (July 27, 1998).

arbitration does not constitute state action and, as a strictly doctrinal matter, is not subject to constitutional requirements of due process.[71] Nonetheless, the protocol functions in a manner not unlike due process requirements, setting forth a series of procedural norms that must be observed in a decision-making process.[72] The employment protocol sets forth a variety of rights including:

- the employee has the right to be represented by a person of his or her own choosing;
- the employer is encouraged to pay at least a share of the employee's fees;
- employees should have access to all information reasonably relevant to their claims;
- before selecting an arbitrator, parties should have sufficient information to contact parties who previously have appeared before him or her;
- arbitrators should have sufficient skill and knowledge;
- arbitrators should be drawn form a diverse background;
- arbitrators should be free of any relationships that would create an actual or apparent conflict of interest;
- the employee's entitlement to the same array of remedies in arbitration as he or she would be entitled to in a judicial proceeding

Although these principles bear some resemblance to constitutional requirements of due process, they function in a different manner.[73] Whereas due process requirements would bind participants in the arbitration as a matter of law (if arbitration were state action), the protocols function more like voluntarily observed private norms.[74]

Initially, providers of arbitration services steadfastly resisted adopting the protocol.[75] Eventually, though, major arbitration service

[71] Paul R. Verkuil, *Privatizing Due Process*, 57 ADMIN. L. REV. 963, 985 (2005).

[72] The content of some of the protections finds its roots in procedural protections attendant to labor–management arbitrations under collective bargaining agreements. *See* Harding, *supra* note 69, at 395–96.

[73] Indeed, the principal architects of the protocol have acknowledged its synergies with constitutional due process doctrines. *See* JOHN T. DUNLOP & ARNOLD M. ZACK, MEDIATION AND ARBITRATION OF EMPLOYMENT DISPUTES 117 (1997).

[74] *E.g.*, U.S. CONST. amend. XIII.

[75] *See* Harding, *supra* note 69, at 403 n.193.

providers, including the American Arbitration Association (the industry leader) endorsed it.[76] By doing so, they certified that they would not administer an arbitration where the parties were unwilling to follow the protocol. That endorsement had powerful effects for other corners of the industry. The National Arbitration Forum developed a "bill of rights" for arbitration participants.[77] The NASD likewise revised its own rules governing the arbitration of statutory employment disputes to reflect the principles embraced in the employment protocol.[78]

The success of the employment due process protocol established a model for subsequent efforts to incorporate due process–like notions into other arbitrations. In the years following adoption of the employment protocol, members of the bar, arbitral institutions, and other advocates hammered out two others – one governing consumer disputes and one governing disputes in the health care industry.[79] Although these subsequent protocols differ in some respects substantively from the employment due process protocols, the basic process behind their creation was the same: creation of a work group of interested parties and industry representatives and eventual acceptance by some of the major institutions administering arbitration in the United States.

The development of the due process protocols presents a puzzle. If arbitral institutions are not constitutionally obligated to subject the arbitrations they administer to protections of procedural due process, why have they chosen to do so voluntarily? At least four possible explanations are possible.

The logical explanation: One might argue that the introduction of due process norms into arbitration is a natural product of the doctrine.[80] This argument finds its roots in the standards for judicial review of arbitral awards. As has been widely reported elsewhere, judicial review of arbitral awards is extremely narrow.[81] Nonetheless, one ground upon

[76] On the industry's adoption of the due process protocols, see Bales, *supra* note 70, at 174; Harding, *supra* note 68, at 403–05.

[77] *See* Harding, *supra* note 68, at 403–05.

[78] *Id.*

[79] On the relationship between the employment due process protocol and the subsequent protocols, see Bales, *supra* note 69, at 175–76; Harding, *supra* note 68, at 405–09.

[80] *See* Maltby, *supra* note 66, at 16.

[81] *See, e.g.*, DRAHOZAL, *supra* note 31, at 494–95; BORN, *supra* note 31, at 795–881.

which parties can seek vacatur or resist enforcement of an arbitral award is some procedural irregularity in the proceeding. For example, Section 10 of the Federal Arbitration Act provides in relevant part that a court may vacate an award "[w]here the arbitrators were guilty of misconduct in refusing to postpone the hearing, upon sufficient cause show, or in refusing to hear evidence pertinent and material to the controversy, or of any other misbehavior by which the rights of any party has been prejudiced."[82] Likewise, the New York Convention provides in relevant part that a court may refuse to recognize or enforce an award falling under the Convention where "the party against whom the award is invoked was not given proper notice of the appointment of the arbitrator or of the arbitration proceedings or was otherwise unable to present his case."[83] In both examples, courts have construed these sections to sanction application of something akin to the forum state's due process standards.[84] Thus, so goes the argument, incorporating due process protections into arbitration is a natural product of efforts by arbitral institutions and other supporters of the arbitration industry to maximize the likelihood that any award will be enforced.

The logical explanation founders, though, for at least two reasons. First, it cannot explain the content of the due process protocols. Although their title suggests the incorporation of due process standards, the due process protocols extend far more protection than a litigant would be entitled to under constitutional standards. For example, whereas the protocols encourage one party in the arbitration (typically the corporate party) to bear a share of the costs, the due process clause would not entitle a litigant in a comparable judicial proceeding to such financial protection. Thus, although the judicial review standards may explain the existence of some type of due process protection in arbitration, they do not explain the scope of that protection.

Second, even granting the partial explanatory value based on the judicial review standards, the logical explanation cannot account for the timing of the development of the due process protocols. Many of

[82] 9 U.S.C. §10(c).

[83] New York Convention Art. V(1)(b).

[84] *See, e.g.*, Parsons & Whittemore Overseas Co. Inc. v. Societe generaly de L'Industrie du Papier (RAKTA), 508 F.2d 969, 975–76 (2d Cir. 1974).

the decisions equating the review standards with constitutional due process norms were already issued in the 1970s. If the integration of due process protections were simply a logical consequence of the judicial review standards, one would have expected them to develop around the same time. Yet, they only developed and were adopted decades after courts began equating the judicial review standards with due process. Thus, the "logical explanation" cannot account for the twenty-year lag between the development of the judicial review norms and the adoption of the protocols.

The sociological explanation: The sociological argument finds its roots in the literature on the socialization of lawyers.[85] According to this argument, lawyers play a dominant role in the governance and management of arbitral institutions such as the American Arbitration Association.[86] Such lawyers, particularly those inclined to work in the alternative dispute resolution field, have been socialized, both by dint of education and practice, to observe certain values. Those values include an awareness of principles of due process, justice, and fairness. Those values, therefore, explain the lawyer's support for the protocols and the principles they embody even if they are not strictly necessary as a matter of doctrine. In Verkuil's terms, the protocols "show that fair process is not the exclusive obligation of government."[87]

Although quite appealing, the sociological argument suffers from several problems. First, like the logical argument, it cannot adequately account for the timing of interest in the due process protocols. Second, the sociological argument cannot account for the initial resistance of the arbitral institutions to adoption of the protocols. If commitment to certain underlying values such as due process and justice explained the

[85] I would like to thank a participant at the Southeast Association of Law Schools' 2006 Annual Meeting for suggesting this line of argumentation. For discussions of how lawyers can be infused with habits including concerns with fair procedures, see John O. Calmore, *Chasing the Wind: Pursuing Social Justice, Overcoming Legal Miseducation, and Engaging in Professional Resocialization*, 37 LOYOLA L.A. L. REV. 1167 (2004); Darryl K. Brown, *Criminal Procedure Entitlements, Professionalism and Lawyering Norms*, 61 OHIO ST. L.J. 801 (2000); Jon O. Newman, *Rethinking Fairness: Perspectives on the Litigation Process*, 94 YALE L.J. 1643, 1648 (1985); Lon L. Fuller, *The Forms and Limits of Adjudication*, 92 HARV. L. REV. 353, 356 (1978).

[86] *See, e.g.*, American Arbitration Association, 2004 Annual Report at 10–11 (identifying the many lawyers who serve as AAA board members).

[87] Verkuil, *supra* note 71, at 985.

institutions' acceptance of the protocols, one would have expected the institutions to adopt them quite willingly; their failure to do so suggests that their acceptance of the protocols was motivated by something other than a commitment to shared values.

Finally, the sociological argument cannot account for the position taken by the arbitral institutions on other matters. For example, the arbitral institutions routinely have allowed arbitrators to hand down awards despite claims of procedural irregularity or a failure by the arbitrators to observe the institution's own rules.[88] Likewise, they have actively resisted attempts to vacate awards on the basis of such procedural irregularities.[89] Under the logic of the sociological argument, one would expect that arbitral institutions would find some way to confess error or correct the irregularity before the award is released. Their failure to do so, indeed their steadfast defense of an award that allegedly results from such procedural irregularities, again casts doubt on the explanatory value of the sociological argument.

The economic explanation: Economics might also explain why arbitral institutions adopted the due process norms. As has been discussed elsewhere, arbitration can be conceptualized as one "product" competing in a larger market for dispute resolution services.[90] In addition to competing with other providers (courts, mediators, conciliators, etc.), arbitral institutions also compete with each other for a share of the "dispute resolution market." As with any market, providers of a product or service compete with other entrants through differentiation of their product. Under this theory, the due process protocols are one means by which arbitral institutions can differentiate themselves from other providers of dispute resolution services.

At first blush, the economic explanation seems remarkably counterintuitive. If one accepts the premise that providers of arbitral services at bottom are economically rational entities seeking to capture a share of the market for dispute resolution services, then it would naturally follow that they would engage in behavior most likely to obtain the business

88 *See* BORN, *supra* note 31, at 843–46.

89 *See, e.g.*, Metallgesellschaft A.G. v. M/V Capitan Constante, 790 F.2d 280 (2d Cir. 1986).

90 For a discussion of a market-based theory of dispute resolution, see Rutledge, *supra* note 11, at 160–65.

of the repeat players and other high-volume consumers in the market. In the areas covered by the due process protocols, those repeat players would seemingly be employers (in employer–employee disputes), producers (in producer–consumer disputes) and health care providers (in health care disputes), each of whom can be expected regularly to enter into contracts and, therefore, potentially engage the services of an arbitral institution. Basic economics suggest, then, that the arbitral institutions should calibrate their rules to attract the business of these customers. Yet in each case, the due process protocols do not favor these entities but, instead, the one-shot player (the employer, the consumer, and the health care recipient). Compared to the employers and other aforementioned repeat players, these entities are far less likely to enter into as many arbitration agreements and, therefore, are seemingly less important "customers" to providers in the dispute resolution market. So why, then, would providers of dispute resolution services willingly accede to requirements that favor the interests of these participants and, arguably, work against the interests of participants who are more likely to purchase dispute resolution services on a regular basis?

Economic principles of bonding might suggest a solution to this conundrum.[91] Although repeat players in the dispute resolution market have an incentive in opting for the dispute resolution mechanism whose procedural choices best advance the firm's interests, that is not their only incentive. In addition, they desire various performance guarantees on the arbitral process, including a guarantee that the arbitration agreement and the award will be enforceable.[92]

The bonding function, moreover, is not limited to providing employers the security that the arbitration agreement and award will be enforceable. As several commentators have noted, the protocol also encourages the *employee* to have confidence in the fairness of the arbitration proceedings.[93] According to Paul Verkuil, the protocols "convey confidence" in the arbitration proceedings. Encouraging the employee's confidence in the process is squarely in the employer's

[91] For a discussion of the role of bonding in the arbitration industry, see Stephen J. Choi, *The Problem with Arbitration Agreements*, 36 VAND. J. TRANSNAT'L L. 1233 (2003).

[92] *See* Bales, *supra* note 69, at 176–77.

[93] *See* Harding, *supra* note 68, at 397–98; Verkuil, *supra* note 71, at 985.

interest – for it reduces the likelihood that the employee will resist the arbitration, either by challenging the enforceability of the agreement or challenging the enforceability of an adverse award. A senior counsel at a major corporation with extensive experience in employment arbitration has described how fair procedures can be in the employer's interest even if they reduce the employer's advantages in the arbitration:

> The enforceability of [arbitration] programs will always be an issue. My philosophy on that is first, you cannot play games with these programs. If you try to use an employment ADR program to limit legal exposure or employee rights or remedies, you are going to get shot down. Second, no matter how fair and reasonable the program, there will always be some risk that a particular court will not enforce it.
>
> Besides, the true key to a good employment ADR program is not legal enforceability. The key to a good program is whether it has sufficient credibility in the eyes of the employees that they willingly use it. If you can get your program to that level, you don't have to worry about enforceability.[94]

Recent empirical research has lent some credence to the bonding theory. It shows that arbitration under the protocols have led to more favorable decisions for the employee, thereby giving the employee and his or her advocates more reason to trust the system.[95] Likewise, judicial decisions bear the bonding thesis, as several have rejected procedural challenges to the enforceability of the arbitration agreements and relied in support of that conclusion on the arbitrations' compliance with the protocols.[96]

Political entrepreneurs might also explain why the arbitral institutions would engage in behavior seemingly contrary to the economic interests of their repeat players. Political entrepreneurs, according to a

94 Richard Ross, How Companies Manage Employment Disputes: A Compendium of Leading Corporate Employment Programs 55 (2002), *quoted in* Bales, *supra* note 70, at 176–77.

95 *See* Harding, *supra* note 68, at 415–16 (citing unpublished research by Bingham and Sarraf); Elizabeth Hill, *Due Process at Low Cost: An Empirical Study of Employment Arbitration under the Auspices of the American Arbitration Association*, 18 Ohio St. J. Disp. Res. 777 (2003).

96 *See* Bales, *supra* note 69, at 178–84.

rich political science literature, overcome the collective action problems of diffuse groups and, by advocating those groups' interests, advance their own agenda.[97] In this context, lawyers representing consumers and employees might function as entrepreneurs for their interests even if any single member of the group does not have a strong incentive to vindicate those interests. Although this bar of lawyers may not be present at the time the employee or the consumer enters into the contract containing the arbitration clause, they nonetheless have the potential to disrupt the stability of arbitration proceedings through repeated and systematic attacks on the overall fairness of the arbitral process. By acceding to a system that serves the interests of these participants in the arbitral process, the institutions reduce the risk of that disruption and, thereby, enhance the security and predictability of arbitral proceedings.

Moreover, the economic argument, unlike the logical argument, better explains both the scope and the timing of the protocols' development. As to scope, the economic argument could justify the relatively greater protections under the protocols compared to those to which a party would be entitled to due process. Much like a contracting party might offer a performance bond in excess of the minimum amount required as a statement of the confidence in its performance, blanketing the arbitration with greater procedural protections than the bare minimum required under the doctrine signals greater security in the award; it reduces the risk that a particularly activist court, seeking to expand the FAA's vacatur standards, might set aside the award. As to timing, the economic argument explains why arbitral institutions paid greater attention to their procedures after *Gilmer*. Once *Gilmer* shifted the focus of judicial review of arbitration away from the subject matter of the arbitration and toward the procedural fairness of the arbitration, arbitral institutions had a newfound incentive to review the vulnerability of their dispute resolution regimes from procedural challenge. The protocols provided a means by which the institutions could signal to their largest customers such as employers that the product remained secure.

[97] For discussions of political entrepreneurs, *see, e.g.*, Clayton P. Gillette, *Plebiscites, Participation, and Collective Action in Local Governance Law*, 86 MICH. L. REV. 930, 976 (1998).

Although the economic argument has some degree of explanatory value, the account is not complete. Specifically, why, for example, did the arbitral institutions achieve the bonding mechanism through the protocols rather than some other means? For example, like some international arbitral institutions, they could have modified their rules to provide for a substantive review of the award for enforceability prior to its release.[98] Alternatively, the due process protections could have been embodied in legislation. Why, then, the protocol? Here, a political argument is necessary to complete the account.

The political explanation: Finally, politics might explain the development of the norms.[99] Private norms such as voluntarily adopted industry standards can regulate private behavior. Public law can form a similar function. That public regulation can take various forms – legislation, judicial decision, or administrative agency oversight. As Eric Posner has explained, depending on the context, each form may be the most efficient.[100] Moreover, groups often may differ over the preferred regulatory mechanism. To take a familiar example, environmentalists may prefer to regulate pollution through strict standards embodied in legislation and administrative regulations whereas industry may prefer either not to regulate the matter at all or, alternatively, to rely on voluntary industry standards.[101]

In this context, regulation by the protocols emerged as a second-best solution for the various participants in the arbitral system.[102] In

[98] *See* Rules of the International Chamber of Commerce Art. 29 (providing for substantive prefiling review of an arbitral award by the Court of Arbitration).

[99] *See, e.g.*, Verkuil, *supra* note 71; Alex C. Geisinger, *Are Norms Efficient? Pluralistic Ignorance, Heuristics and the Use of Norms as Private Regulation*, 57 ALA. L. REV. 1 (2005); Richard J. Pierce, Jr., *The Due Process Counterrevolution of the 1990s?*, 96 COLUM. L. REV. 1973 (1996); Eric A. Posner, *The Regulation of Groups: The Influence of Legal and Nonlegal Sanctions on Collective Action*, 63 U. CHI. L. REV. 133 (1996).

[100] *See* Eric A. Posner, *Law, Economics and Inefficient Norms*, 144 U. PA. L. REV. 1697, 1698 (1996).

[101] *See* Michael P. Vandenberg, *Beyond Elegance: A Testable Typology of Social Norms in Corporate Environmental Compliance*, 22 STAN. ENVTL. L.J. 55 (2003); Neil Gunningham, *Environment, Self-Regulation, and the Chemical Industry: Assessing Responsible Care*, 17 LAW & POL'Y 57 (1995).

[102] For discussions of the economic theory of second-best solutions, see Richard S. Markovits, *Second-Best Theory and Law & Economics: An Introduction*, 73 CHI.- KENT L. REV. 3 (1998); R.G. Lipsey & Kelvin Lancaster, *The General Theory of Second Best*, 24 REV. ECON. STUD. 11 (1956).

the wake of *Gilmer* and the Dunlop Commission report, advocates for employees and consumers in arbitration sought to impose various procedural protections on arbitral institutions through public regulation such as legislation or judicial decision. Both federal and state lawmakers considered legislation that would have regulated employee- and consumer-related arbitration.[103] As with most entities subject to possible governmental regulation, the arbitral institutions ideally wanted no regulation and certainly wanted to avoid extensive public intervention in or oversight of their industry. From the advocates' perspective, the protocols, although perhaps an inferior outcome to pure public regulation, were superior to a completed unregulated system. They provided a mechanism by which the advocates could introduce some of their sought-after norms into arbitration. From the institutions' perspective, the protocols, although perhaps inferior to a deregulated system, were superior to a system of extensive public regulation[104] as through them the institutions could retain some of their independence from governmental oversight. Self-regulation thereby provided both the institutions and the advocates their second-best outcomes.[105]

2. Judicial Interpretation

Private protocols are not the only means by which principles of due process have seeped into arbitration. In some cases, courts have interpreted positive statutory law in a manner to reflect the underlying constitutional principles.

Perhaps the most obvious example has come in international arbitration. Under Article V(1)(b) of the New York Convention, a court may refuse to enforce an arbitral award where "[t]he party against whom the award is invoked was not given proper notice of the appointment of the arbitrator or of the arbitration proceedings or was otherwise unable to present his case."[106] This standard is noteworthy for two reasons. First, unlike most other provisions of Article V, it does not specify an applicable law. Second, it does not explicitly link these standards

[103] *See* Harding, *supra* note 68, at 412–14 (discussing federal and state efforts).
[104] *See id.* at 420, 430–32.
[105] *See id.* at 416–17.
[106] New York Convention Art. V(1)(b).

to any preexisting set of rules governing notice and an opportunity to be heard. Thus, the language might have been understood to create a distinct international standard of notice and opportunity to be heard calibrated to the unique features of international arbitration.[107]

Despite this possibility, courts have taken a different course. Many courts have tied the meaning of these treaty terms to their own domestic constitutional principles. A particularly noteworthy example is the Second Circuit's decision in the *Parsons & Whittemore* case, an important decision glossing the meaning of Article V and handed down shortly after the United States ratified the New York Convention.[108] There, the award-debtor (Overseas), relying on Article V(1)(b), sought to block enforcement of the award on the ground that the tribunal refused to reschedule proceedings because of the inability of a witness to attend them. In rejecting the argument, the *Parsons* court read Article V(1)(b) to "essentially sanction application of the forum state's standards of due process."[109] This conclusion did not follow from the text of Article V((1)(b) and, indeed, rested on rather somewhat flimsy authority, namely a few law review articles, which, themselves, do not meaningfully substantiate either the choice-of-law determination or the linkage between the treaty language and constitutional principles. Nonetheless, that conclusion has been widely embraced by other federal courts subsequently interpreting the convention.[110] Some courts in foreign countries have taken a similar view.[111]

Article V(1)(b) is not the only example of a judicial interpretation importing constitutional principles. Similar examples exist with respect to the Federal Arbitration Act. FAA Sections 10(a)(2) authorize federal courts to vacate arbitral awards "where there was evident partiality or corruption in the arbitrators." That provision was

[107] *See* Gary B. Born, International Commercial Arbitration 2738–46 (2009).

[108] Parsons & Whittemore Overseas Co. v. Societe Generale de L'Industrie du Papier (RAKTA), 508 F.2d 969 (2d Cir. 1974).

[109] *Id.* at 975.

[110] *See, e.g.*, Karaha Bodas Co. v. Perusahaan Pertambangan Moinyak Dan Gas Bumi Negara, 364 F.3d 274, 299 (5th Cir. 2004); Slaney v. Int'l Amateur Athletic Fed'n, 244 F.3d 580, 592 (7th Cir. 2001).

[111] *See, e.g.*, Judgment of 23 April 204, XXX Yearbook of Commercial Arbitration 557 (Oberlandesgericht Cologne) (2005).

the centerpiece of the Supreme Court's seminal decision in *Commonwealth Coatings*, involving a claim that an award should be vacated on the ground that the panel's chair did not disclose a preexisting business relationship with a party.[112] A splintered Court concluded that the award should be vacated, and Justice Black's plurality opinion rested on constitutional reasoning. He relied heavily on the Supreme Court's prior decision in *Tumey v. Ohio* interpreting the Due Process Clause.[113] *Tumey* held that the Due Process Clause prohibited a criminal conviction rendered by a judge whose compensation consisted partly of court fees collected from convicted defendants. Factually, *Tumey* lay far afield from *Commonwealth Coatings*. Yet Justice Black read *Tumey* to stand for the broader constitutional principle that due process required a decision to be "set aside where there is the slightest pecuniary interest on the part of the judge" in the outcome.[114] From this constitutional principle, Justice Black then made an intellectual move not unlike the Second Circuit in *Parsons*. He asserted that "[s]ince in the case of courts, this is a constitutional principle, we can see no basis for refusing *to find the same concept in the broad statutory language that governs arbitration proceedings* and provides that an award can be set aside on the basis of 'evident partiality' or the use of 'undue means.'"[115]

Here, as in *Parsons & Whittemore*, Justice Black's move rested on a shaky intellectual foundation. Certainly, Justice Black might have read the terms "evident partiality" and "undue means" to represent a standard other than that dictated by the due process norms governing judge's compensation. He also might have differentiated between judges as public actors and arbitrators as private ones. (Indeed, Justice White's opinion concurring in the judgment departed from Justice Black on whether constitutional standards governing judges should apply to arbitrators.)[116] Declining to do so, however, enabled Justice

112 Commonwealth Coatings Corp. v. Continental Cas. Co., 393 U.S. 145 (1968).
113 273 U.S. 510 (1927).
114 *Id.* at 148.
115 *Id. See also* Prima Paint Corp. v. Flood & Conklin Mfg. Co., 388 U.S. 395, 416 (1967) (Black, J., dissenting).
116 *Id.* at 150. *See also* Schmitz v. Zilveti, 20 F.3d 1043, 1045–48 (9th Cir. 1994) (discussing the differences between the Black and White opinions in *Commonwealth*).

Black to engraft constitutional principles on Section 10 of the FAA, much like the *Parsons & Whittemore* court did with respect to Article V(1)(b) of the New York Convention.[117]

Although these examples are revealing, it is important not to overstate their significance. These examples of judicial interpretation do not completely incorporate all principles of procedural due process into arbitration. Rather, they incorporate particular components (such as principles of notice or neutrality).

Nonetheless, the important point is not the scope of the incorporation but, rather, the intellectual framework by which the treaty or statute is being interpreted. By explicitly linking the meaning of these various treaty and statutory provisions to principles of constitutional law, judicial interpretation – much like the due process protocols – accomplishes indirectly what could not be accomplished through a frontal argument that arbitration represents state action. Once that intellectual framework is laid, it creates the potential for further incorporation of constitutional principles – not by means of express "constitutionalization" of arbitration but, instead, through further refinements in judicial interpretation of the treaties or statutes. For example, some courts have stretched the general language from *Parsons* (which at its core essentially involved a question of opportunity to be heard) and extended it to a rule that the arbitrator "must provide a fundamentally fair hearing."[118] Such evolutions suggest that the seeds planted by a decision such as *Parsons* will continue to germinate.

3. Treaty Design

A third and final example of the importation of due process norms into arbitration comes from the recent work of the UNCITRAL Arbitration Working Group on transparency in international investment

[117] Although Justice Black's analogy to constitutional principles of due process never gained a full majority of the Court, it nonetheless had an important impact on arbitration practice by enhancing the importance of full disclosure by the arbitrator of any potential conflicts. *See, e.g.*, Sphere Dretke Ins. Ltd. v. All Am. Life Ins. Co., 307 F.3d 617, 623 (7th Cir. 2002); *In re* Andros Compania Maritima S.A., 579 F.3d 691 (2d Cir. 1978); Garfield & Co. v. Wiest, 308 F. Supp. 1107, 1110–11 (S.D.N.Y. 1970).

[118] Generic Ltd. v. Pharm. Basics, Inc., 125 F.3d 1123, 1130 (7th Cir. 1997).

arbitration.[119] The Working Group assists UNCITRAL in the development and refinement of legal instruments governing arbitration such as the UNCITRAL Model Arbitration Law and the UNCITRAL Model Arbitration Rules. During its most recent round of revisions on Model Arbitration Rules, certain nations' delegations raised the issue of transparency in investment arbitration (triggered by the increased use of the UNCITRAL Model Arbitration Rules as the applicable rules in investment arbitrations).

Concerns about transparency arose in light of the significant awards of damages that States can be obligated to pay investors under bilateral investment treaties. Because any payment comes out of public funds, such arbitrations raised the possibility that political elites of a nation would make decisions affecting both the public finances of a country as well as its reputation within capital markets without much meaningful input from its citizenry. Transparency offered a possible antidote to these concerns by creating the conditions for meaningful input by citizens (or, more realistically, political entrepreneurs such as nonprofit organizations) to influence investment arbitration both at the case level and at the systemic level. As the Secretary General's Special Representative on human rights and transnational corporations explained, transparency is "essential if societies are to be aware of proceedings that might affect the public interest and therefore their own welfare."[120]

The transparency mechanisms contemplated by the working group would address several practices in investment arbitration including:

- Publicity regarding the commencement of proceedings;
- Publication of documents used in proceedings (including carve-outs for certain sensitive documents or documents involving national security);
- Publication of the award;

[119] For a discussion of investment arbitration, see Chapter 1, *supra*. In the interest of full disclosure, I should note that I had the privilege of serving for several years as a member of the American Arbitration Association's delegation to the UNCITRAL Working Group. In an abundance of caution, I should note that the views expressed in this book represent my own and not those of the AAA or UNCITRAL.

[120] United Nations Commission on International Trade Law, Working Group II (Arbitration and Conciliation), Rep. on its 54th Sess., Feb. 7–11, U.N. Doc. A/CN.9/717 (Feb. 25, 2011), at 6, *available at* http://www.uncitral.org/uncitral/commission/working_groups/2Arbitration.html.

- Publicly available hearings and transcripts;
- Participation by amicus curiae;
- A registry by which the foregoing documents could be accessed.

Although consensus quickly formed around the topics that any such transparency instrument would address, delegates divided over the precise form such an instrument would take. Options included amendments to existing bilateral investment treaties, design of a joint interpretive declaration to which states could consent, an annex to the UNCITRAL Model Rules, and protocols or guidelines that arbitrators might consult but which would not be formally binding.

Although the transparency debate is not identical to the other examples of due process discussed earlier in this chapter, it shares certain essential elements. Most fundamentally, the transparency debates do not attempt to regulate the relationship between the parties to the arbitration; instead, the transparency debate is primarily focused at the level of the rights of third parties whose interests are affected by the conduct and results of the arbitration At the same time, central to the transparency debate is an attempt to import constitution-like principles to the conduct of an arbitration. As a 2010 report by UNCITRAL explained, a transparency instrument (whatever its form) supplies "a means to promote the rule of law, good governance, *due process*, fairness, equality and rights to access information" (emphasis added).[121] Moreover, as the ongoing debates over the form of the transparency instrument illustrate, decisions about the *form* of any such importation of constitutional norms are as important as debates over the content of any such norms. All of this, moreover, takes place outside any formal "constiutionalization" of investment arbitration by national law or national courts.

Implications for Incorporating Due Process Norms into Arbitration

The preceding part identified several mechanisms by which various components of procedural due process seeped into arbitration

[121] United Nations, Commission on International Trade Law, Report of Working Group II (Arbitration and Conciliation) on the work of its fifty-third session (Vienna, 4–8 Oct. 2010), U.N. Doc. A/CN.9/712 (2010).

jurisprudence despite the absence of an express "constitutionalization" of arbitration (by virtue of the conclusion that arbitration is not state action). This final section offers a normative critique of these developments and compares them as different modes of lawmaking.

What should we make of these alternative forms of incorporating due process principles into arbitration? To answer this question, we can tap into an important literature on the development of due process norms. That literature grew out of a more general narrowing of the state doctrine by the Supreme Court.[122] This narrowing of state action has exempted a variety of potentially public or quasi-public decisions from the strictures of the Due Process Clause. Yet those protections did not disappear entirely. Instead, as scholars such as Richard Pierce and Paul Verkuil have observed, a host of privately designed procedural rights has filled the void.[123]

Verkuil cites as one example the tale of Jerry Tarkanian's battles against the NCAA.[124] There, Tarkanian brought various constitutional and common-law tort claims against the NCAA after it penalized the basketball team at the University of Nevada-Las Vegas. Among Tarkanian's claims was that the NCAA had deprived him of due process. Although the Supreme Court ultimately disagreed, concluding that the NCAA was not a state actor, that did not end the story. Instead, in the years following the Supreme Court's decision, the NCAA undertook an extensive self-study of its hearing procedures and incorporated many changes to those procedures.[125]

Experiences such as those in *Tarkanian* have prompted an extensive debate in the scholarship over regulation via private, rather than public norms.[126] Some scholars, particularly in the law and economics tradition, have argued that private norms provide a superior means of

[122] *See, e.g.*, Edward L. Rubin, *Due Process and the Administrative State*, 72 CAL. L. REV. 1044, 1062–64 (1984) (documenting contraction in the state action doctrine).

[123] Pierce, *supra* note 99, at 1996. *See also* Verkuil, *supra* note 72, at 963.

[124] 488 U.S. 179 (1988).

[125] *See, e.g.*, Verkuil, *supra* note 71, at 973–74; Jody Freeman, *Extending Public Law Norms through Privatization*, 116 HARV. L. REV. 1285 (2003).

[126] *See, e.g.*, Richard H. McAdams, *The Origin, Development and Regulation of Norms*, 96 MICH. L. REV. 338 (1997); Cass Sunstein, *On the Expressive Function of Law*, 144 U. PA. L. REV. 1021 (1996); Lisa Bernstein, *Merchant Law in a Merchant Court: Rethinking the Code's Search for Immanent Business Norms*, 144 U. PA. L. REV. 1765 (1996); Robert D. Cooter, *Structural Adjudication and the New Law Merchant: A Model of Decentralized Law*,

regulating group activity.[127] Others, by contrast, have cast doubt on the trustworthiness, efficacy, and, indeed, the efficiency of regulation via private norms, preferring instead public forms of regulation.[128] This literature supplies a useful lens through which to consider the development of similar private protocols in the arbitration setting and to compare those developments to others (such as judicial interpretation or treaty design) that embed due process principles into arbitration through more formal, public mechanisms.

In some respects, the protocols as a form of private norm regulation are superior to direct regulation. For one thing, compared to direct legislative regulation, they are far easier to implement. A familiar literature in political science has documented the difficulties of enacting legislation due to the multiple decision points where legislative action may fail (committee, floor vote, conference committee, veto).[129] The protocols avoid these impediments to action by involving a single decision point, namely voluntary assent by the associations themselves. Due to the reduced number of decision points, they are also more easily changed and adapted to evolving circumstances.[130]

Additionally, in contrast to judicial regulation, the due process protocols can be more comprehensive and more nuanced. Drafters of the protocols can consider the gamut of available data and experience. By contrast, judicial regulators may be constrained by the record evidence offered by the parties. Likewise, the protocol mechanism allows its drafters to tailor the protocols to the particular needs of the regulated industry, as exemplified by the substantive differences between the protocols for employment, consumer, and health care arbitrations. By

14 INT'L REV. L. & ECON. 215 (1994); ROBERT C. ELLICKSON, ORDER WITHOUT LAW: HOW NEIGHBORS SETTLE DISPUTES (1991).

127 *See, e.g.*, Richard A. Epstein, *Lawyers' Rise or Fall?*, NAT'L L.J., May 31, 2004, at 27; Richard H. McAdams, *Signaling Discount Rates: Law, Norms and Economic Methodology*, 110 YALE L.J. 625, 625 (2001); David Charny, *Nonlegal Sanctions in Commercial Relationships*, 104 HARV. L. REV. 373 (1990).

128 *See, e.g.*, Douglas Litowitz, *A Critical Take on Shasta County and the "New" Chicago School*, 15 YALE J. L. & HUMANITIES 295 (2002) (criticizing the model of group regulation through private norms); Posner, *supra* note 100, at 1726–36 (arguing that in some instances public regulation is more efficient).

129 *See generally* R. DOUGLAS ARNOLD, THE LOGIC OF CONGRESSIONAL ACTION (1990); JOHN W. KINGDON, AGENDAS, ALTERNATIVES AND PUBLIC POLICY (1984).

130 *See* Harding, *supra* note 68, at 371.

contrast, the scope of any judicial regulation may be constrained by doctrines such as standing, bars against advisory opinions, and limits on the remedial powers of courts.

Moreover, as Professor Margaret Harding has observed, the protocol process holds forth the potential for greater participation by interested groups.[131] Whereas access limitations or standing doctrines may limit groups' ability to influence the outcome of legislative or judicial regulation, the process of protocol development and acceptance suffers from no such inherent limitations. To be sure, the validity of this premise depends on the extent to which the protocols' developers choose to include various groups in the development process. Actual experience with the first three protocols, though, suggests that they were in fact developed through an inclusive process.

Finally, the protocols have stimulated a healthy dialogue between courts and stakeholders over best practices in arbitration. A rich scholarship has focused the various "feedback loops" between private and public actors in the development of legal norms.[132] At first glance, this interplay between the due process protocols and judicial evaluations of the fairness of arbitration proceedings might seem to be a positive development. The protocols provide courts a workable benchmark by which to evaluate the fairness of other procedures; moreover, hammered out through dialogue between the industry and advocates for employees and consumers, they arguably offer a relatively balanced metric rather than a biased one. Forged through this process, the protocols stimulate a dialogue between courts and the arbitration industry.

The effects of the protocols have not been limited to the arbitrations themselves. A number of federal and state courts have looked to them as persuasive indicia of the fairness of an arbitration.[133] For example, in *Cole v. Burns International Security Services*, the D.C. Circuit found that an arbitral agreement in an employment contract was

[131] *Id.* at 371.

[132] *See, e.g.*, Geisinger, *supra* note 99; Posner, *supra* note 99.

[133] For a catalogue of cases relying on the Due Process protocols, see Bales, *supra* note 69, at 178–84; *see also* Harding, *supra* note 68, at 409–12.

enforceable partly because the agreement generally comported with the due process protocol.[134] In some cases, courts have relied on the due process protocols even where an arbitration is not formally subject to them. For example, in *Hooters of America, Inc. v. Phillips*, the protocols were relevant to two courts' conclusions not to enforce an arbitration agreement, even though the arbitration agreement was not subject to them. The district court noted that the arbitrator selection procedures differed from those under the protocol, and the Fourth Circuit, in affirming, rested its decision in part on the testimony of an AAA official who said that Hooters' arbitration rules "so deviated from minimum due process standards that [the AAA] would refuse to arbitrate under those rules."[135] Finally, in *Green Tree Financial Corp. v. Randolph*, four justices cited the due process consumer protocol as an example of a fair mechanism by which to allocate costs in an arbitration. These cases illustrate that the due process protocols do not simply influence arbitral practice: They also have an impact on the legal doctrine in cases that, as a technical matter, are not subject to them.

Just as the protocols can influence judicial understanding of fair arbitral procedures, judicial critique can suggest reform pathways to the protocols' developers. This type of dialogue might be a means of addressing not simply questions of procedural fairness but other constitutional questions about arbitration. In *Cole*, Chief Judge Edwards expressed his disagreement with the employment protocol's cost-sharing provisions, which sparked a lively debate over whether the protocol or some other approach should be used to ensure the affordability of arbitration for employees with statutory claims.[136]

[134] 105 F.3d 1465 (D.C. Cir. 1997).

[135] *See* Hooters of Am., Inc. v. Phillips, 39 F. Supp. 2d 582, 598 n.15, 600–02 (D.S.C. 1998). Hooters of Am., Inc. v. Phillips, 173 F.3d 933, 939 (4th Cir. 1999).

[136] *See* Cole v. Burns Int'l Security Servs., 105 F.3d 1465, 1483 n.11 (D.C. Cir. 1997). For exemplary literature on the cost-sharing debate, *see, e.g.*, Michael H. Leroy & Peter Feuille, *When Is Cost an Unlawful Barrier to Alternative Dispute Resolution? The Ever Green Tree of Mandatory Employment Arbitration*, 50 U.C.L.A. L. REV. 143 (2002); Brian Tipton, *Allocating the Costs of Arbitrating Statutory Claims under the Federal Arbitration Act: An Unresolved Issue*, 26 AM. J. TRIAL ADVOC. 325 (2002). The July 2002 issue of the *University of Miami Law Review* dedicated an entire symposium to the issue of arbitration cost allocation in the wake of *Green Tree Financial.*

Although the protocol development process offers certain advantages over regulatory mechanisms, in other respects the due process norms are potentially problematic. One problem, stressed by Carrie Menkel-Meadow, is that the protocols may not achieve as much substantively as direct regulation.[137] This stems from the bargaining toward second-best solutions described previously in the section "Private Protocols." For example, as Menkel-Meadow describes, advocates for the employment protocol necessarily compromised on certain procedural protections in order to obtain the assent of the various industry participants and arbitral institutions. As a consequence of this second-best quality to the protocol-development process, critics have called for strengthened protections.[138] Direct regulatory pathways, such as judicial imposition of due process norms, would not necessitate such compromise.

Other problems stem from the feedback loops generated between the protocols' drafters and courts who consult the protocols. The benefits of the feedback loop between courts and private actors (such as the arbitration industry in this case) mask at least two significant costs. One is a lack of predictability. Specifically, parties are unable to predict precisely how courts will use the protocols. Some decisions cite the protocols as merely indicative of a practice trend; by contrast, others come close to saying that the failure of an arbitration proceeding to comport with the protocols provides a legal reason for denying enforceability of the arbitration agreement altogether. As Richard Bales has explained, the due process protocols function as a guidepost for both employers and the judiciary but, as a consequence, no longer provide predictable guidance.[139]

Compare this with a system in which the due process norms come via another mechanism, whether legislation or judicial decision, as

[137] *See* Carrie Menkel-Meadow, *Ethics Issues in Arbitration and Related Dispute Resolution Processes: What's Happening and What's Not?*, 56 U. MIAMI L. REV. 949, 953 n. 24 (2002).

[138] *See, e.g.*, Bales, supra note 69, at 167; Harding, *supra* note 69, at 371.

[139] Bales, *supra* note 69, at 167; Martin H. Malin, *Ethical Concerns in Drafting Employment Arbitration Agreements After* Circuit City *and* Green Tree, 41 BRANDEIS L.J. 779, 780 (2003).

we saw in the international context.[140] Here, by contrast, the legal effect of the norms is clearer. Unlike the present system, courts are *bound* to apply them (or at least to ascertain the applicability). Thus, compared to a more regulatory model of norm development, the protocol mechanism (so long as courts consult the protocols) creates relatively greater uncertainty over how legal norms will develop.

It is important to stress the limited nature of the claim here. I am not making a normative claim that legislative or judicial regulation would be superior to the current form of private norm development. Nor am I taking a position on whether courts should consult the protocols in cases where they do not strictly apply. Rather, my claim is simply that, if courts do consult the protocols, the uncertainty over their legal effect will inject instability into the content of legal rules.

A further drawback of this protocol process is the lack of transparency.[141] Compared to more regulatory forms of norm development, the protocols are not developed according to any standardized methods by which they are closely scrutinized.[142] In Gillian Metzger's terms, the protocols lack adequate "accountability mechanisms."[143] By contrast, for example, administrative regulation typically would undergo a formal notice-and-comment period followed often by judicial challenge to the reasonableness of the agency's regulation. Likewise, a process of legislative regulation likely would create some sort of legislative record that a court could scrutinize. Even a process of judicial regulation, although the deliberations themselves may be secret, entails a degree of scrutiny. Judges typically reduce their judgments

140 These mechanisms would take various forms. The legislative form is obvious. The judicial form either could come through a conclusion that arbitration did in fact constitute state action or a decision not to enforce an arbitration agreement or an award where the arbitration was not subject to these procedural protections.

141 On the relationship between arbitration and democratic theory, see Richard C. Reuben, *Democracy and Dispute Resolution: The Problem of Arbitration*, 67 LAW & CONTEMP. PROBS. 279 (2004).

142 On the defects in the decision-making process behind the protocols' development, see Leona S. Green, *Mandatory Arbitration of Statutory Employment Disputes: A Public Policy Issue in Need of a Legislative Solution*, 12 NOTRE DAME J.L. ETHICS & POL'Y 173, 215 (1998).

143 *See* Gillian Metzger, *Privatization in Delegation*, 103 COLUM. L. REV. 1367, 1456–76 (2003).

to writing and give reasons for their decisions. Those decisions and the reasoning are then put under a microscope in subsequent cases presenting common issues. By contrast, private norms such as those exemplified by the protocols lack these sorts of institutional checks on the norm-development process.[144]

Here too, it is important to acknowledge limits on the argument. I am not claiming that other forms of regulation – whether administrative, legislative, or judicial – are fully transparent. They certainly are not. But relative to a system of purely private norm development, as exemplified by the protocols, there is a more robust set of institutional checks governing both the process by which those public norms are developed and the scrutiny to which they are subject.

A final drawback is the potential dilution of public law rules. Judicial reliance on privately developed norms to define public standards rests on the belief that those norms represent optimal policy outcomes. Yet, the protocols in several respects represent "second-best" solutions. To the extent imperfect norms shape public law doctrines on fair arbitral procedures, society suffers – whether from inadequate protection (in case of deficiencies in the protocols) or inefficient outcomes (in case of erroneous invalidation of arbitration not heeding the protocols).

CONCLUSION

As a growing number of federal statutory claims were resolved through arbitration, calls to import constitutional norms into arbitration were bound to follow. Perhaps the most important constitutional question, indeed the gateway for many subsidiary ones, has been whether arbitration in some fashion constituted state action. Contrary to the views of several scholars, courts have correctly concluded that it does not. Nonetheless, this conclusion has not ended the constitutional

[144] For the sake of completeness, I should note that private norm-developing institutions are not checkless. If nothing else, market forces – such as the willingness of the market to employ the norms developed by the private institution – may constrain the institutions' behavior. The point remains, however, that these constraints differ in quality and kind from those imposed on processes of judicial, legislative, or administrative regulation. Special thanks to Nic Howell for his thoughts on this point.

debate; instead, the debate has merely shifted to other territory. Other mechanisms including private due process protocols, treaty interpretation, and treaty design have filled the gap created by the judicial conclusion that arbitration does not constitute state action. Developments such as the protocols have extended procedural protections to parties with inferior bargaining positions, in some cases exceeding the protections to which they would be entitled under principles of procedural due process. Moreover, they have influenced the public law norms as a variety of courts have consulted them, even in cases where they technically do not apply. Although some may take a sanguine view of these developments, they are not costless. Privately developed norms risk capture and lack of transparency. More fundamental, though, the dialogue between courts and the protocols' drafters creates doctrinal uncertainty and instability. With this state of affairs, the debate over the relationship between arbitration and constitutional law, particularly the form such developments should take, is bound to endure.[145]

[145] *See, e.g.*, Morton J. Horowitz, *The History of the Public/Private Distinction*, 130 U. PA. L. REV. 1423 (1982); Duncan Kennedy, *The Stages of the Decline of the Public/Private Distinction*, 130 U. PA. L. REV. 1349 (1982).

6 ARBITRATION AND THE JURY RIGHT

"In Suits at common law, where the value in controversy shall exceed twenty dollars, the right to jury trial shall be preserved."[1]

"The right of trial by jury is secured to all and shall remain inviolate."[2]

"Courts of justice shall be open to every person, and speedy remedy afforded for every injury of person, property, or character."[3]

The preceding chapter introduced the idea that arbitration implicates individual liberties. It explained the significance of the "state action" doctrine as a gateway through which such claims, as a formal matter at least, must be assessed, and then delved into the relationship between arbitration law and notions of due process. This chapter builds on that analysis but focuses on another liberty guaranteed by the Constitution, namely the entitlement to a civil jury in "actions at law."[4] To frame the analysis, consider the following hypothetical:

> Alice enters into a contract with her credit card company, Acme. The contract contains an arbitration clause providing simply that "All disputes related to this agreement shall be resolved by a single arbitrator pursuant to the rules of the American Arbitration Association." Alice later discovers that Acme has been charging an

1 U.S. CONST. amend. VII.

2 MONT. CONST., art II, § 26.

3 MONT. CONST., art. II, § 16.

4 There is some confusion over whether state action must be proven in order to state a Seventh Amendment claim. *See, e.g.,* Sarah Rudolph Cole, *Arbitration and State Action*, 2005 B.Y.U. L. Rev. 1 (2005).

> unlawful rate of interest. She commences litigation against Acme, alleging violations of both the contract, and state usury laws and state unfair business practice laws. Her complaint includes a jury demand (to which, let us assume, she would be entitled but for the arbitration clause). Acme moves to dismiss the litigation, on the ground that Alice must arbitrate her claim and, therefore, has no right to a jury trial.

Does the arbitration clause effectively vitiate the parties' jury right? The answer to this question holds potentially quite significant stakes. Not only are juries enshrined in our federal and state constitutions,[5] they have an important impact both on the course of a dispute and the parties' settlement incentives. Juries generally are believed to award more generous damages than judges in bench trials (an empirical proposition that has been hotly contested).[6] Moreover, regardless of the empirical validity of the foregoing proposition, the specter of a jury and the perceived risk of runaway verdicts can press defendants to settle before a jury ever sees the case.[7]

Of course, the stakes can be overstated. Even without arbitration clauses, only a small percentage of civil litigation ever reaches trial,

5 U.S. CONST. amend. VII; ALA. CONST. art. I, § 11; ALASKA CONST. art. 1, § 16; ARIZ. CONST. art. 2 § 23; ARK. CONST. art. 2, § 7; CAL. CONST. art. 1, § 16; COLO. CONST. art. 2, § 23; CONN. CONST. art. 1, § 19; DEL. CONST., art. 1, § 4; D.C. art. I, § 107; FLA. CONST. art. 1 § 22; GA. CONST. art. 1, § 1, ¶ XI; HAW. CONST. art. 1, § 13; IDAHO CONST. art. 1, § 7; ILL. CONST. art. 1, § 13; IND. CONST. art. 1, § 20; IOWA CONST. art. 1, § 9; KAN. CONST. Bill of Rights § 5; KY. CONST. art. 13, § 8; LA. CONST. art 1, § 16; ME. CONST. art. 1, § 20; MD. CONST. art. 23; MASS. CONST. art. XV; MICH. CONST. art. 1, § 14; MINN. CONST. art. 1, § 4; MISS. CONST. art. 3, § 31; MO. CONST. art. 1, § 22(a); MONT. CONST. art. 2, § 26; NEB. CONST. art. I, § 6; NEV. CONST. art. 1, § 3; N.H. CONST. Pt. 1, art. 20; N.J. CONST. art. 1, ¶ 9; N.M. CONST. art. 2, § 12; N.Y. CONST. art. 1, § 2; N.C. CONST. art. I, § 25; N.D. CONST. art. 1, § 13; OHIO CONST. art. I, § 5; OKLA. CONST. art. 2, § 19; OR. CONST. Art. I, § 17; PA. CONST. art. 1, § 6; R.I. CONST. art. 1, § 15; S.C. CONST. art. I, § 14; S.D. CONST. art. 6, § 6; TENN. CONST. art. 1, § 6; TEX. CONST. art. 1, § 15; UTAH CONST. art. 1, § 10; VT. CONST. ch. 1, art. 12; VA. CONST. art. 1, § 11; WASH. CONST. art. 1, § 21; W. VA. CONST. art. 3, § 13; WIS. CONST. art. 1, § 5; WYO. CONST. art. 1, § 9.

6 Stephan Landsman, *The Civil Jury in America: Scenes from an Unappreciated History*, 44 HASTINGS L.J. 578, 610–18 (1993).

7 *See* Peter B. Rutledge, *Whither Arbitration*, 6 GEO. J.L. & Pub. Pol'y 549 (2008). RANDALL KISER, BEYOND RIGHT AND WRONG: THE POWER OF EFFECTIVE DECISION MAKING FOR ATTORNEYS AND CLIENTS 63 (2010) (stating decision errors for plaintiffs and defendants are lower in arbitration than either bench or jury trials, and defendants underprice

much less a jury verdict.[8] This is either because the case is dismissed at a pretrial stage or is settled.[9] At a minimum, however, we can say confidently that the prospect of a jury exerts an important influence on a party's litigation behavior. It follows, therefore, that the waiver of the right to access that institution will affect litigants' incentives.

Synthesizing the foregoing, perhaps it makes more sense to conceptualize the jury as a piece of settlement leverage that parties (often plaintiffs) can use to extract higher settlements and that their opponents (often defendants) can deny them through the use of arbitration clauses. This can come both from the mere possibility of a jury trial as well as the information conveyed in jury verdicts as it enables the parties to predict their likely recovery (or exposure).[10] So, in light of the potential implications of the jury right for the parties' respective settlement positions, does an arbitration clause effectively waive a party's jury right?

The answer turns on a couple of critical propositions. First, it depends on whether the jury right is alienable at all. One could easily imagine a world in which rights, particularly constitutional rights, simply are inalienable.[11] Second, even if the right is alienable in some

their settlement offers in arbitration because of a diminished incentive to avoid adjudicated outcomes in arbitration); Donald Wittman, *Lay Juries, Professional Arbitrators and the Arbitrator Selection Hypothesis*, 5 AM. L. & ECON. REV. 61 (2003).

8 *See, e.g.*, Margo Schlanger, *What We Know and What We Should Know about American Trial Trends*, 2006 J. DISP. RESOL. 35 (2006); Marc Galanter, *The Hundred-Year Decline of Trials and the Thirty Years War*, 57 STAN. L. REV. 1255 (2005); Marc Galanter, *The Vanishing Trial: An Examination of Trials and Related Matters in Federal and State Courts*, 1 J. EMP. LEG. STUD. 459 (2004); Marc Galanter, *The Regulatory Function of the Civil Jury*, *in* VERDICT: ASSESSING THE CIVIL JURY SYSTEM 61, 63 (Robert E. Litan ed., 1993); Schuck, *Mapping the Debate on Jury Reform*, in VERDICT: ASSESSING THE CIVIL JURY SYSTEM 306, 307, 332 nn. 6–7 (Robert E. Litan ed., 1993).

9 Kevin M. Clermont, *Litigation Realities Redux*, 84 NOTRE DAME L. REV. 1919, 1946–59 (2009) (empirical study and findings of pretrial termination averaging 96%); Gillian K. Hadfield, *Where Have All the Trials Gone? Settlements, Non-Trial Adjudications and Statistical Artifacts in the Changing Disposition of Federal Civil Cases*, 1 J. EMPIRICAL LEG. STUD. 705, 728–33 (2004).

10 Galanter *Regulatory Function*, *supra* note 8, at 61, 63: Schuck, *supra* note 8, at 307; *Developments in the Law*, 110 HARV. L. REV. 1408, 1423, 1427 (1997).

11 Lee Anne Fennell, *Adjusting Alienability*, 122 HARV. L. REV. 1403 (2009) (implications of alienability and rights); Daniel A. Farber, *Another View of the Quagmire: Unconstitutional Conditions and Contract Theory*, 33 FLA. ST. U. L. REV. 913 (2006) (discussing the alienability of constitutional rights in exchange for government benefits); Kathleen M. Sullivan, *Unconstitutional Conditions*, 102 HARV. L. REV. 1413, 1476–90 (1989).

circumstances, it depends on whether the right is alienable on a pre-dispute basis, which is to say that parties need not wait for an actual dispute to arise before they can effectively waive their right to a jury trial with respect to claims that fall within the ambit of the arbitration clause. Third, even assuming that parties can prospectively waive their constitutional right to a jury trial on a pre-dispute basis, the argument requires some account of whether the parties have in fact done so. This essentially is a question of contract interpretation: Does a general enforceable commitment to arbitrate effectively waive a constitutional right to a jury trial?

Most debates among scholars and in judicial decisions concern the third issue. As to that issue, most courts conclude that parties can waive the right (absent some showing that the particular pre-dispute written waiver suffers from some defect such as fraud or duress). But one can well imagine alternative approaches turning on the prior two questions (such as whether an arbitration clause suffices to waive the jury right, or whether the jury right is waivable at all!). Perhaps the arbitration clause must expressly make reference to the waiver of the contracting parties' jury rights in order to be effective.

These questions frame the analysis for most of this chapter. Before we turn to those questions, however, two observations are in order – one concerning comparative approaches and one concerning a potential intellectual barrier to the entire undertaking.

The comparative point is obvious but nonetheless important. That is, most countries do not have as robust constitutional right to a civil jury as the United States.[12] By point of example, in many countries, such as Russia and Australia, the right to jury trials is secured only for the most serious criminal offenses. Some countries such as Chile, Mexico, Hungary, Israel, and South Africa offer no jury right at all.[13] A few countries such as England and Canada accord a right to a civil jury in some circumstances, but they generally condition it on

[12] *See Developments*, *supra* note 10, at 1411; John Henry Merryman & Rogelio Perez-Perdomo, The Civil Law Tradition 113 (3d ed. 2007).

[13] Nancy S. Marder, *An Introduction to Comparative Jury Systems*, 86 CHI.-KENT L. REV. 453, 461 (2011); Ethan J. Leib, *A Comparison of Criminal Jury Decision Rules in Democratic Countries*, 5 OHIO ST. J. CRIM. L. 629, 631–35 (2008); NEIL VIDMAR, WORLD JURY SYSTEMS 10–13 (2000).

legislative limitations.[14] Consequently, in most systems, debates over the impact of arbitration (or other forms of civil dispute resolution) on the jury right do not enter the constitutional dialogue. The debate here is largely an American phenomenon.[15]

The doctrinal point concerns the relationship between structural issues, discussed in Chapter 1, and the jury right issues, discussed here. Specifically, to the extent the structural analysis turns on considerations of waiver, is the discussion of the jury not entirely derivative of that analysis? If we posit that the right to an Article III forum is waivable, and the jury right attaches only upon a determination that litigation should proceed, does it not follow then that the effective waiver of an Article III forum necessarily waives the Seventh Amendment right as well? This is more than a hypothetical concern, as several courts have rejected jury right claims on the ground that they were entirely derivative of the Article III claims (which the court had just rejected).[16]

This doctrinal point (one might consider it an objection to the entire undertaking in this chapter) deserves to be taken quite seriously. Surely, there is some overlap – the Seventh Amendment right is the right to a jury in an Article III forum (recall this is one of the few rights that has

[14] *See* Neil Vidmar, *A Historical and Comparative Perspective on the Common Law Jury*, in World Jury Systems, Neil Vidmar (ed.), at 3 (Oxford 2000).

[15] Steve Ware has creatively utilized this exceptional feature of the American jury system to justify a more relaxed standard toward the enforceability of jury waivers. Under Ware's argument, a more relaxed standard reduces the differences in legal systems. Ware responds to Sternlight that enforcement of arbitration clauses is a response to the unique function played by the civil jury in the United States. In this regard, arbitration clauses can be conceptualized as a harmonization mechanism that reduces the differences between the United States and foreign countries over the role played by the civil jury in dispute resolution.

[16] *Syncor v. Conseco*, 2001 WL 223243 at *3 (4th Cir. Mar. 7, 2001); Marsh v. First USA Bank, N.A., 103 F. Supp.2d 909, 921 (N.D. Tex. 2000); Bank One v. Coates, 125 F. Supp. 2d 819, 824 (S.D. Miss. 2001); *Parsley v. Terminix Intern. Co., L.P.*, 1998 WL 1572764 (S.D. Ohio Sept. 15, 1998); Burlington Northern RR Co. v. Soo Line RR Co., 162 B.R. 207, 214 (D. Minn. 1993); Pierson v. Dean Witter Reynolds, Inc., 742 F.2d 334, 339 (7th Cir. 1984) (the "loss of the right to a jury trial is a necessary and fairly obvious consequence of an agreement to arbitrate."); *Geldermann v. Commodity Futures Trading Comm'n*, 836 F.2d 310, 323 (7th Cir. 1987); Cremin v. Merrill Lynch Pierce Fenner & Smith, Inc., 957 F. Supp. 1460, 1471 (N.D. Ill. 1997); National Iranian Oil Co. v. Ashland Oil, 716 F. Supp. 268, 270 (S.D. Miss. 1989).

not been affirmatively incorporated against the states).[17] Yet the underlying considerations are not identical. For one thing, the separation-of-powers considerations drop out in the Seventh Amendment discussion – making the issue less one about the horizontal distribution of power.

For another thing, the answer turns critically on one's theory about the civil jury.[18] One might imagine that the civil jury is essentially an individual right (its placement within the Bill of Rights supports this view as a structural matter).[19] Under this view, the debate over the relationship between arbitration and the jury right becomes one primarily about individual liberty (and thus waiver), creating some risk of overlap with the structural analysis in the preceding chapter. Alternatively, one might imagine that the civil jury plays a more structural role – as a sort of mini-legislature, or even a check on the other branches of government.[20] Under this view, the debate over the waivability of the jury right carries implications broader than matters of individual liberty. Rather, arbitration, as an effective waiver of the jury right, intrudes upon the third-party interests of those who would serve on juries and, more broadly, on the societal interest in the healthy functioning of this institution as an instrument of democratic government. (Here, of course, it should be noted that, under this conception, criticism of the jury-limiting consequence is not limited to arbitration; a host of other instruments in our system of civil procedure, more notably summary judgment and directed verdicts, have a similar effect.) The answer

[17] 2 Ronald D. Rotunda & John E. Nowak, Treatise on Constitutional Law § 14.2(a) (4th ed. 2011); Minneapolis & St. L.R. Co. v. Bombolis, 36 S. Ct. 595, 596–98 (1916).

[18] For a discussion of the possible values served by a civil jury and a survey of the key literature, see Developments, *supra* note 10, at 1421–43.

[19] This stands in contrast to the right to a criminal jury which, curiously, appears twice in the Constitution – in Article III and again in the Sixth Amendment. For an attempt to synthesize the theory underpinning the jury in the two contexts, see Colleen P. Murphy, *Integrating the Constitutional Authority of the Civil and Criminal Juries*, 61 Geo. Wash. L. Rev. 723 (1993). *See also Developments*, *supra* note 10, at 1436 (discussing the relationship between the criminal and civil juries in terms of their common function as a forum of "deliberative democracy").

[20] Juries can serve this checking function through their power to determine the verdict without needing to account precisely for the legal analysis leading them to that result.

to this question informs the justification for an independent inquiry into the relationship between the Seventh Amendment and arbitration law.[21]

Apart from bringing into relief the debate over the role of juries in our constitutional system, separate consideration of the jury right raises a final unique consideration, one that has received virtually no attention in the scholarship or scant case law considering the issue. Namely, assessing the effectiveness of an arbitration clause in terms of the Seventh Amendment jury right provides an opportunity to create a federal standard on the enforceability of arbitration clauses.[22] Recall from the chapter on federalism that one unique feature of the analysis under Section 2 of the FAA was that (at least in the context of domestic/non-treaty arbitrations) state contract law, rather than federal law, governed the scope of contract defenses to the enforceability of the arbitration agreement (that is, whether there was a "ground at law or equity for the revocation of any contract"). Although this approach advanced important federalism values, it undermined uniformity in this area of law. The Seventh Amendment theory avoids this difficulty because the contours of the Seventh Amendment right (including the opportunities for waiver) unquestionably present a federal issue. This creates an opportunity for federal courts to articulate a standard for evaluating the enforceability of an arbitration clause without having to look to the eccentricities of the law of the state in which the court happens to sit.

In sum, there are legitimate reasons for analyzing the relationship between arbitration and the jury right as an independent intellectual theme, separate and apart from the structural issues examined in Chapter 1. With these preliminaries out of the way, we can turn to the tripartite analysis introduced earlier in this chapter – namely (1) should

[21] For classic historical examinations of the jury right, see Edith Guild Henderson, *The Background of the Seventh Amendment*, 80 HARV. L. REV. 289 (1966); Charles W. Wolfram, *The Constitutional History of the Seventh Amendment*, 57 MINN. L. REV. 639 (1973).

[22] One decision has drawn these linkages. In *Walker*, the court confronted a plaintiff's claim that an arbitration clause violated his federal constitutional right to a civil jury. The court held that federal law governed the question of the jury waiver; it cited the Sixth Circuit's strict standard for the effectiveness of waivers of (constitutional/jury) rights. [Walker v. Ryan's Family Steak Houses, Inc., 289 F. Supp. 2d 916, 936 (M.D. Tenn. 2003); Morrison v. Circuit City Stores, Inc., 317 F.3d 646, 668–69 (6th Cir. 2003).]

the jury right be alienable at all; (2) if so, should it be waivable on a predispute basis, and (3) if so, does a general agreement to arbitrate represent an effective waiver?

ALIENABILITY OF THE JURY RIGHT

Should the jury right be alienable at all? If the answer is no, then the implications for arbitration (at least in jurisdictions such as the United States where most civil disputes give rise to a jury right) are fatal. Yet in most respects the trend in constitutional jurisprudence is to recognize the possibility of waiver. Criminal defendants routinely waive their pretrial and trial rights such as the right to the presence of counsel during a post-indictment lineup or interrogation. At least in the criminal context, any such waiver must be knowing, voluntary, and intelligent.[23] Whether that same standard applies with respect to rights in civil proceedings is less clear, a topic to which we return later in this chapter. What is clear is that parties in noncriminal matters likewise can waive their rights. Indeed, with respect to the jury right, the legendary civil procedure scholar Fleming James could confidently declare nearly a half-century ago that the jury right "has been uniformly construed as a right which may be waived by the parties."[24]

Given the universal acceptance of the possibility that the jury right can be waived, one might reasonably ask why it even becomes necessary to contemplate its inalienability (what I call the "inalienability" position). The short answer is that alienation of a constitutional right, even if allowed, is not costless. A recognition of these costs influences the view about how easy it should be to effect the waiver. Considering the possibility of inalienability enables us, thereby, to focus on the costs of alienation, which helps us consider the waiver discussion later in this chapter.

To begin to focus on the costs of alienation, consider the example of the ultimate inalienable right, the right to be free from involuntary servitude. Even if I entered into such a contract freely, of my own

[23] Johnson v. Zerbst, 304 U.S. 458, 468 (1938).

[24] Fleming James, *Right to a Jury Trial in Civil Actions*, 72 YALE L.J. 655, 656 (1963).

will and with all the procedural protections one could imagine, anyone would be hard-pressed to accept the idea that I can voluntarily enslave myself.

This is so for several reasons. For one thing, we might have serious doubts about the voluntariness of this decision. Who in their right mind would not only agree to work for nothing, but actually accede themselves as property to another human being? Apart from the damage to the person, of course, society suffers as well in various ways. The mere acceptance of voluntary enslavement legitimates a process that society has condemned (and thereby offends that society's norms).

Although I am not suggesting that waivers of the Seventh Amendment entail the same costs as waivers of the Thirteenth Amendment, the jury right plays a significant role in our society. This certainly was true at the time of the Founding.[25] Even in the twentieth century, scholars and judges have stressed the instrumental and democratic values of the jury. For example, in one famous case, the Supreme Court observed that "The trial by jury is justly dear to the American people. It has always been an object of deep interest and solicitude, and every encroachment upon it has been watched with great jealousy."[26]

Consequently, alienation of the jury right, like alienation of the Thirteenth Amendment right, entails costs – both to the party alienating the right and to society as a whole. When one waives the jury right, we might worry about whether that decision was truly voluntary (who would give up the right to be judged by his or her peers)? We also might worry about the costs borne by third parties. Here, however, the cost entails a reduction in the opportunity for democratic deliberation entailed by the jury right. In other words, waiver of my right to the

[25] *See* Federalist 83 ("The friends and adversaries of the plan of the convention, if they agree in nothing else, concur at least in the value they set upon the trial by jury; or, if there is any difference, it consists in this: the former regard it as a valuable safeguard to liberty; the latter represent it as the very palladium of free government."); Developments, *supra* note 10, at 1429 (noting that jury's function "as a check on oppressive officialdom and a 'security against corruption'... was an important part of the Anti-Federalist case for the Seventh Amendment.") (footnotes omitted).

[26] Chauffeurs, Teamsters & Helpers Local No. 391 v. Terry, 494 U.S. 558, 581 (1990) (quoting Parsons v. Bedford, 28 U.S. (3 Pet.) 433, 446 (1830).

jury affects those who otherwise would have the opportunity to serve on my case and, thereby, in some small way shape the process whereby disputes in our society are resolved (and law is shaped).

Thus, we can understand the inalienability argument along the following lines. Rights should be inalienable when the costs of alienation (whether to the individual, to society, or both) are too great. By referring to costs, I do not mean costs in strictly economic terms. The damage to democratic deliberation and other values that are either unmeasurable or incommensurable might justify a strong form argument against alienability, as the argument against slavery demonstrates. Conversely, though, when the costs are not so great, then the argument against inalienability weakens, and the possibility of alienation can be more easily imagined.

At this point in the analysis, it is worth pausing to consider an irony in any argument against alienation. One might reasonably argue that the concept of an inalienable right is an oxymoron (with apologies to the drafters of the Declaration of Independence).[27] A right is an individual entitlement, a bulwark that protects the individual from intrusion by the state. To alienate that right, far from imposing costs (at least on the individual), is its ultimate manifestation. One has freely chosen to forego an entitlement as to which one holds the absolute discretion about its disposition.

Consider, for example, the right to vote. All citizens over eighteen and not laboring under a felony conviction (in most states) enjoy that right.[28] But many do not exercise it (especially in elections that do not involve selection of the U.S. president).[29] Do we conceive of this "inaction" as a social wrong? If so, then perhaps we should, as some

[27] "We hold these truths to be self-evident, that all men are created equal, that they are endowed by their Creator with certain inalienable Rights, that among these are Life, Liberty and the pursuit of Happiness." The Declaration of Independence para. 2 (U.S. 1776).

[28] U.S. CONST. art. I, § 2; U.S. CONST. amend. XV, XIX, XXVI; The Voting Rights Act of 1965, 42 U.S.C. §§ 1973–73bb-1 (2008); Reynolds v. Sims, 377 U.S. 533 (1964), Richardson v. Ramirez, 418 U.S. 24 (1974).

[29] The percentage of the voting age population participating in the selection of the U.S. president was 57.1% in 2008 and 55.7% in 2004. However, the percentage of the voting age population for an election of only U.S. Representatives was 37% in 2010 and 36.1% in 2006. U.S House of Representatives, Office of the Clerk, *Statistics of the Presidential and Congressional Election*, biennial.

countries have done, require citizens to exercise their right to vote upon penalty of some fine or other legal consequence.[30] But if that proposal strikes us as anathema (how can someone be *forced* to exercise a right?), then waiver (at least in some contexts) is something to be celebrated, not abhorred.

The key phrase, then, is "in some contexts." Which contexts? Several considerations might inform our answer to that question. One key consideration would be the duration of the alienation. For example, a firefighter who agrees to a single drug test is waiving "fewer" rights than one who agrees to standing drug tests over the course of her career. A second consideration might be the nature of the right waived (one that entails relatively little third-party costs versus one that entails many). A third consideration would be the quality of information that the individual has before the waiver becomes effective (thus waivers of the right to a criminal jury without the opportunity to consult with counsel are more suspect than counseled waivers). A final consideration might be the revocability of the waiver (thus, someone who renounces his citizenship may not easily undo that decision, as opposed to someone who declines to vote in one election but chooses to do so in the next one).

Applied to waivers of the jury right, the foregoing considerations cut in different directions. Jury waivers, once made, are hard to revoke. At the same time, they only affect a single case (or in case of a contractual jury waiver, a set of disputes). Whether the waiver is informed will, of course, be a fact-specific inquiry. And the social values at stake depend critically on one's conception of the purposes of the jury right.

How we resolve this depends critically on our conception of the jury. If we accept the idea that the jury is a liberty designed to protect the individual, then the arguments about the social value of the jury (and the relative need to police alienability) are weaker. On the other

[30] Australia and Belgium both impose compulsory voting with penalties of small financial amounts, one to three francs in Belgium and twenty to one-hundred dollars in Australia. Lisa Hill, *Compulsory Voting in Australia: A Basis for a 'Best Practice' Regime*, 32 FED. L. REV. 479, 494 (2004). Twenty-three countries have compulsory voting. Central Intelligence Agency, *Suffrage*, The World Factbook. Note, *The Case for Compulsory Voting in the United States*, 121 HARV. L. REV. 591 (2007).

hand, if we view the jury as a structural feature of our society (a bulwark against tyranny if you will), then the argument for alienability becomes harder to make.[31]

So far, we have analyzed the alienation question at a unidimensional level – focusing principally on the Seventh Amendment's jury guarantee. Federalism principles complicate matters (as they have elsewhere in the book).[32] Although the Seventh Amendment remains one of the few guarantees of the Bill of Rights not incorporated against the states,[33] state constitutions contain their own jury guarantees. Even if the federal constitutional right is alienable, the state right might not be. Periodically, state courts have made broad pronouncements declaring the jury guarantees in their state constitutions to be unwaivable, and a few have invalidated arbitral schemes (though these tend to be mandatory court-ordered schemes as opposed to the contractual ones examined here).[34] So how does one think about the alienability question in the context of a two-tier system of government?

FAA preemption might create an escape hatch from this dilemma. Recall from Chapter 3 that, by virtue of the Supremacy Clause, the

[31] Justice Nelson makes this argument in his concurring opinion in Kloss v. Edward D. Jones Co., 54 P.3d 1 (Mont. 2002). He then weakens the force of this argument by conceding that parties of equal bargaining power should be able to waive the jury right. This proposition stands in some tension with his spirited defense of the jury right. If the jury right is so important, then there may be good reason not to allow its alienability regardless of the sophistication of the parties or their relative bargaining position. Moreover, it is far from clear whether the key criterion should be equal sophistication as opposed to a minimum threshold of sophistication. One could have sophisticated parties that have unequal bargaining positions (a Harvard-educated investor and a bank with a lot more resources), or one might have two unsophisticated parties with equal bargaining positions (two local joes who sign an arbitration agreement because they have heard something about arbitration).

[32] Jean R. Sternlight, *The Rise and Spread of Mandatory Arbitration as a Substitute for the Jury Trial*, 38 U.S.F. L. Rev. 17, 26 nn. 46–47 (2003).

[33] Minneapolis & St. Louis R.R. v. Bombolis, 241 U.S. 211, 217 (1916).

[34] For example, in *Lisanti v. Alamo Title Ins. of Texas*, the New Mexico Supreme Court struck down arbitration mandated by state statutory/regulatory scheme as violative of jury right. 55 P.3d 962 (N.M. 2002). That case involved a statutorily imposed arbitral scheme. GTFM LLC v. TRN Sales, Inc., 2000 WL 364871 (S.D.N.Y. Apr. 10, 2000). Moreover, the court had not agreed to review any question of FAA preemption. In *Bank S., N.A. v. Howard*, the Georgia Supreme Court invalidated all prospective waivers of jury right. 444 S.E.2d 799 (Ga. 1994). Yet curiously it did not doubt the enforceability of arbitration agreements even though such agreements unquestionably had precisely the same effect. *Howard*, 444 S.E. 2d at 800 n.5 (addressing arbitration).

federal standard almost always will prevail over the state standard, even when that state standard is grounded in the state's constitution. Thus, to the extent a state constitutional jury guarantee impedes enforcement of the arbitration agreement, Section 2 and *Southland* would dictate that the state guarantee cannot stand, even in state court.[35]

Or do they? That depends critically on whether the state jury right is considered a "generally applicable contract defense" or, instead, a doctrine that "singles out/discriminates against" arbitration.[36] One could plausibly argue that state constitutional guarantees of jury rights do not discriminate against arbitration but equally apply absent the arbitration clause. Put another way, take the basic hypothetical introduced at the beginning of this chapter but assume that, instead of agreeing to arbitration, the dispute resolution clause simply contains a bilateral waiver of both Alice's and Acme's jury right (thus envisioning a bench trial in state court). As a matter of state constitutional law, such an alienation of the parties' jury right might be equally unenforceable even in the non-arbitral context. Consequently, the FAA does not preempt generally applicable state constitutional guarantees that, as a matter of state law, are not alienable. Several courts and scholars have endorsed this argument.[37]

The problem with this argument, as Steve Ware insightfully observed, is that it cannot be reconciled with Section 2 of the FAA. Section 2 preserves only grounds at law or in equity for the revocation of "any" contract. The critical term here is "any." State constitutional involving the alienability of the jury right are not blatant anti-arbitration rules insofar as they do not single out arbitration agreements.[38] Rather,

[35] *See, e.g.,* Bradley v. Harris Research, Inc., 275 F.3d 884, 890 (9th Cir. 2001) (holding that FAA-preempted state law prohibited venue shift in cases even though law did not mention arbitration specifically).

[36] For a complete discussion, see Chapter 3.

[37] Kloss v. Edward D. Jones & Co., 54 P.3d 1 (Mont. 2002): For scholarship, see Sternlight, *supra* note 31, at 17, 37 (2003); David S. Schwartz, *State Judges as Guardians of Federalism: Resisting the Federal Arbitration Act's Encroachment on State Law*, 16 WASH. U. J. LAW & POL. 129 (2004).

[38] Compare the laws at issue in *Allied-Bruce Terminix* and *Doctors Associates*. Doctor's Associates, Inc. v. Casarotto, 517 U.S. 681 (1996); Allied-Bruce Terminix Cos., Inc. v. Dobson, 513 U.S. 265, 271–74 (1995).

in Ware's terms, these grounds apply only to some contracts, namely only those containing arbitration clauses and contracts containing jury waivers.[39] Consequently these are not grounds for the revocation of "any" contract and, therefore, do not survive Section 2 analysis. To survive Section 2 analysis, it is not sufficient that the defense only applies to a category of contracts; instead, it must be something akin to universality.[40]

Other efforts to circumvent FAA preemption and rooted in the state jury guarantee are possible. Suppose that a state declares that the resolution of trials by jury is an important public policy (whether in a statute, in the constitution, or in jurisprudence interpreting the constitution). Accordingly, contracts (whether arbitration agreements or otherwise) that strip parties of that jury right are unenforceable because they violate public policy. The public policy doctrine, so the argument runs, is a generally applicable contract defense that survives the Section 2 preemption analysis. Thus, a state constitutional jury guarantee can render an arbitration clause unenforceable.

Although this line of argumentation has not garnered much support in the case law, it is not without force. In contrast to the preceding argument, public policy is a "ground" for the revocation of "any" contract and, thus, satisfies Ware's universality criterion. The problem, as Chief Justice Burger recognized in *Southland* and Justice Scalia recognized more recently in *Concepcion,* is that the defense is too malleable.[41] Almost any idea can be creatively smuggled into public policy, thereby undercutting too far the uniformity goals of the FAA. In that respect, the public policy argument suffers from the same defect as the unconscionability argument that the Supreme Court recently rejected in its *Concepcion* decision discussed in Chapter 3. To embrace a broad version of the defense allows state governmental institutions hostile to arbitration to smuggle anti-arbitration doctrines into the jurisprudence by disguising them as generally applicable contract defenses. That

[39] 38 U.S.F. L. REV. at 46.

[40] 38 U.S.F. L. REV. at 47.

[41] Even Justice Nelson, one of the most ardent defenders of the jury right as a defense to enforceable arbitration agreements acknowledges the persuasive force of *Southland* as a limit to this argument. *See Kloss*, 54 P.3d at 14 n.3.

approach cannot be squared with the FAA's goal of promoting the enforcement of arbitration agreements.

To summarize, this section has sought to evaluate the contours of any argument that the jury right is inalienable. Although virtually all courts and commentators have accepted the possibility of alienability at least in some circumstances, the exercise has proven useful by bringing into relief the fundamental values underpinning the jury right and, consequently, the costs of alienation. Our view turns critically on the extent to which we conceptualize the jury guarantee as simply an individual right or, instead, a more structural feature of democratic government – one that enables deliberative democracy and stands between the state and an individual before property or assets can be forcibly repossessed. Moreover, as in other contexts, the federalist feature of our system of government complicates the analysis by introducing the possibility that state values may re-enforce the jury right. All of these considerations, therefore, serve as a backdrop to the real battleground, namely the circumstances under which waiver is possible. The next section begins to tackle that issue.

EFFECTIVENESS OF PRE-DISPUTE WAIVER

If we accept the premise that the jury right can at least under some conditions be alienated, the focus then turns to identifying those conditions. The most cautious position would be one under which the jury right cannot be waived prior to an actual dispute arising (I call this the "no pre-dispute waiver" position.). This is effectively the approach taken by many European countries that preclude the enforcement of pre-dispute arbitration (and forum selection) clauses in consumer and employment contract.[42] It is also the approach taken in the United States with respect to certain niche industries (such as contracts

[42] Zivilprozeßordnung [ZPO] [Civil Procedure Statute, Art. 617–18 CCP; European Union Directive on Unfair Terms in Consumer Contracts, Council Directive 93/13/EEC, 1993 O.J. (L 095) 29; Christopher R. Drahozal & Raymond J. Friel, *Consumer Arbitration in the European Union and the United States*, 28 N.C. J. INT'L L. & COM. Reg. 357 (2002) William M. Howard, *Arbitrating Employment Discrimination Claims: Do You Really Have To? Do You Really Want To?*, 43 DRAKE L. REV. 255 (1994).

between automobile manufacturers and dealers, credit card contracts with military service personnel, poultry wholesale agreements and, most recently, certain residential real estate loan contracts).[43] Moreover, at the time of this writing, the newly created Consumer Financial Protection Bureau has been authorized to consider and, if appropriate, issue regulations banning the use of pre-dispute arbitration agreements in a broader array of consumer credit agreements.[44] The proposed Arbitration Fairness Act would have adopted this view.[45] Central to the rhetoric of such rules and proposals (particularly in the United States) is that arbitration clauses effectively surrender a valuable constitutional right and, therefore, such a right should not be alienable before a dispute arises.[46]

This view of the waiver question exemplifies a classic case of decision making in the face of incomplete information. The argument against pre-dispute waiver rests on the assumption that, until parties know the complete contours of a dispute, they lack the necessary information to make a fully informed choice whether to exercise, or waive, their right to a jury trial. Pre-dispute arbitration clauses force parties to make a decision about that important right before they have full (or at least adequate) information about the nature of their dispute. Consequently such clauses should be *per se* unenforceable. Parties remain free, however, to waive their right to a jury trial *after* a dispute has arisen, just as they may do so even in the absence of an arbitration clause.

[43] CompuCredit Corp. v. Greenwood, 2012 WL 43514 *6 (U.S. Jan. 10, 2012) (recognizing the restriction for arbitration in: 7 U.S.C. § 26(n)(2) (2006) for commodity whisteblowers; 15 U.S.C. § 1226(a)(2) (2006) for automobile manufacturers and dealers; and 12 U.S.C. § 5518(b) (2010) for providing authority to the newly created Consumer Financial Protection Bureau to regulate predispute arbitration agreements).

[44] 12 U.S.C. § 5518(b) (2010).

[45] Arbitration Fairness Act, H.R. 3010 and S. 1782, 110th Cong. (2007).

[46] Arbitration Fairness Act of 2011, S. 987, 112th Cong. (2011) (finding that consumers and employees have little or no meaningful choice about submitting claims to arbitration and often are unaware they have given up their rights); Public Citizen, *The Arbitration Trap: How Credit Card Companies Ensnare Consumers, available at* www.citizen.org/documents/ArbitrationTrap.pdf (2007) (stating waivers of the right to trial by jury usually are required to be knowing, voluntary, and intentional, but courts uphold arbitration agreements at lower standards); Jean R. Sternlight, *Rethinking the Constitutionality of the Supreme Court's Preference for Binding Arbitration: A Fresh Assessment of Jury Trial, Separation of Powers, and Due Process Concerns*, 72 TUL. L. REV. 1 (1997).

Although this argument has a certain surface appeal, it has received little support from courts. Generally courts easily conclude that a jury right can be waived on a pre-dispute basis. Unfortunately, most decisions offer little in the way of analysis to support this conclusion, so it is worth elaborating on the precise theoretical argument behind this judicial rejection of the "no pre-dispute waiver" position.[47]

For one thing, the objection ignores the fact that, as a society, we enforce decision making in the face of incomplete information all the time. For example, in employment contexts, employees may be required to make decisions about benefits choices such as insurance or pension plans without fully knowing their future health or retirement needs. Similarly, in the consumer context, consumers can enter into enforceable future commitments in the face of incomplete information. For example, when I rent a car, I must decide whether to purchase the "prepaid fuel" option or to fill the tank myself before returning the rental car even though I may not know, ex ante, how far I plan to travel or how easy it will be to fill the tank during my journey. Of course, these (and many other) examples may be distinguished on the grounds that, compared to the jury right, the individual interests at stake are far lower. But this is not the only flaw with the "no pre-dispute waiver" position.

Even assuming one can distinguish waivers of the jury right from waivers of other rights in the face of incomplete information, problems remain. In some cases, the problems are simple line-drawing ones – how do we decide whether a dispute has begun? In other cases, the problems are informational ones – begging the question whether a particular definition of the dispute actually solves the underlying informational deficit. Yet in other cases, the proposed definition of the commencement of the dispute can undermine the very viability of arbitration.

[47] Geldermann v. Commodity Futures Trading Comm'n, 836 F.2d 310 (7th Cir. 1987) (concluding that commodities brokerage waived jury right by opting into licensing scheme that entailed arbitration); Bank One N.A. v. Coates, 125 F. Supp. 2d 819 (S.D. Miss. 2001), *aff'd*, 2002 WL 663804 (5th Cir. 2002); Marsh v. First USA Bank, N.A., 103 F. Supp. 2d 909, 921 (N.D. Tex. 2003) (concluding that agreement to arbitrate waived jury right); Cremin v. Merrill Lynch Pierce Fenner & Smith, Inc., 957 F. Supp. 1460, 1461 (N.D. Ill. 1997).

To begin to flesh this out, consider three possible standards for definition of when the dispute begins:

- When all of the elements of the first claim have ripened?
- After the litigants have had an opportunity to consult with counsel?
- Only after a complaint has been filed?

Now consider the consequences of these possible standards:

- *When all of the elements of the first claim have ripened?* If that is the standard, the line is incredibly hazy (making it difficult for parties who want to arbitrate to know when precisely they can make a proposal that, if accepted, would be enforceable). That standard also does little to overcome the informational deficit because, even once those elements have ripened, the individual (Alice, to use the example from the beginning of the chapter) may not even realize that she has her claim and may not know the contours of her rights.
- *After the litigants have had an opportunity to consult with counsel?* This overcomes some of the informational deficits presented by the preceding definition (assuming, of course, a minimally competent counsel). Of course, informational gaps may remain, which can only be filled in during the litigation once discovery has occurred. This definition retains, however, the blurriness because the parties may not know when precisely each other has consulted with counsel. Finally, we must acknowledge that this definition introduces a new cost into the equation, namely that the introduction of counsel may interject principal–agent problems where the agent (i.e., the party's attorney) may have a self-interest in pushing his or her client to a dispute resolution form (litigation) that enhances the payoff for the lawyer (through higher fees generated through litigation) even if that form, seen from the client's perspective, may be suboptimal.
- *Only after a complaint has been filed?* Unlike the prior two options, this approach does not suffer from a lack of clarity (except for the extreme hypotheticals about whether a suit has been properly commenced, matters that typically occupy obscure annals of civil procedure jurisprudence and the creative veins of a law professor's mind). Relative to the initial point when a party has had the opportunity to consult with counsel, the informational deficit may have

> shrunk further (as the party and his or her counsel do the vetting necessary to test a case). Although relatively clear, however, this approach may well reduce the possibility of arbitration altogether. This may occur for one of two reasons.[48] It may occur because, by the time litigation has commenced, the parties' have dug into their positions and, therefore, may be unwilling to agree upon anything (seeing a proposal for arbitration as an attempt by one party to secure some procedural advantage). It may also occur because, ironically, the parties have *too much* information about their dispute and, therefore, the reduction in their ignorance gives them relatively less reason to bargain.

In other words, of the several possible standards, several involve line-drawing problems. To the extent the line-drawing problems can be overcome, informational deficits may remain. Even when those are overcome, several of these proposals entail independent costs that may affirmatively undermine the efficacy of arbitration.

In light of its complications, it is unsurprising, therefore, that this position has attracted little support except with respect to special-interest legislation. A closer examination of that legislation demonstrates the perils of its underlying logic. As noted above, in a few specialized areas, Congress has actually taken the exceptional step of declaring pre-dispute arbitration agreements unenforceable. The model for this legislation was a 2002 act that prohibited such agreements in contracts between automobile manufacturers and automobile dealers. The bill passed with much fanfare as an essential protection for the party in the inferior bargaining position (i.e., the automobile dealer). Yet a few years after its passage, the act was used in an unusual situation – namely by an automobile manufacturer who sought to block

[48] For an elaboration on this point and a citation of the relevant literature, see Peter B. Rutledge, *Whither Arbitration* and various essays in the *Cardozo Journal on Conflict Resolution*. Peter B. Rutledge, *Whither Arbitration*, 6 GEO. J.L. & PUB. POL'Y 549 (2008); Amy J. Schmitz, *Nonconsensual + Nonbinding = Nonsensical? Reconsidering Court-Connected Arbitration Programs*, 10 CARDOZO J. CONFLICT RESOL. 587 (2008); Paul Bland & Claire Prestel, *Challenging Class Action Bans in Mandatory Arbitration Clauses*, 10 CARDOZO J. CONFLICT RESOL. 369 (2009).

an arbitration agreement that a dealer tried to enforce.[49] In other words, notwithstanding the dealer's alleged insufficient sophisticated to enter into an agreement on a pre-dispute basis, the dealer eventually wanted to enforce the agreement once the dispute arose, only to be thwarted by the manufacturer. As this example demonstrates, it is difficult to anticipate, ex ante, the informational deficits of contracting parties and regulate the dispute resolution market in a way that is designed to help overcome those deficits.

To summarize this part, even if it is assumed that the jury right is in some instances waivable, it is difficult to defend a position under which pre-dispute waivers are unenforceable. As a theoretical matter, that position is difficult to square with the general tolerance of such decisions, presents line-drawing problems, does not address informational deficits (or disparities), and ultimately undermines the efficacy of arbitration. As a practical matter, the limited legislative and judicial experience with this approach demonstrates the unforeseen consequences and flimsy analytical justification for the view. It is therefore unsurprising that the most serious debates have turned not on the categorical possibility (or impossibility) of pre-dispute waiver but, instead, the conditions under which such waiver can be effective. The third and final subpart of this chapter turns to that issue.

QUALITY OF THE WAIVER – IS GENERAL LANGUAGE SUFFICIENT?

The foregoing subsections have shown how the analysis of the jury question cannot easily be disposed of, either at the level of absolute principle (i.e., the inalienability of the jury right) or by means of a categorical rule that precludes all pre-dispute waivers of jury rights. Rather, the analysis at bottom must turn upon an assessment of the quality of the waiver.[50]

49 Volkswagen of America, Inc. v. Sud's of Peoria, Inc., 474 F.3d 966, 969 (2007).

50 For commentary arguing that arbitration violates the Seventh Amendment, *see, e.g.*, Sternlight, *supra* note 31, at 21–26 (2003); Jean Sternlight, *Mandatory Binding Arbitration and*

To sharpen our thinking on this point, let us return to the example introduced at the beginning of this chapter but refine it slightly by introducing two variations on the basic fact pattern:

> Variation 1: The dispute resolution clause into which Alice and Acme enter simply provides that "all disputes arising under this agreement shall be resolved exclusively by arbitration."
>
> Variation 2: In addition to the foregoing language set forth in Variation 1, the dispute resolution clause also provides that: "THE PARTIES VOLUNTARILY AND KNOWINGLY WAIVE ANY RIGHTS THEY HAVE TO A JURY TRIAL, EITHER PURSUANT TO ARBITRATION UNDER THIS CLAUSE OR PURSUANT TO A COURT ACTION BY YOU."[51]

Intuitively, one might believe that the two fact patterns present an important difference. Although the first example simply makes a generic reference to arbitration without any mention of the jury right, the second example expressly informs the parties at the time of contracting that one consequence of arbitration is the surrender of any otherwise available jury right. The juxtaposition of this information in all capital letters, next to an arbitration clause with normal capitalization, also enhances the likelihood that these implications will be drawn to the reader's attention at the time of contracting.

Several premises are embedded in this intuition. One premise would appear to be that parties actually read the language of contracts before those contracts become effective (either by signature or conduct). Some empirical research suggests that parties (particularly commercially unsophisticated ones) do not read agreements before entering

the Demise of the Seventh Amendment Right to a Jury Trial, 16 OHIO ST. J. DISP. RES. 669 (2001) (arguing that arbitration clauses should be subject to a "knowing, voluntary and intelligent" standard that typically governs waiver of constitutional rights in criminal proceedings); Sternlight, *supra* note 46, at 99 (arguing that arbitration clauses may violate the Seventh Amendment). For commentary rejecting the Seventh Amendment attack, *see, e.g.*, Stephen J. Ware, *Contractual Arbitration, Mandatory Arbitration, and State Constitutional Jury-Trial Rights*, 38 U.S.F. L. REV. 39 (2003); Stephen J. Ware, *Arbitration Clauses, Jury-Waiver Clauses and Other Contractual Waivers of Constitutional Rights*, 67 L. & CONTEMP. PROBS. 167 (2004).

51 *Syndor*, 2001 WL at *3.

into them.[52] To the extent that empirical assessment is valid, so the argument goes, the two variations actually present no meaningful differences in terms of the quality of the waiver.

Although that premise might be sufficient to support a distinction between the two variations, it is not necessary. Alternatively, one could draw on a normative principle to support a distinction between the two cases. Under the normative principle, even if parties do not in fact read contract terms in detail before entering into the agreement, the law will presume that they do so.[53] Such a presumption is necessary for several reasons. For one thing, if the law were otherwise, problems of proof would abound. Proof that a party actually read a contested contractual term would likely boil down to the party's own testimony, and in the case of a dispute, the party contesting the arbitration clause has a natural incentive to claim that he or she did not read the agreement. For another thing, the presumption is necessary in order to facilitate contractual relations. Parties offering goods or services could not have the confidence that they will receive the benefit of their bargain if the written words to which those bargains are reduced lack enforceable effect simply because one cannot prove that the other party read the document. The result would be a remarkable chilling effect on contractual relations, to the general detriment of society.

Even assuming the correctness of this normative proposition, the intuition that the two variations present materially different circumstances turns on a second premise, namely that whatever standard we apply to the effective waivers of the jury right, *written words* will suffice to satisfy that standard. One could imagine a view under which no written submissions whatsoever suffice to waive the jury right, instead

[52] David Horton, *The Shadow Terms: Contract Procedure and Unilateral Amendments*, 57 U.C.L.A. L. REV. 605, 662 (2010) ("[S]tudies reveal that a maximum of about five product characteristics will be 'salient' to any given consumer"); Jean R. Sternlight, *Creeping Mandatory Arbitration: Is It Just?*, 57 STAN. L. REV. 1631, 1648 (2005).

[53] Upton v. Tribilcock, 91 U.S. 45, 50 (1875)("A contractor must stand by the words of his contract; and, if he will not read what he signs, he alone is responsible for his omission"); Omri Ben-Shahar, *The Myth of the "Opportunity to Read" in Contract Law*, 5 EUROPEAN REV. 1, 7 (2009) (explaining the general duty to read a contract as people are presumed to have read them); SAMUEL WILLISTON, A TREATISE ON THE LAW OF CONTRACTS § 1577 (rev. ed. 1937) (citing the presumption of knowing the terms of a contract).

requiring some additional forms of procedural safeguards beyond objective manifestations of assent to written words.

Criminal trials provide a useful analogy here. For example, certain criminal procedural rights such as the right to presence of counsel at trial can only be effectively waived upon a colloquy with the judge in open court;[54] by contrast, other rights, such as certain Fourth Amendment rights or the rights to *Miranda* warnings prior to any custodial interrogation, can be effectively waived through acts of assent to written terms.[55] Against this backdrop, the question in this context then becomes: Why should waivers of jury rights in this context be susceptible to effective waiver in written form (such as the pretrial criminal rights) and not be susceptible to waiver only in open court (such as the criminal trial rights)?

To explore this analogy further, it is helpful to imagine how one would transpose the "criminal model" into this context. That is to say, assuming that written words, standing alone, do not effect a predispute waiver of a jury right, what additional procedural protections might be required? Several come to mind:

- *A cooling-off period:* This protection, which finds support in European consumer protection law, would afford the party waiving her jury right the opportunity to reexamine the decision for a period of time after affixing her signature to the waiver. The underlying rationale is that the cooling-off period allows the party an opportunity to examine the implications of her decision without the pressure or stress of the moment of executing the agreement. The problem,

[54] Von Moltke v. Gillies, 332 U.S. 708 (1948) (requiring the trial court undertake a "thorough inquiry" to ensure the accused has made an informed decision); Iowa v. Tovar, 541 U.S. 77, 81 (2004) ("The constitutional requirement is satisfied when the trial court informs the accused of the nature of the charges against him, of his right to be counseled regarding his plea, and of the range of allowable punishments attendant upon the entry of a guilty plea.") Although it seems it is generally true that one must waive the right in open court in order to allow the trial court to give the requisite advice, this position is tenuous. *See* 3 CRIM. PROC. § 11.3(a) & b) (3d ed.).

[55] North Carolina v. Butler, 441 U.S. 369, 373 (1979) ("An express written or oral statement of waiver of the right to remain silent or of the right to counsel is usually strong proof of the validity of that waiver, but is not inevitably either necessary or sufficient to establish waiver. The question is not one of form, but rather whether the defendant in fact knowingly and voluntarily waived the rights delineated in the *Miranda* case.").

of course, with the cooling-off period is that its efficacy turns on a psychological assumption, namely a belief that the person entering into the contract will in fact use the cooling-off period for the purpose for which it was intended. This is particularly problematic in situations such as pre-dispute arbitration agreements (as opposed to consumer purchases) where the prospect of a dispute (as opposed to the prospect of a using a new consumer gadget) may not be salient on the individual's mind (especially so when no dispute arises during the cooling-off period).

- *Witnesses:* Various contracts employ the use of witnesses in order to ensure the accuracy of the contractual undertaking and, in some cases, to ensure the full capacity of the person entering into the commitment. Applying that safeguard in this context however raises various problems. For one thing, it simply transposes the problem of the irrational contracting party to the witness himself. Why should we assume that the witness is any more capable than the contracting party of appreciating the impact of the undertaking (particularly where the witness, unlike the contracting party) has no stake in the outcome? For another thing, it adds a transaction cost to the undertaking (locating the witness, ensuring his presence and capacity to be a witness, etc.), which increases the overall price of the transaction. That may be a transaction cost worth undertaking (particularly if the aggregate improvements in contracting exceed the aggregate cost increases), but one should nonetheless not be oblivious to those costs.
- *Attorneys:* Various legal acts, whether involving waivers of rights or otherwise, require attorneys. The role of the attorney may vary. Under one approach, the party must have an opportunity to consult with an attorney before a waiver can be effective.[56] Under another approach, the waiver must occur in the presence of an attorney. Under yet a third approach, the attorney may serve a function not unlike a witness, affirming through the affixation of her signature the capacity of the individual effecting the waiver. Transposed to

[56] Michigan v. Jackson, 475 U.S. 625 (1986), *overruled by* Montejo v. Louisiana, 556 U.S. 778 (2009).

the context of civil jury waivers in arbitration agreements, each of these approaches can address some of the perceived shortcomings in relying on written words as a manifestation of a party's informed desire to waive his jury right.[57] Yet these approaches also replicate some of the problems precipitated by a witness requirement. They resurrect the agency problem – although admittedly, in contrast to the witness, the attorney may actually have better information and have a more direct interest in ensuring an accurate waiver. They also clearly enhance the transaction costs as no attorney will do this out of his or her own sense of goodwill. And, borrowing on a theme developed in the preceding section, they introduce principal–agent problems as the attorney may have self-interests (which the witness lacks) to discourage the use of a form of dispute resolution that may undermine the attorney's own pecuniary interest.

- *Pendency of the litigation:* In contrast to the preceding two safeguards (but conceptually similar to the "cooling-off" concept), this approach turns on a triggering event rather than the participation of particular individuals. Unlike the cooling-off period, the triggering event is not the passage of time but, rather, the commencement of litigation.[58] The underlying theory is that the commencement of litigation signifies a point where the claimant has more information about the nature of her claim (concretized by virtue of the fact that she has filed her complaint). At that point, she has

[57] Notably, the contract in the *Walker* case, discussed *supra* note 21 , gave the employees an opportunity to consult with an attorney before signing the arbitration agreement. The court nonetheless found this opportunity to be "unrealistic." Walker v. Ryan's Family Steak Houses, Inc., 289 F. Supp. 2d 916, 936 (M.D. Tenn. 2003). Although I have disagreed with the analysis of the *Walker* court generally, its conclusion confirms the idea that the introduction of an attorney interjects a transaction cost (which either results in someone not availing themselves of the right or scuttling the transaction altogether).

[58] The Georgia Supreme Court adopted this approach with respect to jury waivers generally. Bank South, N.A. v. Howard, 444 S.E.2d 799 (Ga. 1994). Notably, the Court excepted arbitration clauses from this general rule even though such clauses undoubtedly effect a waiver of a jury right in a manner no different from an express waiver of the right. *Id.* at 800 n.5 (cite) The Georgia Supreme Court justified this exception on the ground that the Georgia legislature had enacted an arbitration act (thereby legitimizing arbitration as a form of dispute resolution). Yet the existence of a legislative enactment should not be dispositive with respect to a constitutional issue. A constitutional conclusion about the effectiveness of a jury waiver would, by its very nature, prevail over a conflicting legislative enactment.

sufficient information to be able to appreciate the full consequences of the waiver. If she chooses to waive at that point, the waiver is more fully informed and, thus, more appropriately enforced. The problem, however, is that this standard essentially guts pre-dispute arbitration agreements altogether. To the extent we believe that arbitration, to be effective, must be committed to on a pre-dispute basis (that is, before irreconcilable antagonisms arise and disputing parties become unable to agree on anything), this approach is no different from the "no pre-dispute waiver" approach – it sounds the death knell for arbitration.

- *Judges:* At the extreme end of the alternatives, we might adopt the criminal model wholesale and require the waiver to occur in the presence of a judge. This presupposes the commencement of litigation and thereby succumbs to the same criticism regarding preceding list items. To the extent protocols develop to ensure meaningful waivers of the jury right (not unlike meaningful waivers of various criminal trial rights in the context of a guilty plea), our concerns dissipate over whether the individual has full information to effect a decision. Nonetheless, the transaction costs become even more profound when compared to the mere involvement of the attorneys. Moreover, this proposal entails third-party costs as well (namely the backlog in the judicial system as other cases, not subject to arbitration, must wait while courts clear out the "arbitration colloquies"). By contrast, a mechanism of ensuring enforceable agreements without the mandatory need for judicial intervention reduces these third-party costs (albeit at the expense of some of the judicial safeguards that the presence of a judge would offer).

As these increasingly burdensome examples demonstrate, the problem with piling more procedural safeguards onto an essentially private commercial transaction is that, at a certain point, the transaction no longer makes economic sense. In theoretical terms, the contracting costs outstrip the marginal benefits of the transaction to at least one of the parties and, consequently, the transaction is never consummated (at a net cost to society in terms of the benefits to its welfare that come from the exchange). Consequently, we see that either we should conclude that waiver simply is not possible (which takes us back to the absolutist position explored in the preceding section and the attendant social costs of that position) or we admit that a written waiver is possible notwithstanding its imperfections (which carries its own social costs). By upholding written waivers, what we really are saying is that one set of trade-offs between contracting costs and social costs is more tolerable than another. As a normative matter, therefore, the ideal standard of waiver is one that achieves the maximum increase in net social welfare from the transaction at a minimum of contracting costs.

Assuming, then, that we can justify the premises on which the distinction between our two variations is based, does it follow that all written references to arbitration suffice to waive effectively the jury right? The majority of courts take this view.[59]

A few courts and scholars have articulated a competing viewpoint,[60] which starts with the assumption, first explored in the "inalienability" section above, that the jury is an important component of our civil justice system.[61] From this premise, the argument then moves to the proposition that courts ordinarily assess jury waivers using the knowing, voluntary, and intelligent standard.[62] This argument then faults courts for failing to apply this same general standard to arbitration clauses that effectively waive access to a jury.[63]

Although this competing viewpoint can be credited with exposing the sloppy intellectual development behind the dominant position, it

[59] *See* Dillard v. Merrill Lynch, Pierce, Fenner & Smith, 961 F.2d 1148, 1155 n.12 (5th Cir. 1992); United States v. ASCAP, 708 F. Supp. 95, 97 (S.D.N.Y. 1989). Several district courts have addressed this issue. *See* Cremin v. Merrill Lynch Pierce Fenner & Smith, Inc., 957 F.Supp. 1460 (N.D. Ill. 1997); Ilyes v. John Nuveen & Co., Inc., 949 F. Supp. 580 (N.D. Ill. 1996); Marsh v. First USA Bank, 103 F. Supp. 2d 909, 920–21 (N.D. Tex. 2000); Bank One N.A. v. Coates, 125 F. Supp. 2d 819 (S.D. Miss. 2001).

[60] The California Court of Appeals in *Badie v. Bank of America* made this point about what an arbitration clause had to contain in order to amount to an effective waiver of the state jury right. 79 Cal. Rptr.2d 273 (Cal. Ct. App. 1998). In *Walker v. Ryan's Family Steakhouse*, a federal district judge actually accepted the argument that the enforcement of a pre-dispute arbitration agreement (here in the context of an employment agreement) violated the jury right.

[61] This harkens back to the inalienability position discussed in the first section of this chapter. Here, it is hoped that the reader will see how the inalienability position, although not accepted as a dispositive principle, nonetheless influences the debate over what forms of waiver will be acceptable.

[62] Sternlight, *supra* note 31, at 22 (citing Med. Air Tech. Corp. v. Marwan Inv., Inc., 303 F.3d 11, 18–19 (1st Cir. 2002).

[63] 16 OHIO ST. J. DISP. RES. at 727–29.

suffers from serious intellectual flaws. Scholars such as Steve Ware have noted that the knowing, voluntary, and intelligent standard is more familiar in a criminal context than civil context. He then argues that courts frequently use contract analysis for civil law constitutional waivers, and claims that jury waiver cases are an outlier. He then concludes that the Court should jettison the knowing consent requirement for jury waiver clauses.[64]

The flaw identified by Ware is not the only problem with the counterargument. A deeper flaw is its basic circularity. Even accepting the major premise that waivers of jury rights should be evaluated under the "knowing, voluntary, and intelligent" standard, this proposition simply begs a minor premise that the counterargument never fully addresses. That is, why does a written arbitration agreement not supply sufficient evidence of a knowing, voluntary, and intelligent waiver? If it does, then the counterargument collapses under the weight of its own standard. In other words, if a general arbitration clause were deemed to constitute a knowing, voluntary, and intelligent waiver, then the counterargument's complaint is misplaced.[65]

So how does one begin to answer the unaddressed premise of the counterargument? This returns us to the idea developed earlier in this chapter that one's view on the conditions under which a jury waiver will be enforced ultimately boil down to an assessment of costs and tradeoffs – namely maximizing the social benefits that come from enforcing agreements while minimizing the costs borne by those who may have agreed to arbitration without fully appreciating the consequences. To unpack this issue, it helps to consider several different types of language that might be used in an arbitration clause:

- At one end of the spectrum might be a clause that expressly included the jury waiver in its description of the arbitration right.[66] Such

64 Ware, *supra* note 50. The Connecticut Supreme Court appeared to embrace this approach in L&R Realty v. Connecticut Nat'l Bank, 715 A.2d 748, 753 (Conn. 1998).

65 *Marsh* holds that it should not (without proposing clearly an alternative approach – other than a general contract approach). Marsh v. First USA Bank, N.A., 103 F. Supp. 2d 909, 921 (N.D. Tex. 2003).

66 Kloss v. Edward D. Jones & Co., 54 P.3d 1 (Mont. 2002) (precise facts of case were complicated by the fact that Kloss signed a detachable card, not actual contract containing this clause; moreover, there is some suggestion in the record that Kloss did not see agreement before she signed the card).

formulations contain the clearest evidence that the assent to arbitration includes an assent to waiver of the jury right.

- An intermediate case would be an arbitration clause that talks about giving up the right to litigate claims "through a court" without expressly mentioning a jury.[67] Such formulations do not contain clear evidence that assent to arbitration necessitates assent to waiver of the jury right. Nonetheless, as several courts have found, such formulations are reasonably read to imply assent to waiver of the jury right, for the jury right only becomes triggered when one invokes judicial process. To the extent one waives the right of judicial access, the jury right is necessarily included in that waiver.[68]
- At the other end of the spectrum might be a case that involves a general commitment to arbitrate (perhaps imposed as a condition of employment) without elaboration on the consequences of the agreement.[69] These cases require the greatest inference from courts. To be effective, it must be assumed that, when a party was agreeing to arbitration, it understood what arbitration meant. Specifically it understood that arbitration necessarily implied foregoing access to the court and the procedural entitlements made available in courts, namely juries.

Courts have taken different views on which forms suffice. Some courts have proposed quite specific formulations for a written waiver to be effective. According to one skeptical court, the waiver must be "clearly apparent in the contract and its language must be unambiguous and unequivocal leaving no room for doubt as to the intention of the parties."[70] Another court implicitly requires reference to the jury right.[71]

[67] *Marsh,* 103 F. Supp. at 921; Bank One, N.A. v. Coates, 125 F. Supp. 2d 819, 824 (S.D. Miss. 2001).

[68] Geldermann, Inc. v. Commodity Futures Trading Com'n, 836 F.2d 310, 323–24 (7th Cir. 1987).

[69] Cremin v. Merrill Lynch, Pierce, Fenner, & Smith, Inc., 957 F. Supp. 1460, 1471 (N.D. Ill. 1997).

[70] *Badie,* 79 Cal. Rptr. at 289.

[71] Walker v. Ryan's Family Steak Houses, Inc., 289 F. Supp. 2d 916, 934–36 (M.D. Tenn. 2003)rev'd, 400 F.3d 370, 382 (6th Cir. 2005)("[A]lthough the waiver provision does not refer to relinquishing the right to a jury trial, this Court has held that "a party who enters

Other courts have been more reluctant to require a particular form of words.[72] This reluctance is grounded in a concern about second-guessing parties' commercial expectations. The Fourth Circuit's decision in the *Syndor* case illustrates this point. There, the plaintiffs signed a document indicating that they knowingly and voluntarily waived their jury right. They claimed, however, that the waiver was ineffective because the counterparties (a contractor and lender) did not affirmatively inform the plaintiffs of the jury waiver. The court rejected this with the statement that parties have a duty to inform themselves of the contents of an agreement before executing it and, short of fraud or overreaching, will not be allowed to impeach the contents of their commitments by claiming they did not know what they signed.[73] Underlying *Syndor* is the idea that there is an important value in the enforceability of written commitments regardless of the content of those commitments, and courts should be reluctant to peer beneath the content of those commitments for fear of upsetting broader commercial expectations and general autonomy principles.

If no single form of magic words can be logically derived,[74] perhaps a more helpful way to reframe the question is to ask where the burden should lie. Should one party bear the burden of specificity in contracting (thus making only the first example sufficient to constitute a waiver)? Alternatively, should one party bear the burden of knowing

an arbitration agreement necessarily consents to the clear and obvious consequence: the surrender of his right to go to trial.").

72 79 Cal. Rptr. 2d at 289.

73 2001 WL 223243 at *3.

74 Even if a form of magic words could be identified, residual difficulties would arise. One residual problem might be a claim that one party did not know what she was signing. *See Walker*, 289 F. Supp. 2d 916. Second, the person signing the agreements might lack the proper capacity to enter into the agreement. This may be due to intelligence limitations or language limitations. Again, the problem here lies not specifically with arbitration agreements per se but, rather, is a broader question of how capacity doctrines will be defined in a particular legal system. Third, doubts may arise in particular cases over the lack of assent. The hypotheticals that have driven the argument so far have all concerned bilateral contracts with clear moments of offer and assent. Difficulties arise however where assent is harder to measure. This might occur, for example, where the arbitration agreement is "stuffed" into a bill sent to a customer who indicates his assent by paying the bill or engaging in some other act that manifests his assent to the terms (even where serious doubts may exist whether he has even seen those terms). *See* David Horton, *The Shadow Terms: Contract Procedure and Unilateral Amendments*, 57 U.C.L.A. L. REV. 605 (2010) (opposing unilateral modification of the procedural terms of arbitration clauses).

the consequences of its commitment even if they are not spelled out explicitly in the contract (thus making all three of the preceding examples equivalent)? This latter view was essentially the one embraced by the appellate court in *Syndor*. Seen through this lens, the proper approach to the "magic words" question comes not from scientifically identifying what form of written waiver suffices but, instead, from a policy-laden debate balancing judicial enforcement of commercial expectations on the one hand against paternalistic oversight of parties' contractual commitments on the other hand. Regrettably here, as in other contexts such as the federalism discussion, the doctrine has not adequately grappled with the values underlying the constitutional questions.

Perhaps the approach taken in the context of the due process protocols provides a model for stimulating that consideration of the underlying values. There, we saw how privately developed protocols stimulated a debate between courts and private stakeholders over the degree to which a given model satisfied the courts' concerns about procedural due process in arbitration. In some cases, courts singled out particular clauses for praise as models of due process; in others, they criticized a model for riding roughshod over such principles. A similar dialogic approach might be undertaken in the jury waiver context as well – with private entities developing model clauses designed to ensure complete waiver of the jury right, and courts supplying feedback on the adequacy or inadequacy of those waivers (based upon the underlying policy considerations identified here). Over time, model clauses might provide "safe harbor" language assured to pass judicial muster, whereas more adventurous clauses risk closer judicial examination and scrutiny. In the long run, perhaps this provides the surest model of addressing the values underlying questions about what forms of written words suffice to waive the jury right in an arbitration.

CONCLUSION

In sum, this chapter has addressed the relationship between arbitration and the jury right. The extreme position under which the jury right is inalienable is untenable. Equally untenable is the position that the jury right cannot be waived on a pre-dispute basis. Although untenable, these positions are important because the principles underlying them inform the main battleground debate, namely the conditions under which the jury right can be waived. The majority of courts rightly conclude that general consent to an arbitration clause should be deemed sufficient to waive the jury right, but the intellectual underpinnings of that conclusion are woefully underdeveloped. Nonetheless, the solution is not to embrace the counterargument but, instead, to put the dominant jurisprudential view on a surer footing through development of a dialogue between courts and private stakeholders over the forms of written words that balance the competing values.

CONCLUSION

The introduction of this book offered the metaphor of a wall to describe the relationship between arbitration law and constitutional law. At various historical phases, that wall was quite firm. Over time, though, as arbitration has come to occupy more fields of disputes, cracks began to develop in that wall – permitting the seepage of principles from one discipline into the doctrine and dialogue of another. To be sure, the wall endures today, but it is not as firm as it was a century or even half-century ago. The past six chapters have sought to describe the contours of the wall, the areas of seepage, and the consequences of that seepage. This conclusion aspires to identify some crosscutting themes and to chart the course for future research.

CROSSCUTTING THEMES

Theme 1: Limited doctrinal impact – Perhaps the central lesson of this book is that constitutional values have not influenced arbitration at the level of direct doctrinal incorporation. Arbitration has not offended horizontal separation-of-powers principles (either with respect to the judicial power, as discussed in Chapter 1, or with respect to executive power in the case of trade and investment arbitration, as discussed in Chapter 2). Nor has arbitration seriously implicated civil liberties (either with respect to due process rights, as discussed in Chapter 5, or with respect to the jury right, as discussed in Chapter 6).

The one exception to the general pattern against express doctrinal incorporation has been the vertical separation of powers. As Chapter 3 explained, doctrines of FAA preemption have significantly constrained the ability of state legislatures to regulate the field, particularly with respect to the arbitrability of certain claims. Despite the weak textual basis for this conclusion (as set forth in Justice O'Connor's dissent in *Southland*), this anti-federalism jurisprudence has largely cemented in the constitutional law of arbitration. Despite the strong penchant for states' rights among a majority of justices on the current Court, only Justice Thomas remains steadfast in the view that *Southland* should be overruled.

Yet the federalism story – the one area where constitutional law has worked a direct doctrinal effect on arbitration law – is a more complex one than the mere displacement of state law by federal law. As Chapter 3 explained, state law still plays an important role through the development of generally applicable contract principles that apply, at least, in domestic arbitrations. That residual role has an important impact on the horizontal allocation of power at the state level, arguably making state judges more important policemen of arbitration agreements than elected state representatives. Just as state courts can influence the impact of state law on the FAA preemption analysis, so too can parties. Although heavily criticized, the Supreme Court's decision in *Volt* remains good law, creating the possibility that, through state choice-of-law clauses, parties may be able to invoke some mechanisms under state arbitration law unavailable under federal law.

While the doctrine continues to leave a role for state rights in the preemption analysis, that role may well be declining. The Supreme Court's decision in *Concepcion* trimmed even the ability of state courts to influence the regulation of arbitration agreements. It polices purported applications of state contract law in order to ensure that they are not simply repackaged anti-arbitration doctrines that the FAA was designed to eliminate. So too has the Court shown greater skepticism toward party efforts to reinvigorate state law through party choice. Both the Supreme Court's decisions in *Mastrobuono* and *Preston*, although not expressly overruling *Volt*, have largely cabined the decision and limited parties' ability to rely on general choice-of-law clauses to invoke provisions of state arbitration laws at odds with the FAA.

Theme 2: Subdoctrinal influences – Although arbitration law has largely remained immune from the application of express constitutional limits (excepting federalism), the absence of express doctrinal incorporation does not mean that constitutional values have been missing from the development of arbitral institutions. Rather, they have influenced the development of those institutions in softer, more subtle ways.

One means has been through interpretation of positive law other than the Constitution. For example, Chapter 5 showed how some U.S. courts in enforcement actions under the New York Convention have interpreted Article V(1)(b) to incorporate American due process norms even though that provision of the treaty neither dictates an applicable law nor refers to a system's constitutional jurisprudence. So too Chapter 1 explained how the manifest disregard of the law doctrine could be understood as an application of the canon of constitutional avoidance – by preserving a residual role for courts to police the substance of arbitration awards. This enabled them to avert a frontal attack on arbitration grounded in Article III and the private rights doctrine.

A second means whereby constitutional principles have seeped into arbitration law is through system design. Chapter 2 showed how this had occurred in the context of NAFTA's fallback mechanism, designed to address the concerns of some legislators that, without it, NAFTA's implementing legislation potentially created problems under the Appointments Clause of Article II. Chapter 2 also showed how constitutional concerns had influenced system design choices about the extent to which the United States would allow its officers to enter into binding commercial arbitration. As the Dellinger Memorandum demonstrates, even though the risk of constitutional invalidation is slight, the Justice Department has hewed to a policy generally prohibiting U.S. officials from entering into binding commercial arbitration on behalf of the United States. Whereas the NAFTA fallback mechanism exemplifies how constitutional analysis of an arbitral scheme shapes systemic design at the level of legislation, the Dellinger Memorandum demonstrates how constitutional analysis of an arbitral scheme shapes systemic design at the level of executive branch behaviour.

A third means of influence comes in the development of private norms. As Chapter 5 explained, the due process protocols have represented important developments in this regard. Despite the lack of "state action" in arbitration (thereby eliminating due process requirements as a matter of formal constitutional doctrine), these privately developed protocols are underpinned by principles quite similar to those that guide procedural due process. Similarly, the development of transparency protocols in the investment arbitration process represents another attempt to import constitution-like values into a system that, as a formal doctrinal matter, is not subject to them.

Theme 3: Dialogic influence – The foregoing theme about the sub-constitutional levels at which constitutional norms influence arbitration leads naturally to a third theme. That is, because the debate over constitutional principles in arbitration takes place at the sub-constitutional level, it facilitates a far greater dialogue between institutions of the state as well as with private parties than if the constitutional doctrine occupied the entire field. As discussed in Chapter 5, the D.C. Circuit's criticism in *Cole* about cost-shifting rules in arbitration prompted significant rethinking on the issue by private providers administering consumer and employment arbitration pursuant to the protocols. Similarly, Justice Ginsburg's opinion in *Randolph*, singling out a particular set of arbitral rules for praise as a sensible system of cost regulation, sends an important signal to the provider community about what sorts of schemes can pass judicial muster. The Supreme Court's decision in *Concepcion*, approving AT&T's arbitration clause despite the presence of a class waiver, likewise stimulates thinking about companies using arbitration clauses in their consumer contracts and the extent to which their clauses should track the "sweeteners" in AT&T's clause in order to ensure the enforceability of their own clause. All of these examples illustrate how the manner in which these constitutional principles are ventilated – through the forms other than express doctrinal incorporation – has facilitated a healthy dialogue between the judiciary and the relevant constituencies (arbitral institutions, companies, and consumer advocates) over the acceptable "norms" governing this form of dispute resolution.

FUTURE DIRECTIONS

Areas for future research stem from both the limits on this project identified in the introduction as well as from the analysis contained in the preceding six chapters.

One obvious area for future research is a comparative undertaking. As noted at the outset of this book, I made the explicit decision not to investigate systematically how other countries approached these questions (relying, instead, on international examples only for illustrative purposes or where they were helpful for reinforcing a point). Nonetheless, such a project would, I believe, reveal a great deal about how other systems deal with these issues. In conversations with colleagues from around the world as well as my own cursory review of some of the comparative literature, I do believe a story can be told about how other legal systems mediate the relationship between arbitration law and constitutional law. A good comparativist, or perhaps better yet a collection of authors from different legal systems, might undertake this project.

A second area for future research is to understand an institutional puzzle presented by this book – namely why the form of constitutional influence varies with the issue. Put in concrete terms, why precisely do horizontal separation-of-powers issues tend to manifest themselves in judicial interpretation of statutes and treaties whereas concerns about individual liberties manifest themselves in private developed protocols such as the due process protocols for consumer and employment arbitration, or the transparency protocol in the area of investment arbitration? By contrast, vertical separation-of-powers values have been the one area where direct doctrinal incorporation of constitutional law has had an impact on the field.

My instincts are that the answer lies in some combination of two powerful influences – namely a strong desire for a uniform national arbitration scheme dating back to the FAA's enactment in 1925, coupled with a strong conception of freedom-of-contract principles in the United States making individuals (even when they occupy inferior bargaining positions) masters of their agreements. This combination of ideas may well explain the desire to leave many doctrinal matters on a nonconstitutional level (to leave the maximum flexibility by Congress), a strong anti-federalism jurisprudence (to avoid a circumvention of the uniform system by the states) and a weak individual rights jurisprudence (to avoid watering down the sanctity of contract). Yet that account does not adequately explain why precisely the horizontal separation-of-powers issues tend to be resolved at the level of statutory or treaty interpretation whereas the individual liberties issues tend to be resolved through private norm development. A fuller explanation must, regrettably, await another project.

A third and final direction for future research would be to investigate at a higher level of abstraction the influence of norms on a legal system or an area of the law. For example, one could easily imagine how constitutional principles influence areas of the law beyond arbitration despite the absence of an express application of constitutional doctrine. Likewise, this project can tap into ongoing debates about the extent to which international law might creep into a domestic legal system even absent express domestication of the international norm through positive law.

Far from being daunting, these areas for future research should be inspiring. In a world of increasingly complex and specialized legal systems, chasms can easily develop between different fields of the law, causing us to lose sight of the subtle but important connections between those fields. This is neither a phenomenon unique to the relationship between arbitration law and constitutional law, nor is it one unique to the U.S. legal system. This book has sought to bridge one such chasm, but many others can be built. It is my sincere hope that others will take up the tools offered in this book and apply them to other fields of law and to other legal systems. As you do so, please let me know of your efforts.

INDEX